# THE HORSE IN THE WEST

# The spread of the hors

YAKIMA
1730

NEZ PERCE
1710

BLOOD
1730

CAYUSE
1720

BLACKFEET
1750

PLAINS
CREE
1770

CROW
1730

MISSION
SAN RAFAEL 1817

SHOSHONE
1690

MANDAN
1750

MISSION
DE CARMEL 1770

1720

1770

EL CAMINO
REAL

UTE

MISSION
SAN DIEGO 1769

NAVAJO
1650

SIOUX

PUEBLO

APACHE

COMANCHE
1720

KIOWA
1600

1690

CADDO
1550

CONCHO
1650

1530

1519

January, 1494

SPANISH EXPLORATION AND TRADE ROUT

1525-35

1527

# o the western world

500 B.C.

CELTS

1000-600 B.C.

1600 B.C.

MESOPOTAMIAN TRADE ROUTES

2000 B.C.

800 B.C.

1600 B.C.

MOORS
711

1700 B.C.

COLUMBUS' SECOND VOYAGE 1493

D. RENZ STOLP

# THE HORSE IN THE WEST

*Written and photographed*
*by Bradley Smith*

*A Gemini Smith Book*
*Published by The World Publishing Company, New York and Cleveland*

*Color Photography* BRADLEY SMITH

*Graphics Director* D. RENZ STOLP

*Technical Editor* SYD LOVE

*Editorial Research* HELEN REED SMITH

*Editorial Assistant* FLORENCE KRONFELD

*Production Supervisor* NANCY G. HENDERSON

COVER:      *Champion Arabian mare \*Naganka running with her foal at Varian Arabians, Arroyo Grande, California.*

END PAGES: *Spring roundup at Eaton Ranch, Wolf, Wyoming.*

PAGE 1:      *Yearlings after drinking and bathing at 6666 Ranch near Guthrie, Texas.*

PAGES 2-3:  *Map by D. Renz Stolp showing movement of horses from Europe to the New World and their spread through New Spain to the Indians of North America.*

PAGES 4-5:  *Untamed stallion, mares, and foals race across the valley in the Pryor Mountains of Wyoming.*

Published by The World Publishing Company
2231 West 110th Street, Cleveland, Ohio 44102
Published simultaneously in Canada by Nelson, Foster & Scott Ltd.

First Printing—1969

Library of Congress catalogue card No. 76-93746
All rights reserved. Printed by Frye & Smith, Ltd., in the United States of America.

**WORLD PUBLISHING**
**TIMES MIRROR**

# CONTENTS

# THE WESTERN HORSE IN HISTORY

The West is not merely a geographic region. It is a legendary place created out of Western traditions. It has no boundaries. If today it is also geographically an area of superhighways, industrialized sections, and suburban tract houses, it is still both the real and traditional home of the Indian and the cowboy, the pioneer and the horse.

It is impossible to imagine the Western United States without the horse. To think of this spacious country with Indians and cowboys on foot, of pioneers without scouts, and of stagecoaches without horses creates a picture the mind cannot accept. Yet, three hundred years ago, the West was horseless. Its only people were the Indians, their only transportation was by foot.

The West had no written histories, no songs, no legends until the horse became a part of the lives of the Indians and the pioneer settlers. Then a whole new world was founded from the horse's back. The horse supplied not only transportation for exploration and conquest, but it became the weapon and the instrument that made it possible for a small band of *conquistadores* from Spain to subdue vast nations in Mexico and the southwest regions of the present United States. The horse also permitted the original Indian population west of the Mississippi River and north of the Rio Grande to become mobile and to grow in numbers from small, isolated, slow-moving groups to swift-riding bearers of a new equestrian culture.

But the Spaniards who brought the modern horse to the Western world had no such plans. Their greatest explorer, Christopher Columbus, the Admiral of the Ocean Sea, discoverer and colonizer of the New World, foresaw the importance of the horse. On his first voyage the Genoa-born navigator noted in his journal that horses were entirely unknown to "the Indians." Having seen the sweeping distances to be explored and having been exposed to the pedestrian culture of the people he called Indians, he realized how important the horse would be for transportation and for conquest. Therefore, on his second voyage, as his son wrote in his *The Life of the Admiral, Christopher Columbus, by His Son Ferdinand*, the discoverer spoke of the great importance of horses in the first settlements of the New World. Columbus' first New World biographer, Washington Irving, wrote, "Horses, both for military purposes and for stocking the country, [and] cattle and domestic animals of all kinds were likewise provided." On the second voyage Columbus brought both stallions and mares and landed them on the north-central shore of Hispaniola near the present boundary between Haiti and the Dominican Republic, the first region colonized by the Spanish in the New World. From this first breeding farm

9

and from subsequent shipments from southern Spain, breeding farms were established in Jamaica and Cuba.

As Spanish exploration of the New World increased, the Spanish Crown demanded that permanent settlements be established. Horses were of prime importance. After 1504, prices rose to a new high when a special license became required for export. Nevertheless, we know that such a license was issued for 106 mares to be shipped to the Indies on February 15 of that year. Transportation to the islands, a sea journey of from twenty-five to fifty days, was incredibly difficult. Stalls were built on the decks of the small sailing vessels, leaving almost no space for crew and passengers. Often half of the horses perished in transit.

In this connection it is interesting to speculate on the horse latitudes and the reason for their name. These sectors of the Atlantic Ocean are in the vicinity of thirty-five degrees north latitude and thirty degrees south latitude, between the trade winds and the prevailing westerlies. In the horse latitudes, atmospheric pressures become quite high. As a result, long calm periods with very light variable winds—or periods of no wind at all—frequently dominate those regions. Ships often were becalmed there. Some writers have speculated that because of the heat and the length of time the ships were powerless, horses died and had to be thrown overboard. Therefore, the appellation horse latitudes. Other writers have suggested that because the sailors were working "off the dead horse"—which meant that they had received pay up to that time and were working on pay that had been advanced to them—this was responsible for the name. These interesting conjectures have no basis in fact. The area was named by early Spanish navigators, who called it El Golfo de las Yeguas (The Gulf of the Mares) because the winds there were as fickle as the temperament of a female.

Gonzalo Fernández de Oviedo, the first historian of the West Indies and a mayor of Santo Domingo, confirmed Columbus' earlier statement by writing that when the Spaniards arrived, no horses of any kind were on the island of Hispaniola and that the first mares and stallions were shipped from Spain to that island. He also observed that others were shipped to various West Indies islands including Jamaica and Cuba.

The breeding stock that first came to the New World was from the stud farms of Córdoba and Sevilla. These Arabian horses were directly descended from the animals brought to Spain by the Moslems when they crossed the Strait of Gibraltar in 711 A.D. to begin their thrust into the Iberian Peninsula. Moorish horse breeders may be said to have had the greatest influence on the development of the modern horse. In the immense desert regions the speed, stamina, and maneuverability of the horse were essential in transportation and in warfare. The sheiks bred for all of those qualities, and the mounts they had so carefully developed made the conquest of the Iberian Peninsula possible. In southern Spain during the Moorish occupation, thousands of horses were bred from Arab stock. Such animals were the most prized possessions of their owners. Drawn from this early Arab blood were the horses that first reached the Americas.

And 150 years later, that same original Arab breeding stock provided England with the founding sires of the Thoroughbreds. So the Moors must also be credited with breeding toward the most important strain of racehorses in the modern world.

Today in the Western United States all horses, with the possible exception of some of the draft horses, such as the Clydesdale, and the ponies, Shetland and Welsh, have some Arabian blood.

But the Arabs were by no means the first people of Europe to domesticate and breed horses. It is generally believed that the modern horse descended from two wild ancestors native to Europe and Asia. They are known as the Przewalski horse, after the Russian scientist who identified them, and the tarpan. Both of these animals were relatively small, ranging from eleven to fourteen hands high, compared to heights of fifteen to sixteen hands common for some of today's breeds. Each had a straight broad back, a fairly large head, small ears, an upright brushlike mane, and a long bushy tail. The Przewalski horse, which still exists, has a pink-white muzzle and a black tail. The overall color of the horse is medium brown with a tinge of red. This horse has survived, though in very small numbers, in Mongolia where a few have been seen in recent years. It has been rebred (there are over one hundred today) and placed in zoos throughout the world, including the Hellabrunn in Munich and the San Diego Zoo in California.

The tarpan was a mouse-gray horse which, considering his small body, had a large coarse head. Although the tarpan has now become extinct, many of his characteristics are found in the modern horse.

Some zoologists believe there may have been a third ancestor, a heavier wild horse. The weight of the evidence seems to indicate no such ancestor. But the theory of cold-blooded and hot-blooded horses has persisted through a considerable number of generations. Outstanding authorities, ranging from O. Antonius, the early German zoologist, to Lady Wentworth, owner of the famed Crabbet Stud in England, have insisted upon such a heavy cold-blooded ancestor to the large-boned horse breeds represented by the Percheron and Clydesdale. Lady Wentworth went farther than any of the other authorities in insisting that this ancestor may be classed as *equus caballus frigicalidus*, representing the cold-blooded horse, and *equus caballus ardens*, where the hot blood is in excess. Lady Wentworth insisted that varying degrees of hot- or cold-blooded mixtures have resulted in all of the types of horses that range from the relatively pure hot-blooded Arabian to the relatively pure cold-blooded Percheron. Yet there is little actual archeological or historical evidence that such an ancestor for the heavier breed ever existed.

If such an ancestor could be found of the heavy cold-blooded horse, the problem of tracing the descent would be greatly simplified. But it is more probable that in certain areas horses were, after domestication, bred for weight and pulling power, as in the case of the draft horses and the large animals that carried armor-clad knights, rather than for speed and stamina, as in the Arabian group.

Man has proven, both in ancient and modern times, that he can control the evolutionary direction of the animals he domesticates. Horses have been bred in many directions, and this experimentation has given us all the various modern breeds and types. Selective breeding began in pre-Biblical and even prehistoric times. It is believed early horse migration started in central Europe and moved toward Asia and that those horses migrating toward Asia and bred by the Asiatics formed a distinct series of types that have been well recorded in sculpture and painting through the various Indian and Chinese dynasties. The horses that migrated toward the south into the Mesopotamian Valley also probably came from north-central Europe. They later found their way into Egypt, where they may be seen in early murals.

In the Old Testament, chariots and horsemen are described in Genesis 48:17, when Joseph gave the Egyptians bread in exchange for horses: "And they brought their cattle unto Joseph. And Joseph gave them bread in exchange for the horses . . . ." Again, a few chapters later, when the burial of Jacob is described: "And there went up with him both chariots and horsemen; and it was a very great company."

But perhaps the earliest evidence of horses used in warfare was in the fifteenth century before Christ when a people migrating from southern Russia moved into an area between the Tigris River and the Mediterranean Sea. They are called the Mitanni, and they introduced the horse to Asia Minor and popularized its breeding. These people, known as Aryans, were the first to introduce rapid transport using a domesticated horse and light-wheeled chariots for transportation, for sport, and for war.

This horse-drawn war chariot completely changed

MESOHIPPUS

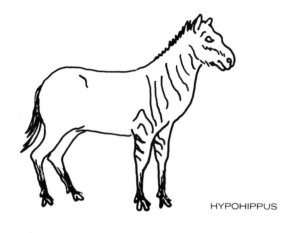

HYPOHIPPUS

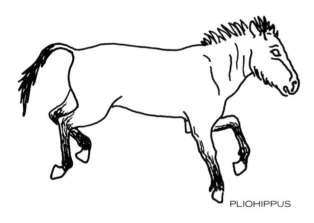

PLIOHIPPUS

PRZEWALSKI

the form of armies and military tactics. All of the countries of Europe and Asia soon recognized the value of the horse as an offensive weapon.

From Egypt the horse spread to the Arabic nations, and there in the desert he slowly evolved into the most important ancestor of the modern horse. Evidence as much as twenty-five thousand years old demonstrates that the horse was well known to early man. He painted the horse on the walls of the caves of Lascaux in Dordogne, France, and along the northern coast of Spain in the caves of Altamira and El Castillo. It is probable, however, that domestication did not begin until about five hundred years before the Aryans commenced their widespread use of the horse, and that earlier the horse had been hunted for food like any other wild game.

Long before this, over ten thousand years ago, a remote ancestor to the European horse roamed the North American Continent. Although he little resembled a horse, being not much larger than a greyhound, he belonged to the same species as the modern horse, the odd-toed ungulates. This formerly large family encompassed at least one hundred and fifty mammals whose characteristics included having three toes. That first horse, however, the eohippus, actually had four toes on its front feet, three on each of its rear feet. Now all but three members of that family — the tapir, the rhinoceros, and the domestic horse — have become ex-

*It has taken over 58,000 years for the modern horse known as* Equus *to evolve. Here are shown some of the stages in his development from a small greyhound-dog-size to the present superbly structured and muscled domesticated horse. The earliest horse, eohippus, had four small hooves, or toes, on his front feet and three on the back. Mesohippus, which belongs to the Oligocene age, existed some fifteen thousand years later. He was larger, with a bigger brain and had only three toes on each of his front and back feet. Hypohippus followed about three thousand years later, and the animal began to take on some characteristics of the present horse. Finally came* Equus przewalski, *the modern wild horse.* Equus caballus, *the domesticated horse of today, followed. All horses now living, including zebras and asses, belong to the* Equus *group of the odd-toed ungulate family that also includes the tapir and the rhinoceros.*

tinct. The rhinoceros and the tapir are fast disappearing, but the domestic horse survives in ever-mounting numbers. The small ancestor of the modern horse doubtless became extinct as a result of being hunted by the first Americans. These early men migrated over a broad land bridge from Siberia, presumably crossing sometime before 10,000 B.C. This was the epoch of the last great glaciation, when sea levels receded as a great deal of water was absorbed by and locked into the glaciers and ice sheets. Across the fertile plain, traversing what is now the Bering Strait, bison and antelope and mammoths preceded or accompanied man to the New World. These men were the ancestors of the people Columbus erroneously called Indians.

In Spain, the horse in general was known for a long time by the Catalán word *Zenete*. This was a term the Catalán people of Spain used to describe the Berbers, a Moorish race who normally were on horseback, at least the first time they were encountered. But when one of those horses was a purebred Arab, he was referred to as *asil*, which in Arabic means purebred. *Zenete*, by way of the Middle English and Middle French tongues, has reached today's English-language dictionaries as jennet. *Caballo* is the Spanish word for a male horse. This means a full horse; that is, one that has not been gelded. And the word for a horseman, and for a gentleman as well, is *caballero*.

In the early American West, every good man was said to have possessed a horse. And usually he could acquire one easily, for they were omnipresent and for that reason were inexpensive. One of the reasons for the early spread of horses is that the Spaniards in their first years in the New World did not geld.

Cortés had been a successful breeder of cattle and horses in Cuba before embarking on his great adventure. His rival, Diego Velázquez, governor of Cuba, had become affluent through the raising of fine horses, the original stock of which he had personally brought from Hispaniola. In fact, the Velázquez stock comprised many of the first breeding animals to reach Cuba. These included eight horses and mares. And at least one of the first horses to reach New Spain, now Mexico, came from Velázquez' breeding farm at Bayamo, Cuba, where large ranches had developed rapidly. Cortés for his conquest selected sixteen horses from the finest Cuban stock, and those were the animals he landed with at Vera Cruz harbor on April 21, 1519. Fortunately, through the careful chronicle of Bernal Díaz del Castillo, a great deal is known about the colors and other characteristics of that seminal group.

Díaz was one of the conqueror's captains. Born in Old Castile in the year that Columbus discovered America, Díaz survived the lengthy and bloody conquest to die at eighty-nine at Guatemala, where in his seventies he wrote his journal, a narrative which historians and other scholars today still seek and cherish at the Archives of the Indies in Sevilla. Bernal Díaz, who outlived all the other conquerors, wrote in his *Historia Verdadera de la Conquista de la Nueva España:* "At that time [before leaving Cuba] horses and Negroes were worth their weight in gold, which is the reason why more horses were not taken."

After landing, in the first battle against the Indians, he recounted that: "During all this time Cortés and his horsemen failed to appear, and we feared that they had met with disaster. But then we caught sight of them, though the Indians did not at once see them coming toward their rear. As the plain was level ground, the horsemen were good riders, and the horses were fine gallopers, they quickly speared the enemy as they chose, while we fell on them with such force that they quickly turned tail. They had never seen horses up to this time and thought that the horse and its rider was all one animal."

In the most routine fashion he notes that the Spanish bound up the wounds of the injured soldiers and doctored the horses by searing their wounds with the fat from the body of a dead Indian they cut up.

Like a good reporter Díaz recorded conversation between the *conquistadores* and the natives. "When the Indians questioned the Spaniards about their guns and horses, the Spaniards told them that with the stones they put into the guns they could kill anything they wished, and the horses ran as fast as deer and could catch anything they told them to run after."

While horses thrived in Hispaniola, Jamaica, and Cuba, they were even happier with their environment on the mainland of North America. Breeding farms expanded rapidly in New Spain. Soon it was necessary to have Indians take care of the horses and even to mount them so they could control the extensive herds of cattle. These were the first cowboys, called in New Spain *vaqueros* (*vaca* = cow; *ero* = pertaining to). Yet within the confines of the land which was to be known as Mexico, the Spanish for many years kept the Indians from acquiring their own horses. Ordinances forbade Indians to ride except by special dispensation. And so, from 1519 when the first animals arrived, until the colonization north of the Rio Grande was begun by Juan de Oñate in 1598 near the present city of Santa Fe, New Mexico, the Indians of North and South America were on foot.

The nomadic Apaches were the first Indians to obtain horses in considerable numbers from Spanish settlements. As most of the other tribes would later, the Apaches completely adopted the horse. They rode them, drank their blood, used their hides for shelters, and dined on horseflesh. Soon horses became their most important article of trade.

Indians knew that horses could carry them away from slavery and into a new species of freedom on the plains. Beginning with the Pueblo revolt in 1680, the Indians began to possess horses in considerable numbers. In that uprising, led by Popé, thousands of Indians killed four hundred colonists and missionaries and drove the Spaniards out of New Mexico to the region of El Paso.

Then, for the next two hundred years, the Indians north of the Rio Grande conducted retributive attacks against their Spanish conquerors. Yet the spread of horses among the Indians was gradual. Even as late as 1680 few horses were in Texas and almost none were north of New Mexico. But from 1700 on, mounted Indians began to move across the plains and mountains.

In the early days of the *conquistadores*, however, the Spaniards tried desperately to nourish the myth that the white man and his horse belonged to a special divine race. At first the Indians were astounded by the size and ferocity of the horses, and they believed that the animals were, indeed, gods. One time on the island of Petén, off the Guatemala coast, Cortés was forced to abandon a crippled stallion, a favorite he called El Morzillo. Several years later a band of Franciscan monks arrived at Petén to find a temple built to that horse. The Indians had worshiped El Morzillo as long as he lived, then had stuffed the skin, built the temple for him, and had brought offerings, as to a deity.

The northward spread of the horse was gradual, but the greatest thrust was the exploratory expedition of Francisco Vázquez de Coronado in his search for the gold that many Spaniards thought was held in the legendary Seven Cities of Cibolá. On that great northward adventure in 1540 from the region of Mexico City to the present site of Santa Fe, New Mexico, he took approximately one thousand horses. There is, however, almost no mention of mares being part of the expedition, though two are noted. Because this was a toil of conquest to find those cities of storied wealth, it is reasonable that the horses were taken strictly as mounts for the soldiers, and that mares for breeding purposes would have been unnecessary.

The expedition was a disaster. Instead of golden cities, Coronado and his men found the seven primitive villages of the Zuñi Indians. Nevertheless, he explored the region of the present border of New Mexico and Arizona. Coronado did this for two weary years. Few if any of those one thousand horses survived the journey, many of them being killed and eaten by the Indians. And it would be half a century before another Spaniard went into that sector.

Friar Alonso de Benavides, one of the earliest priests in New Mexico, wrote that no horses nor signs of horses were in New Mexico in 1598 when Oñate arrived. The priest speaks of the Apache Indians but records that they traveled with pack dogs dragging the triangular sled which the early French fur traders had called a *travois*.

Yet in time the Indian got his horse from the Spaniard. As soon as the country was secure against major Indian uprisings, Hernán Cortés and others of his captains started extensive breeding farms or ranches on the huge land grants with which the Spanish Crown rewarded them.

But soon after the New Mexico frontier was established, the Spanish began to lose horses to the Apaches and to the Pueblos. Within twenty years a few Indians learned from their Spanish masters how to care for stock, even how to break and train and breed it. Bartering, stealing, and breeding of horses became the Indians' way of life. Those first settlers of the West, struggling for survival, were clever and able. They captured Spanish soldiers and colonists and traded them back for horses. The fastest horses and mares were stolen in the night and were returned to the invaders in exchange for knives, beads, axes, and members of their tribe who had fallen into enemy hands.

Every effort was made to acquire guns along with horses. But the Spaniards could see how dangerous the acquisition of horses by the Indians was becoming. Trade in firearms was forbidden. However, the French in the eighteenth century had no such scruples. Neither did the English. As French and English traders moved slowly westward from Louisiana into Texas and to the Middle West, they willingly traded guns for horses, food, and slaves. The French especially had no love for the Spanish and were not at all unwilling to arm the Indians against them.

But the French and Spanish settlements, except for the extreme outposts, were far apart, so the major commerce in horses continued to be between Spaniard and Indian. The devout trail-blazing Father Eusebio Kino, who founded and served the earliest mission in New Mexico, wrote in 1701 that each year in January and February the Apaches arrived for their usual animal stealing. He added that after stealing horses they performed other serious damage. The good padre knew his horses and his Indians as well. One of the great endurance riders of all time, Father Kino spent almost half of his waking hours on horseback. He made more than forty trail rides, and many of them were well over one thousand miles long. One arduous ride totaled one thousand five hundred miles from Misión Nuestra Señora de los Dolores, about one hundred miles below the present Arizona-Mexico border, to the Spanish capital at Mexico City. Along the way he said mass and baptized Indians daily. This hard-riding priest was then fifty-one years old. The distance was covered in fifty-one days, an average of almost thirty miles a day.

But Father Kino's Apaches were by no means the only Indians with horses in the beginning of the eighteenth century. The Navajos and Utes were well mounted. Later the Comanches, who became early chieftains of the horseback-riding Indians, were beginning to acquire mounts in west Texas. The Hasini, Caddo, Bidais and, in the plains, the Pawnee, Osage, Kansas, Wichita, and those same Comanches began a new life in a changed environment with the horse as its center.

The Indian not only needed the horse, but at times he even loved him. Here is one Indian's eulogy of the animal, a poetic description called "The War God's Horse Song," translated from the Navajo by Dane and Mary Roberts Coolidge:

"My horse has a hoof like striped agate;
His fetlock is like a fine eagle plume;
His legs are like quick lightning.
My horse's body is like
an eagle-plumed arrow;
My horse has a tail like
a trailing black cloud."

Soon Indian trading parties made long difficult journeys across hundreds of miles to Spanish settlements. Carrying furs, slaves, and buffalo meat and hides, they traded for horses, knives, beads, and saddles. Often a weaker tribe banded together with a stronger one to form such a trading caravan. Encamping within a Spanish settlement or as close to it as possible, they settled down to leisurely pipe-smoking and horse-trading sessions. Typical of such centers was Taos, New Mexico. Friar Serrano wrote that as many as two hundred Indian tepees were pitched adjacent to the Spanish community. Indians with their barking dogs, piles of animal hides, and their wives and children, he said, swarmed over the entire presidio.

The Indians offered male, female, and child slaves plus hides of deer and buffalo for their most coveted possession—horses. The shortsighted Spaniards are recorded as selling a horse for as little as three buffalo hides, the conquerors no doubt forced into such transactions by the cold New Mexico winter. And a healthy ten-year-old Indian girl slave was often given to a Spaniard in exchange for one riding horse or two pack animals. Much of this trading was in direct opposition to ordinances sent out by the Spanish Crown forbidding the enslavement of the Indians by the Spaniards. For despite the royal fiat, Indians at the outposts of the new empire were enslaved in considerable numbers to be trained at the missions as agricultural and domestic workers. Spain, however, did not introduce slavery to the aborigines. Indian custom had included making chattels of those unfortunates captured in intertribal warfare.

The myopia of the Spanish horse-trading policy soon began to catch up with the conquerors, and it militated against them. Not only did the Indians purchase as many horses as they could, but they stole whatever they could grab by the mane and throw a leg over. The Spanish colony in New Mexico became so short of horses that new stock had to be imported from below the Rio Grande. Then began a perpetual cycle of horse stealing. As the Indians became stronger, they raided more often than they traded. No Spanish settlement was safe.

Horses taken by the Indians bred at least as fast as those of the Spanish, while the Indian population multiplied along with the horse population. For, with horses, many more deer and buffalo could be killed, and with more food available the Indian nations grew rapidly. Most tribes used the less fit animals for food, keeping only the best for riding and breeding.

The Spaniards retaliated with stern but ineffectual measures. The death penalty for stealing a horse became well known throughout the West. But no threat could stop the flow of horses and guns to the Indians. By 1750 the Comanches in the Southwest had thousands of horses and had organized their warriors into efficient raiding units.

This Indian nation within less than fifty years became the greatest owner and breeder of horses in the West. Comanche children played with ropes or rawhide lariats along with their bows and arrows. Children were expected to ride almost as soon as they could walk, and riding became the most important skill within the Indian nations. Bridles were little used then, a single strand of rope or sinew or leather serving this purpose when it was tied around the horse's muzzle. And Spanish saddles, traded and stolen for many years, gave way to homemade saddles or simple pads or blankets.

Comanche raiders became so bold that they surrounded the Spanish settlements in San Antonio and, in the face of sanguine opposition from the military garrisons, moved into army corrals and drove the horses away. Comanche cavalry also mounted long desperate forays into the interior of Mexico as far south as Chihuahua and Coahuila. Huge haciendas were surrounded, and the finest horse stock was driven off. Hacienda owners, threatened with death, were told to make sure that the horses left by the raiders were well cared for so that a healthy herd would be available when the raiders returned.

Horse trading was not confined to the Spanish

and the French. Intertribal exchanging of horses was at least as common. As with the Spanish, slaves and women—along with buffalo robes and deer hides—were most generally bartered for horses. By the middle of the eighteenth century, chiefs and warriors often owned hundreds of mounts.

The Comanches boasted that they had more horses than there were stars in the sky. Their economy (as well as that of other Plains tribes) became based almost purely upon the horse.

Horses flourished so in Indian country that by 1770 a dramatic reversal was noted in many areas. For now the Indians—in addition to continuing to supply horses to the French and English for guns— began to make that same trade with the Spanish. Firearms increasingly became part of the mounted life of the tribes. And even in those tribes that did not possess many horses, braves soon learned that a gun eliminated the difference between the man on foot and the man on horseback.

It must not be supposed that the Indians in any manner considered horse stealing an immoral or unethical act. Horses were not conceived of as being God-given instruments of the Spanish. The Indians convinced themselves that horses were meant to be distributed to them. Soon horse stealing became a status symbol in most Indian nations. A young brave could show his courage by going on foot to a Spanish settlement, quietly waiting through the night, untethering or roping a fine mount, silently leading it away, then riding back to his encampment. Thievery of horses was often done on an individual basis and was considered almost as great a test of manhood as the taking of a scalp.

Some night raids involved large numbers of warriors. In at least one instance, young braves made their way to a Spanish stockade where horses and mules were kept behind high walls. They stealthily scaled the walls during the night and waited in the shadows until the stockade gates were opened in the morning. Then, at a signal from the leader, they leaped upon the backs of the horses they had chosen (and which they had silenced by gently stroking during the night) and rode swiftly through the open gate.

But the Indian did not steal exclusively from the Spanish. Horses belonged to whoever could take them and keep them. And the horse gave the Indian a greater opportunity for warfare than ever before. Some nations prospered on warfare, and almost every tribe was at war with a neighboring tribe—usually over horses. Meriwether Lewis and William Clark noted some of these wars as they made their historic march across the Western United States in 1804-6.

Their guide, the Indian woman Sacajawea, who took over when her French trader husband Chaboneau had led them through all the region he was familiar with, had been stolen from the Shoshone. With a remarkable sense of direction, she led Lewis and Clark over an anfractuous trail to her people where, exhausted and foot-weary, they obtained horses. These horses, sold to Lewis and Clark by the Shoshone for knives, guns, and medals, enabled them to travel across the Rocky Mountains and over the Lolo Trail into Idaho. Without the horses they would never have made it, for not only did the animals supply transportation, they were eaten one by one by the exploring party when all other food was exhausted.

One of the most exciting moments on the expedition came when Captain Lewis saw an Indian "mounted on an elegant horse without a saddle, and a small string attached to the under jaw answered as a bridle." This Indian took alarm and did not respond to the signs of friendship that Lewis gave. Two days later, however, they fortunately encountered three Indian women. Convinced the white men meant no harm they accepted some beads, pewter mirrors, and paint, then led Lewis and Clark toward their camp. After proceeding about two miles, the explorers and their new guides were met by "a troop of nearly 60 warriors mounted on excellent horses riding at full speed" toward them. The women showed their ornaments and explained that the white men had not harmed them.

The Shoshone chief and his captains cordially accepted Lewis and Clark.

While in the encampment Captain Lewis learned of the fast horses the Indians hunted deer with. Armed with bows and arrows, some twenty Indians would encircle a herd of antelope. The circle would be slowly tightened until the hunters had gained advantageous positions around the game. At top speed, one group would then ride toward the herd. The antelope soon outstripped the horses, but when the prey reached the other rim of the circle, they were chased back by hunters on fresh horses. Each time they turned, new hunters awaited them. In one of these instances, described in the Meriwether Lewis journal, the antelope succeeded in breaking out of the circle, and the hunters came home without game. It is easy to see how desperately such a people would crave guns for killing game, for, as the journal relates, forty and fifty hunters would sometimes have to ride for half a day without obtaining more than two or three antelope—and sometimes none at all.

The first three horses traded to Lewis and Clark were obtained in exchange for an army uniform coat, a pair of leggings, a few handkerchiefs, three knives, and some other small articles. The journal recounts: "...the whole of which did not, in the U.S., cost more than $20.00." They purchased the fourth one for an old checkered shirt, a pair of used leggings, and a knife. Indians and explorers were pleased with the exchange. There is no doubt that the Shoshone had obtained their horses from the Spaniards, because Captain Clark records that as he was entering the mountains after reconnoitering, he met an Indian with two mules and a Spanish saddle. The Indian was polite enough to offer the explorer use of a mule to ride over the hills. Captain Clark accepted the offer and gave him a waistcoat as a reward for his civility.

By 1805 Spanish horses had fanned out in three directions from old Mexico. In California, Spanish missions had been established as far north as San Francisco. Dolores Mission had been founded there in 1776, and San Jose Mission had been established nearby in 1797. Horses were an important part of the operation at all of the missions. Indians were trained to handle the stock and to tend the fields. From Santa Barbara southward, Spanish and later Mexican ranchers staked out large land grants. Thousands of horses grazed over the luxuriant hills and valleys. And horse stealing again became widespread. One group of Indians became so addicted to robbing ranchers of their horses that the tribe was known throughout the West as the Horse Stealing Indians.

The second stream of horses advanced northward from Santa Fe into Colorado, Wyoming, Idaho, and Montana. The third group, and the largest, extended across New Mexico eastward into Oklahoma, Kansas, Missouri, and Arkansas and southeast into Texas.

When Lewis and Clark met the Shoshone, they were encamped not far from Three Forks, Montana. A completely nomadic people, the Shoshone moved from the shores of the Columbia River, where they fished during the summer, to the Three Forks area, where they hunted buffalo. In speaking of the social life of the Shoshone, the Meriwether Lewis journal records that an infant girl often was betrothed to a grown man, for the man himself or for his son, and that compensation for the girl, who would be delivered to her husband when she was thirteen or fourteen, was made in horses or mules.

Sacajawea had been contracted for in this way before she was taken prisoner. When she returned to the camp with Lewis and Clark, she was immediately claimed by the man to whom she had been promised. However, when he learned she had a child by her common-law husband, the French trader Chaboneau, he rejected her.

Women among the Shoshone assisted in caring for the horses when the tribe was moving. Captain Lewis tells how one woman, who was leading two pack horses, turned the animals over to a friend and stayed behind the pack train. When he asked the chief why she was missing, Lewis was told she had stopped to have her baby. Lewis records his surprise when, about an hour later, the woman passed him carrying her newborn child—both of them apparently in perfect physical condition.

On all expeditions women were in charge of the baggage and loading and unloading the horses. A warrior cared only for his own riding horses. He performed no labor except hunting and fishing, which he did not regard as woman's work. Lewis and Clark recorded that no wild horses were in the regions they traversed but that the original stock was procured from the Spaniards and bred by the Indians. "The horses are generally very fine, of a good size, vigorous and patient of fatigue as well as hunger. Each warrior has one or two tied to a stake near his hut both day and night so as to be always prepared for action."

By the time of the Lewis and Clark explorations, the Indians had learned to emasculate the poorer specimens among their stallions to produce geldings. Meriwether Lewis, after receiving a handsome gelding as a gift from a Chopunnish chief, wrote: "The stone horses [stallions] we found so troublesome that we have endeavored to exchange them for mares or geldings, but although we offered two for one, they were unwilling to barter."

Therefore, it was decided that the stallions should be castrated. But Meriwether Lewis was intent upon determining which method of gelding was better, that used by the Virginia horse breeders or this Indian nation. Consequently, "two were gelded in the usual manner, while one of the natives tried the experiment in the Indian way, without tying the string of the stone [which he assured us was much the better plan] and carefully scraping the string clean and separating it from the adjoining veins before cutting it." Lewis then reported that all the horses recovered but that the horses gelded in the Indian manner did not swell or suffer as much as the others and that they recovered sooner. He concluded: "We are fully persuaded that the Indian method is preferable to our own."

The Shoshone told the explorers they could reach a Spanish settlement in ten days' march by following the Yellowstone River. But the Indians complained that the Spanish refused to let them have firearms, telling them that these were dangerous weapons which would induce them to kill each other. So, having few guns, the Shoshone continued to use the bow and the arrow, the lance, and the buffalo-hide shield.

One other weapon was important to them—the paggamoggon, which consisted of a wooden shaft about two feet long covered with leather. At one end a leather thong two inches long was tied to a leather cover which contained a round stone weighing about two pounds. The other end had a leather loop through which the wrist was slipped so the instrument could not be dropped. They fought from horseback, and with this formidable weapon, swung with force at high speed, a man could easily stun his enemy, and sometimes he could kill him.

A type of armor that would at least deflect the arrow if not the bullet was developed by many of the tribes. The Shoshone used folds of antelope skins stuck together with glue and sand. A large skirt of similar material was made to protect the horse's vital parts.

Indians made halters of buffalo hair plaited or twisted together until it was the size of a man's finger, although sometimes a thong of rawhide was employed for this. The lead was long and, because the horse was in constant use or readiness, was never removed from its neck. One end was tied in a knot around the neck, then brought down to the under jaw, around which it was formed into a noose passing through the mouth. The end was then drawn up on the right side and held by the rider in his left hand while the rest trailed after him. When the horse was put out to graze, the noose was taken from the mouth.

Saddles, copies of the Spanish and French pack and riding saddles, were used mostly by women and older men. A young warrior rode on a leather pad stuffed with buffalo hair and secured by a hide thong running under the horse's belly.

The Indians were the first great ropers in the West. The Lewis journal records that Indians made a noose in the rope, and even though horse and quarry would be running at great speed, the rider rarely failed to throw the rope around the prey's neck. To the Indian the horse became a personal companion, and as it became an important adjunct to warfare, it also became an extension of the Indian's personality — an expression of his wealth, his virility, and his attitudes. Favorite horses were painted, and the ears were often cut, sometimes perhaps to allow the owner to identify his horse in the dark, but more likely for ornamentation. The Indians never cut the manes nor trimmed the tails of their mounts, but they did plait feathers into them as decorations.

It is probable that Lewis and Clark were the first non-Indians to see the horse later to be known as the Appaloosa. The explorers encountered this animal when their route took them over Lemhi Pass, across the almost impassable Lolo Trail in the Bitter Root Mountains. Here they were forced to eat some of the twenty-three horses they had spent so much time gathering from the Shoshone. Others of the horses strayed away.

Travel across the trail was intensely difficult, and for Thursday, September 19, 1804, the journal records that Captain Clark proceeded up the creek along which the road was steeper and stonier than any he had passed. After six miles he reached a small plain in which he fortunately found a horse on which he breakfasted. He hung the remainder on a tree for the party in the rear.

Their path continued through Nez Percé country into the Weippe Prairie and up to Clearwater River. The Nez Percé Indians had horses, and they seem to have been the first to breed the spotted horse that became known throughout the West as the Appaloosa.

The trail followed by Lewis and Clark took them down the Clearwater River past the present twin cities of Lewiston, Idaho, and Clarkston, Washington. They then followed the Snake River and crossed the source of the Palouse River, after which the spotted horses were finally named. In the journal the explorers describe the horses of the Nez Percé, which is what the French traders called those Indians, although the natives' noses were not pierced, as that French designation implies. The native name for this tribe was Chopunnish.

The explorers found the Nez Percé selfish and avaricious, and recorded that they parted very reluctantly with every article of food or clothing that was traded, while expecting to be recompensed for every service no matter how small.

A branch of this tribe lived along the Palouse River, and in time the early colonials came to call that tribe the Palouse Indians. The Appaloosa strain of spotted horse was intensively bred by this tribe. For many generations Appaloosas were bred for spots, and even today on the reservation near Moscow, Idaho, descendants of the Nez Percé — Palouse Indians still breed and race the Appaloosa.

It was not long after the horses came to the New World that the Spanish brought long-horned cattle into Mexico. As the cattle herds increased, horses were bred and trained to handle them. The Spanish Crown continuously encouraged both cattle and horse ranches throughout New Spain. Permanent grants, which included thousands of acres of choice land, were given to anyone who would start a breeding farm or a cattle ranch.

After Mexico won her independence from Spain in 1821, the new government pursued the policy that had been originated by the Spanish Crown. So in the Mexican states of Texas and Coahuila, ranchers who agreed to settle on the land were given grants of 2,451 acres each.

If a farsighted leader organized one hundred families and brought them into the region, not only was each family given the above acreage but the organizer was given five leagues of good grazing land, 22,140 acres. Under Mexican law, settlers coming from Louisiana and Arkansas were welcomed and given grants of first-rate land.

At the same time, the Mexican government in

California was also granting extensive estates to ranchers. Great haciendas were thus created, and large herds of cattle and hundreds of good horses grazed over the fertile California countryside. Again, the horses were descended from Spanish stock.

By the time Texas proclaimed itself independent from Mexico in 1836, ranchers of Anglo-Saxon lineage possessed immense holdings of cattle and horses. When the actual independence was effected, all Texas residents except Indians and Negroes automatically became citizens, and the head of each family was entitled to 4,605 acres (one loyal) of land. Single men were allowed 1,476 acres, while special grants were given to officers and soldiers who fought in the Texas army against Mexico. This liberal land policy contributed greatly to increasing the cattle and horse population of Texas.

Many horses were required to handle the cattle on the open range, which was the land held in the public domain. The government allowed ranchers to graze cattle there so long as they did not fence those lands. Everyone used the open range, which is why branding became so important and why it was necessary to have cowboys keeping suspicious eyes on the herds.

Every possible visual symbol was used, and a great deal of ingenuity was exercised in trying to find designs that could not be easily copied. Although many brands reproduced initials of the owners, and numerous brands used digits such as 6666, there were also more imaginative markings, such as the outline of a hatchet or tomahawk, a question mark, a pistol, or a dollar sign, or even the outline of a horse's head.

To become a successful rancher, it was necessary only to own some breeding stock and a string of good horses, and to hire cowboys at from $10 to $30 per month. A top hand could buy a saddle with a month's wages. Or he could buy three horses. In those days a man usually did not buy land when he arrived in Texas. He invested in cattle, horses, and men, fed his livestock on the free range, then drove the cattle to market. And he saved money by using range beef to feed the men who worked the cattle. Range cattle just after the Civil War could be bought for as little as $1 to $4 per head, and Texas had plenty of them. The cattle drives brought great wealth to the Texas ranchers. But those long trips to the rail heads required tremendous toil of the trail horse and brought a Stetson full of misery to the cowboy who had to nursemaid the cows across almost uncharted wilderness and through perilous Indian country. Big drives after the war consisted of herds numbering from 2,500 to 4,000 head of cattle, which could be handled with twelve to fourteen men. Each man had four to six mounts and at least four mules were needed to haul the chuck wagon with the bedding and the biscuit flour. A drive often included two teams of four mules each.

The cattle moved ten to fifteen miles a day, and if they were properly handled they gained weight along the way. Including the cowboys' wages, food and, in fact, all expenses, a three-month drive from Texas to Abilene, Kansas, cost around $1,500. Profits often were ten times that sum.

Cattle drives from Cook County, Texas, to Abilene followed trails forged by bold men like Jesse Chisholm, the half-breed Cherokee whose wagon wheels cut the famous Chisholm Trail in 1866 when he freighted a load of buffalo hides to his trading post near Wichita. On these epic cattle movements the foreman scouted the land ahead, posting his two most important cowboys on "point," that is, one on either side checking the terrain and assuring that the lead cattle took the best route. Two more cowboys rode "swing" about one-third of the way back along the herd. They would be sure that the cattle would swing in the direction of the lead cattle. Then, about three-quarters of the way back on either side came the "flankers." Bringing up the rear, which was known as "the drag," came the dust-eating, youngest, poorest-paid cowhands. It is probable the expression "it's a drag" came from this unpleasant kind of work.

Cattle drives today are not nearly as big as they once were. But some spreads, such as the 6666 Ranch and the Pitchfork, both in the Guthrie, Texas, area, are vast. Cattle drives last several days.

The cowhand's duties on a working ranch have always been well defined. The horse wrangler has complete charge of the cowboys' mounts when they are not riding them. His specific job is to see that the horses do not scatter too much when they are left free to graze because they have to be rounded up again and roped and saddled each morning. They usually are kept grazing not too far from the chuck wagon, and that wagon is always located near a spot where the horses can water. The horse wrangler usually scouts ahead to find a good grazing spot with water, and the chuck wagon follows. In the old days the connection between horse wrangler and chuck wagon was very close, for it was he who was responsible for getting the fuel for the cook's fire. This fuel was often wood kept in a sling under the chuck wagon, and when wood was not available, cow droppings, called cow chips, were burned. The wrangler also had to put up with the two teams of four mules each to pull the chuck wagon. These were traditionally Spanish mules descended from ancient stock and preferably of a dun color.

In the old days, and even until fairly recently in the West, the cowboy worked sixteen hours a day and usually put in two more hours of night duty. A wrangler rode twelve to fifteen miles a day either in his search for a camp site or to keep the *remuda* (the extra horses) moving with the chuck wagon. Because of a mustang's innate wildness, every cowboy promptly learned never to unsaddle his horse until he had roped the mount he planned to ride next and had everything ready for saddling him.

A good cow horse holds his head high and is always alert. Some cowboys believe you can tell how intelligent a horse is by the way he handles his ears. They say that when he moves one ear forward and the other backward and then quickly reverses the process, it gives some indication of his thinking ability. At least it shows that he has good reflexes. The horse which, when he hears a noise, puts both ears forward and never flicks either back, is not considered by most cowboys to be as valuable.

A wrangler, after a comparatively short time working with the *remuda*, learned to identify horses, even at some distance, by the shape of their heads or the way they moved. Because of the loneliness of the cowboy's life on the range, the relationship between horse and man grew very close. They learned to depend upon each other. There are many stories about how horses have taken their disabled riders to safety and how they found food or water when man's directional instinct had given out. But there are few accounts about how dependent a horse can become upon a man.

One such tale tells how a cowboy had a horse that wandered away from his overnight encampment and, when he tried to catch him, kept moving just out of reach. So the cowboy gave up, went back and put out the fire, packed all his gear and, in high-heeled discomfort, began walking away from the camp carrying everything with him. The horse looked up and watched for a couple of minutes, then quickly cantered back past the camp site, caught up with the departing cowboy and stood quietly while he was bridled and saddled. Of course, the stories are numerous, too, about the horses that are liable to buck and bite and kick and dance no matter how lengthy their relationship with a man.

The cowboy's most important equipment after finding himself a good horse is a good saddle with a pommel that will take the tremendous pull of a two-year-old heifer when the heifer is jumping on the end of a rope. All cowboys take great pride in the quality of their boots and hats.

Old-time cowboys always undressed from the bottom up and dressed from the top down. A cowboy would first take off his boots, never removing the spurs, then take off his socks, strip off his hide-hugging pants, take off his shirt, and finally remove his hat and set his boots carefully on the rim — it just might blow away. When he dressed, he started at the top, putting on his hat, shirt, pants and, finally, socks and boots.

The ordinary cowboy's job consisted of picking up cattle and horses that wandered away from the herds and needed feeding, of putting out salt, greasing the windmills and repairing them, classifying the cattle, separating the cows and calves, moving the cattle to good summer pasture, branding the stock in early and midsummer, cutting out the yearling steers and two-year-old heifers, seeing that the bulls had access to the cows for breeding purposes, and putting up and repairing fences. Two roundups, one in the spring and another in the fall, were the busiest times of the year, just as they are on the large ranches today. Most calves are born in the spring, and in the summer a special branding is set aside for the calves. After the fall roundup, the stock goes into the winter pastures.

On some early cattle ranches breeding was not selective. But on others, especially in Texas and New Mexico, fast horses were mated to fast horses, and good-working, alert, or smart animals to other good workers. How a horse appeared was not important. What mattered was how fast he could run, whether he knew how to stand during calf roping, and whether he could outthink a bull calf.

Although most of the Indians were on reservations by the time the major Texas cattle drives began, they were still a hazard. As the buffalo population was wiped out between 1870 and 1880, the government began to provide free beef for the Indians on the reservation. But the Indians did not always react favorably to their subsidized way of life and would often stampede cattle being driven so that they could be hired to round them up. Indian territory and the reservations had also become refuges for white renegades, who stole cattle and horses.

If a horse thief was apprehended in Texas in the 1890's he got five to fifteen years in the penitentiary, if he was lucky. If not, he was promptly shot or lynched. In contrast, a thief who stole money or other goods was rarely sentenced to more than two years. But horses were considered a very special kind of property, an extension of the cowboy himself.

As the cattle were filling up the grazing lands, the buffalo were being methodically exterminated. They were killed off not by the Indians, who hunted them for meat and hides, but by well-organized white hunters, who were primarily interested in buffalo hides and buffalo robes that were bringing good prices in the Eastern towns and cities. Between 1870 and 1880, as the railroad cut the track of a new era across the virgin plains, it carried in hundreds of hunters and shipped out thousands of buffalo hides.

One of the great pioneers in the West, Charles Goodnight, one of whose ranches was near Amarillo, Texas, had so many buffalo around his ranch that he decided to try crossing Longhorn cows with them. He matched buffalo studs with the Longhorn cows and created a long-horned brindled calf with a buffalo hump. He had hoped to develop a new kind of cattle that would withstand the Texas heat and that could forage as the buffalo did. But although a few calves were born, the mothers almost invariably died. The experiment was a failure.

It remained for the King Ranch to develop the only new strain of Texas cattle, called Santa Gertrudis. They were formed by breeding shorthorn cows to Brahman bulls from India. They imported shorthorn cows because the Longhorns could not stand the heat of southern Texas as well as the Brahman-shorthorn combination. The Brahman bulls were developed and reared in the hot sultry plains of southern India, so they adapted perfectly to the Texas climate. But, of course, they could not ever replace the buffalo.

So by 1880 — in one decade — the buffalo in the southern regions of the United States was gone. It took about five more years for the northern buffalo to be exterminated. With the death of the buffalo, the Indians were without food, clothing, and shelter, for the buffalo had provided all three. As a result, a considerable number of ranchers made a great deal of money out of government contracts to supply beef on the hoof to the reservations. The Indians had no choice but to become dependent upon these government handouts. In 1870, for instance, the government purchased 12 1/2 million pounds of beef for the Indians. A year later the purchases were over twice as much. And by 1872 the relief supply was up to forty million pounds of beef on the hoof, of which the Sioux alone accounted for twenty-six million pounds.

Yet this was not enough to keep the Indians happy. Horse and cattle raids continued to be staged, especially in northern Texas. In Bandera, Texas, as early as 1854 a Mormon colony headed by Lyman Wight had been moving across the country when the Comanches killed one of their heifers and stole eight horses. The Mormons sent men to pursue them. After hard riding for two days, the boys overtook the Indians, killed one and wounded three others. They came back with all of their animals and six of the Comanches', including their bows, shields, and lances.

Lyman Wight wrote to Major Robert S. Neighbor, Indian agent, on March 18, 1855: "Two more Indian depredations of the most savage character [occurred] on the 16th instant. They took the opportunity while we were at dinner and drove off sixteen horses, all we had but one, and that was gone from home. This prevented our following them as they had got an hour or more head start and our neighbors 11 miles off and no way of sending an express as most of us was down with sickness. The 17th we spent in hunting our cattle and got them into a yard late in the evening. This morning the 18th we found two of them cut to pieces in a savage manner and twenty-five oxen drove off. We thought last fall when we gave you such a list of Indian depredations that we were perfectly broken up as that was our feeling then.

"While Congress is spending six or eight months to find out whether it is best to reinforce the army or not, the Indians are killing men, women and children and driving off large quantities of stock and nothing to hinder. We make this one more appeal to Government and if this fails we have but one alternative and that is to abandon the frontiers all together. The horses we have had stolen this time are worth $60 a piece."

Major Neighbor's reply from San Antonio, Texas, March 26, 1855: "Gentlemen: I am in receipt of your communication of the 18th instant and much regret that the Indians have done your settlement such serious damages. The Indian agents have done all in their power to quiet the Indians; but so long as the military branch of the government continue to harass the friendly Indians and make indiscriminate war on them we must expect a continuance of Indian depredations. By General Smith's orders the Lipans have been driven away from the control of the Indian agents and are now in Mexico, and in connection with and encouraged by thieving Mexicans, are continually depredating on the frontier. By the movements of the troops under Capt. Calhoun from Ft. Chadbourne all the Southern Comanches have been driven to hostilities and are now depredating our frontiers. It is impossible for the Indian agents to make peace, or quiet the Indians until the troops stop making war with the Indians. It will also be impossible for me to make any progress in settling down and quieting the Indians until the troops are brought out of the Indian country—they are now in the Comanches' hunting ground and the Comanches are compelled to live in or near our settlements where there are no troops to harass them. So you may thank Gen. Smith for the presence of Comanches in your homes." If more men in those days had possessed and demonstrated the foresight and compassion that Major Neighbor did, the ravages by men white and red might not have been so frequent and enduring.

Upon hearing that the Choctaw Indians were stealing horses in the region of Kickapoo Creek in Young County, Texas, John Middleton went out after some of the horse stealers. He divided his men and they approached on different sides of the encampment. The chief came out and said they were there to hunt peaceably and wished no harm to anyone. Middleton answered that the Choctaws had been horse stealing all over the countryside. The chief said the horse stealing was being performed by wild Indians, not by his civilized tribe. Middleton replied he did not know wild Indians from tame ones and they had better get out of the area. They left that day, moving into Palo Pinto County. But there another group of Texans accused them again of horse stealing and made them move on.

There is no question but that some of the Texans were as callous as any Indian — and certainly as bloodthirsty. A story is told about Colonel John R. Baylor, who was riding with some of his friends when they saw seven Indians riding some distance ahead. The chief was wearing a headdress with silver plates mounted on a wide leather strap that reached from his head to his feet. Baylor told his party to watch while he shot off one of the plates. He fired, knocked off the plate, and wounded the Indian. Then they charged the Indians, and when one of them tried to carry the wounded chief away, he was shot down. The chief died soon afterward. When the body of the chief was found near a stream, the strap with the silver plates was sent to Colonel Baylor as a memento.

And this: A Texan named Van Burns fighting in one of the minor Indian battles and riding a very fast mare left the party to chase an Indian and, according to John Middleton, returned within five minutes with the Indian's scalp.

Indians, therefore, were not the only savages doing the scalping during the horse raid wars in Texas. During those fights many white men dyed their faces and arms, dressing as Indians so the Indians would be blamed for the horse stealing. Middleton points out that in a Comanche area an Indian horse stealer was killed, his arm was cut off and carried down to the settlement, and when

washed thoroughly it proved to be that of a white man. Occasionally, white men masquerading as Indians led Indian groups on such raids.

There were even instances when Indians stole the horses from the settlers, the settlers recovered them from the Indians, and then the Indians stole them a second time.

In a hand-to-hand battle with a Texan named Culver, an Indian was wounded, but after being shot jumped into the saddle on Culver's horse and escaped. By the blood the Indian was losing, however, Culver trailed him until nightfall and most of the next day. At the end of the trail, Culver found the Indian lying dead on a rock. Hitched to a tree nearby — for Indians knew the value of good horses — Culver found his mount.

When the Indians stole horses and the settlers pursued them, if the horses were recovered they were distributed to their original owners. But the pursuers also took all of the Indians' horses and distributed them among the pursuing party, some of them going to settlers who earlier had lost their horses in Indian raids.

After the Civil War deserters from the Confederate Army moving through Texas toward California were responsible for a considerable amount of horse stealing, for they liberated as many horses as they needed while they traveled through.

In east Texas, escaped Negro slaves sometimes stole horses and drove them into Mexico where they could feel relatively free. Occasionally, heinous mistakes were made, however, as in one case cited by R. H. Williams. "Five of us," he said, "were sent off by our commander [in the Confederate Army] to catch up with seven armed Negroes who were supposed to be driving stolen horses into Mexico. After chasing them for three days, we finally discovered that they were only two Negroes and that they were driving their master's horses under orders to a hacienda across the Mexican border."

When the Confederate Army held San Antonio, Texas, atrocities were committed against the

Mexicans and the Indians as well as against other citizens who refused to take the oath of allegiance to the Confederacy. Captain Duff had given orders to his soldiers that raiders were to be given no quarter; no prisoners were to be taken.

With the advent of barbed wire after the Civil War, stockmen on large ranches, whose cattle were being grazed for market, began to fence large areas of public-domain land. The cowboys did not like fencing, for this unnatural prohibition meant that horses were often cut and scratched by running into the barriers, and in addition it was necessary to put up the fences and ride along them to see that they were not cut. On some ranches cowboys were known to have put up fences during the day and taken them back down at night — to keep their jobs and to maintain the range free and open. Yet on the whole a fenced range was economical for the ranchers in two ways. It actually required fewer hands to guard the cattle, and the owner knew that if he had good bulls they were servicing his own cows rather than someone else's.

Ranchers got by with fencing public lands for some years, and when the government during the Theodore Roosevelt administration insisted that all fences be taken down, many stockmen tried grazing their cattle within the Indian reservations. The Indians were given a small rental fee and were paid either in money or in cattle. One such contract was for three million acres at two cents per acre per year and this enabled the rancher to fence the reservation land. However, the Department of Indian Affairs frowned upon this practice, and although the cattlemen pressured the government, the practice was finally declared illegal.

Texas fever was one of the problems faced by cattle raisers as they drove their herds north. Texas cattle brought the disease north into Kansas and Missouri. After a couple of serious outbreaks, the ranchers in those states organized to stop the cattle drives. Often with guns ready they met the cowboys coming north and would not let the cattle or cowboys enter the state. The disease seemed to strike only in the summer so the drovers were sometimes forced to wait on the plains until winter to continue the northward drive. This resulted in the death of thousands of cattle and slowed down the movement of beef from Texas to the Northern states.

The confrontation became quite dangerous between the ranchers bringing their cattle north and the farmers in Kansas and Missouri. In some cases, the Northern men not only threatened to kill, but actually shot the Texas cattle — and sometimes gunned down the men driving them.

The Western ranges became an arena of violence, not only for the men who opposed one another, but for the thousands of wild stallions. One such encounter was dramatically narrated by Sewell Ford in a memorable short story about a black Thoroughbred that had reverted to a wild state and a buckskin mustang that opposed his leadership.

He wrote: "There ensued such a battle as would have brought delight to the brute soul of a Nero. With forefeet and teeth the two stallions engaged, circling madly about on their hind legs, tearing up great clods of turf, biting and striking as opportunity offered. At last, by a quick, desperate rush, the buckskin caught the thoroughbred fairly by the throat. Here the affair would have ended had not the black stallion, rearing suddenly on his muscle-ridged haunches and lifting his opponent's forequarters clear of the ground, showered on his enemy such a rain of blows from his iron-shod feet that the wild buckskin dropped to the ground, dazed and vanquished.

"Standing over him, with all the fierce pride of a victorious gladiator showing in every curve of his glistening body, the black thoroughbred trumpeted out a stentorian call of defiance and command. The band, that had watched the struggle from a discreet distance, now came galloping in, whinnying in friendly fashion.

"Black Eagle had won his first fight. He had won the leadership. By right of might he was now chief of this free company of plains rangers. It was for him to lead whither he chose, to pick the place and hour of grazing, the time for watering, and his to guard his company from all dangers."

No matter how feral a once-domesticated horse may become in his free state, or how long the wild state lasts, if he is returned to captivity, he becomes domesticated quickly. It seems very easy for this formerly free animal to take up the habits of the tame ones around him. Within days, and sometimes within hours, providing the horse had formerly been domesticated, he can be led about on a halter and soon ridden.

In wild-horse country, the sight of a stallion alone, yet still standing with dignity, indicates a crisis has occurred in a herd. A younger stallion, or maybe even an older one, might have defeated him in a fight, forcing him to leave his mares and to roam alone, at least until — by theft or in personal battle — he acquires another string of mares.

When stallions fight they bite, kick, and even wrestle one another, holding with their forelegs. The weaker one is often forced to the ground. He seldom gets up to triumph.

As leader of a herd the stallion allows no interference from outside with his females or their foals. After young males grow to full strength, however, they often dispute his leadership. Then a fight is inevitable. But many of the young horses, rather than challenge a strong and established sire, or submit to his domination, will quit the herd to start searching for a weaker herd leader to attack.

Today's wild horse is often called a mustang — a word probably derived from corrupting the Spanish *mesteño* (of the ranch) or *mostrenco* (strayed). He generally is larger than either of his ancient ancestors, the tarpan or the Przewalski. Yet mustangs are not as large as horses bred in captivity. They are self-sufficient and live on difficult ranges, sometimes as high as seven thousand feet. Water is their biggest problem because to survive they must have water at least every two to three days.

Professional hunters of wild horses use a variety of techniques to catch the powerful and alert animals, which like to stay in their own territory. Most of these "mustangers" carry supplies enabling them to camp near the herd and, if possible, between the horses and their water supply. Mustangers hunt and capture wild horses either to break them or sell them. And sometimes that sale is for only what the mustangers can receive for the horse's hide, or for the entire animal at the slaughterhouse. They learned from the Indians to encircle the quarry on their own mounts, causing the wild animals to make increasingly shorter turns until they can be driven into a box canyon or surrounded by men and be roped.

Another method of capture used to be creasing. But Ramon F. Adams, in his book *Western Words*, says creasing was rarely successful. He wrote:

"The act consists of shooting with a rifle so that the bullet grazes only the cords in the top of the animal's neck just in front of the withers, about an inch or so deep, close to the spinal column. This causes a wound which temporarily paralyzes a nerve center connected with the spinal cord and the brain and knocks the horse down. He is thus stunned long enough for the hunter to tie him down before he recovers. Success with this method calls for expert marksmanship and an abundance of luck … For every horse captured in this way, fifty were killed."

J. Frank Dobie, in his work *The Mustangs*, also stresses the barbarity of this method, which he called "a kind of a sport — without sportsmanship." Dobie wrote:

"If a rifleman wanted to kill a horse, he did not aim to crease it; if he aimed to crease, he frequently killed … Most bullets either missed or killed. Some men aimed at a spot close to the withers, some 'about a foot' behind the ears." Dobie said creasing apparently was brought to the West from the Old South. He added: "Woodsmen learned that the solution from a rain-soaked sack of salt hung in a tree would bring wild horses as well as deer to lick the ground beneath. A man would secrete himself near one of these prepared salt licks to kill deer and crease horses. One ambusher, a Frenchman, knocked a horse down, ran with halter, fastened it on the victim's head, tied the rope to the tree under the salt sack, waited for the horse to rise, and then discovered that he had broken its neck."

Among other methods practiced was snaring. In this procedure — much more successful than creasing — a cowboy made a noose with his lariat and placed it near a lure, such as a salt lick, then drew it up when the horse stepped into it. Sometimes a noose was dropped from a tree, where a mustanger sat hidden.

But the most common method was, and still is, the chase. And the chase usually is long, and it is in the theme of a cat-and-mouse game being played by man and animal. For a wild horse moves with great swiftness and agility, and although he is curious about man he also is wary enough not to let the stranger come too close. The old-time mustangers kept at the chase day and night, leaving the wild ones little time to eat or sleep. They did allow them to reach water at reasonable intervals, however, because taking on water slowed them down.

Wild stallions have been known to attack men, charging at them and driving them off. But they would rather keep moving away as long as possible. Cornered, they will use hoofs and teeth to fight, whether man is on horseback or on foot. Sometimes, however, they can be led into a dead-end trap by running a tame horse or two into the wild band, then roping the mustangs when they follow the tame lure into a trap. This technique has been successful for generations in India where tame elephants are used to lead the wild ones into captivity.

When rounding up horses in rough country, two men are a lot better than one, for a long, hard relay run is usually required to exhaust the heart of a mustang and permit him to be cornered.

One way to tame a wild horse is to trim his feet so close that it is painfully difficult for him to walk, much less to run or buck. Many years ago mustang-

ers started resorting to this procedure in order to get an animal accustomed to the corral. They still do it.

But after considerable breaking to the corral and the saddle, and to man himself, some horses are just too ornery to ride. Bret Harte's description of a tameless mustang is a timeless classic. In "Chu Chu" he wrote: "I approached her gently. She shot suddenly into the air, coming down again on perfectly stiff legs with a springless jolt. This she instantly followed by a succession of other rocket-like propulsions, utterly unlike a leap, all over the enclosure. The movements of the unfortunate Enríquez were equally unlike any equitation I ever saw. He appeared occasionally over Chu Chu's head, astride of her neck and tail, or in the free air, but never IN the saddle. His rigid legs, however, never lost the stirrups, but came down regularly, accentuating her springless hops. More than that, the disproportionate excess of rider, saddle, and accoutrements was so great that he had, at times, the appearance of lifting Chu Chu forcibly from the ground by superior strength, and of actually contributing to her exercise! As they came toward me, a wild tossing and flying mass of hoofs and spurs, it was not only difficult to distinguish them apart, but to ascertain how much of the jumping was done by Enríquez separately. At last Chu Chu brought matters to a close by making for the low-stretching branches of an oak tree which stood at the corner of the lot. In a few moments she emerged from it — but without Enríquez."

Wild mares (and tame ones too, for that matter) always try to return to where they dropped their foal the previous year. Most foals, wild or tame, are born at night, probably because the possibility of other animals attacking is less at night. By sunup mare and foal are both ready to move at a fairly rapid stride.

A well-fed horse sleeps only a few hours out of each twenty-four, rarely more than three or four, and that sleep usually is taken between midnight and daylight. Most of the time he sleeps standing, although young horses, and occasionally older ones, may lie down in the sun for a nap. So they graze all day and most of the night too, for a horse on the range is often hungry, and when he is hungry he is restless. He crops the grass closer than a cow does but not as close as a camel. In Arabia it is said a horse would starve where a camel would find feed.

Drama and romance entered the life of the Western horse when the Pony Express galloped onto the scene in 1860. To carry the mail swiftly across the Rocky Mountains through hostile Indian country was an enterprise that took iron-bottomed horses and rawhide men. As a business enterprise it was a failure. But it was an undying success as Western tradition and legend.

A Californian, Senator William H. Guin, originated the idea six years before the service was inaugurated. While traveling on horseback between San Francisco and Montana on a business trip Guin realized that mail and important messages could be delivered speedily if a relay of riders could make a nonstop trip between St. Louis, Missouri (the railroads went that far), and San Francisco.

Three years after Guin's historic trip, gold was discovered in Colorado. The Rocky Mountains were in great need of communication and, like California, could pay for it. Guin's idea was adopted in 1860 by the largest freight-carrying firm in the West, Russell, Majors, and Waddell. This company financed a new venture, The Central Overland California and Pike's Peak Express, to be known forever after as the Pony Express.

Riders carrying the mail westward mounted their horses in St. Joseph, Missouri, raced on to Julesburg, Colorado, then across to Fort Laramie, Wyoming, and on to Fort Badger, Wyoming; Salt Lake City, Utah; Carson City, Nevada; and finally to Sacramento, California, a sprint of almost two thousand miles. From Sacramento the rider with his mail pouch took the river boat to San Francisco. When Indian trouble or weather interfered, an alternate route took the mail to Denver, Colorado, up

to Fort Halleck, Wyoming, on to Fort Bridger, and into Salt Lake City. A Pony Express rider was in the saddle fifty to one hundred miles, depending upon the distance between major rest and remount stockades. The horses could not stand the pace for long, so new mounts were available at remount stations every fifteen to twenty miles, and stockades were necessary around those stations in or on the edge of hostile Indian country. By the first day of the mail run, eighty riders had been employed, and they had the use of four hundred of the toughest, fastest cow ponies ever bridled. The first two riders, one in St. Joe, the other heading east from San Francisco, began the first race across country on April 3, 1860. They passed each other in Carson City, Nevada, but there was no time for greetings. Both riders kept moving in opposite directions. The first venture required thirteen days. Thereafter, the mail was carried once a week in each direction.

The precious cargo, often including gold certificates and negotiable securities as well as important news, was carried in four leather-covered, watertight pockets that fitted over the pommel of the saddle. It was held in place by the saddle horn and the rider's legs. This mail pouch, called a *mochila*, had four locks. Three compartments contained the transcontinental dispatches and could be opened only with the proper key. And that key was in company hands — at the end of the run. The other pocket, which was also locked, could be opened with a key held by the postmaster at each important mail drop along the way. A *mochila* fully packed weighed twenty pounds. It is a great credit to the men who carried them that few were ever lost or stolen.

When the Pony Express started, postage was $5 per half ounce. Later the rate went down to as low as $1 per half ounce, the cheapest mail rate Pony express ever offered. But this was the airmail of the time. The horses were said to fly over the miles between Missouri and California.

From Sacramento the mail was rushed onto the fast river steamer, the *Antelope*, for the voyage to

San Francisco. The first thirteen-day deliveries from St. Joe to San Francisco included this boat ride. Thanks to experience and shortcuts, the service was improved considerably. Just eleven months later Abraham Lincoln's inaugural address was delivered in seven days and seventeen hours. On the first trip the *mochila* contained only twenty-five letters. On the last one, 150 were enclosed. On one of the record runs, news of the opening shots of the Civil War sped across the West in just eight days and fourteen hours.

Buffalo Bill Cody claimed he was only fourteen years old when he signed on as a Pony Express rider, and no one has successfully contested the claim. He is said to have made the fastest endurance ride on record: 322 miles in twenty-four hours and forty minutes. Not surprisingly, he used up twenty-one horses on that run. The well-armed riders and fast ponies could usually cope with Indian attacks by outrunning, outshooting, or outmaneuvering them. But a few riders never finished their runs. Indians delighted in stealing the fast horses from the less protected remount stations and occasionally attacked a major stockade, burning it to the ground. One of the best-known Indian fighters among the Pony Express riders was Pony Bob Haslam, who carried the mail and fought off Indians all the time the service lasted.

But a new kind of competition was developing that could outrun any horse. In the race against the magnetic electric impulse of the telegraph, the horse could not win. Each day telegraph poles continued their inevitable march across the plains and mountains. Thin lines of wire were stretched from the West to meet the lines coming from the East. As the distance between them lessened, the length of the Pony Express route shortened. Finally, after the telegraph lines met on October 24, 1861, the Pony Express became extinct. Yet it lived on in the Wild West shows, in lurid paperback novels dramatizing the exploits of the riders, and in the tall stories of the old-timers.

There were many extraordinary riders in the old West and among the legendary ones was Ellie Newman, a man outside the law and a storied horseman. Newman once rode 150 miles on a Spanish mustang without even letting the horse stop to graze. He was a firm believer that in endurance running as much depended upon the rider as upon the horse. Newman, quoted by the late J. Frank Dobie, once said, "The last six inches in a man's backbone must be flexible enough to ease the horse as it moves." Some riders are a dead weight while others sit lightly in the saddle.

The flamboyant Colonel John C. Frémont, who became a California hero deservedly or not, once rode from Los Angeles to Monterrey, Mexico, a distance of 850 miles, in nine days. He used up seventeen horses. But of all the great riders in Western history, none ever measured up to Francois Xavier (Little) Aubry, sometimes called Little Audrey. It is possible that the Little Aubry (or Audrey) stories famous throughout the West for many, many years — tales describing the impossible feats of a diminutive cowboy — were based on some of Aubry's exploits. Although he made many incredibly fast horseback journeys, his greatest feat was riding from Santa Fe, New Mexico, to Independence, Missouri, a distance of eight hundred miles, in six days. He was carried by a favorite yellow mare called Dolly, which in one stretch sped him for twenty-six hours without a stop. Later, Dolly was wounded in an Indian fight, and Aubry noted, "She gave out on account of her wound." Because starvation was an immediate prospect, he was forced to eat his favorite mount. However, he did express a certain amount of regret.

A still-standing record for a race on a Western horse goes to Frank Hopkins, who rode a dun stallion the 1,799 miles from Galveston, Texas, to Rutland, Vermont. This magnificent horse had been captured in a wild herd. He had black mane and tail, hard black hoofs, and a heavy dark line (like many Appaloosas have) down his back. The 1,799-mile ride took Hopkins thirty-one days, an average of fifty-eight miles a day. This race from Galveston north offered a considerable stake to the winner. Hopkins' dun stallion, seven years old and sinewy, passed every rider. They arrived in Rutland two days before the second rider rode wearily into town.

But most Western horses were used for more mundane tasks. Among other feats, they pulled the Conestoga wagons carrying the pioneers and their possessions. And the stagecoach that carried the great bulk of Easterners who reached the West in the fifties and sixties was drawn by six matched horses.

Corresponding with those movements was the activity of the freight caravans moving north from Mexico, carrying household goods shipped from Spain, altars for the Catholic missions, and carvings of saints. And this freight was pulled — not by horses nor steam engines — but by mules. Also, it was the mule that brought the plows, the delicate English and French antiques, the lace curtains and all manner of valuables from East to West. Besides the drumming of the hoofbeats of the mustangs and the staccato cadence of the cowboy's running horse, the crack of the muleteer's whip and the hoarse cry of "hi-yah" or "giddap" rang across the silent mountains and valleys.

The sure-footed, lethargic, but dependable mules were a giant contrast to the fleet, sensitive, and high-strung horses of the West. The contribution of the mule to the movement of civilization to the Western states was an important one, notable enough to deserve a book devoted to the mule alone. But mine is a book about horses, and although there is a slight family resemblance, the mule is not a horse. He is the product of breeding a male ass to a female horse. This is not easily accomplished, for asses and horses do not normally breed with one another.

Cross breeding to produce a mule was probably discovered in pre-Biblical times, for in the thirty-sixth chapter of Genesis in the King James version of the Bible, the Edomites and Hosites are recorded as having bred mules.

Genesis 36:24 reads: "And these are the chil-dren of Zibeon; both Ajah, and Anah: this was that Anah that found the mules in the wilderness, as he fed the asses of Zibeon his father."

From this evidence and the fact that ancient Egyptian kings and queens are shown with mules, we can say it is probable the practice of mule breeding began in Southwest Asia and spread throughout the Mediterranean regions.

Christopher Columbus was given a mule to ride to the court of Isabel and Fernando but not — as many historians have recorded — as an insult to the Admiral of the Ocean Sea. Indeed the opposite was true. Their Catholic Majesties, believing that their emissary had been badly treated, furnished him with a mule, the safe and easy riding animal used in fifteenth-century Spain by bishops and kings.

At the time of the conquest of Mexico, Spain had raised the practice of mule breeding to an art. Techniques for isolating mares in heat and forcing them to breed with asses were developed. Thousands of asses were exported to the Western colonies to be bred to mares. But because the mule is sterile he was of less value to the Indians than the horse. Because of his excellent sense of balance and sure-footed gait, however, he was of inestimable worth to the early settlers from Spain and to the European pioneers who crossed the United States from East to West.

Yet even in those days, when the Concord coaches were carrying men and money across the Western mountains, thousands of once-domesticated horses that had become wild were still thundering across the hills and valleys in an effort to elude the thrust of civilization. Travelers' diaries record that great herds could be seen, and great pyramids of manure along the trails indicated the areas frequented by the feral horses.

Wild horses by the hundreds even today roam the hidden hills, steep canyons, and lonely mesas of the Far Western states. One of the largest concentrations of these free-ranging animals covers a wide stretch of the most rugged terrain in the United States. This pocket of safety, this land of freedom for horses, is in the northern tip of Wyoming where the Montana border cuts through the colorful Pryor Mountain range. It is a land where automobiles and jeeps or men on foot are at a disadvantage. It takes sharp hoofs and highly developed muscles of four-legged animals with an instinct for survival to cope with the awesome forces of nature in this far-away country. Water holes are infrequent. The steep cliffs are inaccessible to man. The horses own the country at an altitude of from six thousand to ten thousand feet, and there is little level land except on the mesas. Foraging for food is always difficult. In addition to the hardships inherent in the elements, predators — mountain lions and bears — often attack young horses. Elk, deer, and antelope eat the plant life. Survival is a constant struggle against nature.

Some three hundred mares, foals, and stallions (the number constantly changes) have frequented this high country over the years. Some herds may go back to the earliest Spanish stock, but most of them have mixed with domesticated animals that have escaped from ranches within the past generation. In recent years this range has been generally protected by ranchers in the surrounding area, men who have from time to time captured and redomesticated some of the wild ones for ranch use.

Now this free range, the only one of its kind in the world, is officially protected by the United States government. A 31,000-acre wild-horse refuge has been established in the Pryor Mountain area. Here the horses will be free from intrusion by man. They will live out their lives in a natural state, breeding, fighting, and dying without interference. On this open range bounded by the Custer National Forest on the northwest, Crooked Creek on the west, the Pryor Mountains on the south, and Big Horn Lake and the Big Horn Mountains on the east, visitors will be able, through their binoculars (and sometimes without them), to see these free, high-spirited horses in a natural environment.

But this region is not the only home of the wild horses of the New World. Herds still roam the Mexican highlands and, in the United States, herds are well established in both the Northwest and the Southwest.

While the wild-horse population may be expected to increase, it will be nothing like the phenomenal increase in the total number of horses in the West during the past ten years. In every section the horse population has more than doubled since 1959. It seems impossible but the recent surveys by the U.S. Department of Agriculture show that the total horse population in the United States increased approximately three times between 1959 and 1968. More than one million foals are born each year. There are now over seven million horses in the United States, with the majority of them in the West. At the present time, Texas and California lead the country in the number of horses within their borders.

This, then, is a sketchbook about the horses of the West — their past and their present. The following chapters will take up the major breeds individually. Almost every Westerner has some preference. But be it Quarter Horse or Arabian, Thoroughbred or Appaloosa, the horse is increasing rapidly in the regions to which he first brought civilization some 375 years ago.

No longer does the horse in the West belong to tradition and legend. He is not a relic of the past but belongs to the present. On small farms (usually referred to as ranches no matter how small) extensive breeding farms, cattle ranches, rental stables, and in back yards, the horse is part of the social and economic life of today's West. In some areas he has been fenced in. Highways and freeways cut through green hills and rock-strewn mountains. But bordering them and within the ever-rising towns and cities are man's most important link to nature, the horses of the West.

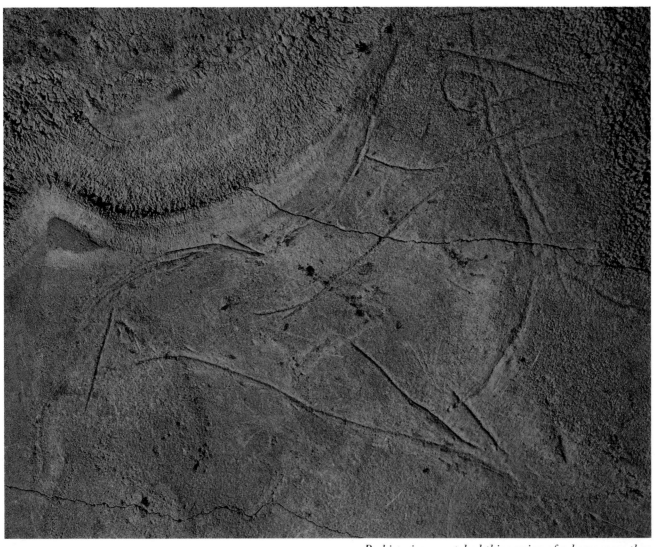

*Prehistoric man etched this version of a horse more than ten thousand years ago in a cave at Altamira in northern Spain.*

# THE HORSE IN ART, FROM EUROPE AND ASIA TO THE NEW WORLD

Cro-Magnon man first recorded the horse in the latter part of the Stone Age, the high Paleolithic period which is dated roughly from twenty thousand years to eight thousand years before Christ. Within this epoch, cave art represented the animals men hunted or possibly worshiped. Paintings, which included horses, bison, mammoths, deer, and goats, reached a high level in caves of western Europe, especially in what is now southwestern France and northwestern Spain. From them we know that wild horses quite similar to the modern horse roamed western Europe some twenty thousand years ago. Horses were not domesticated for another fifteen thousand years. Sometime between 5000 B.C. and 2000 B.C., after the reindeer, elephant, and cattle had learned to live with man, the first horses were tamed. From that earliest beginning, the horse has been used in war, pleasure, work, and recreation.

*A horse trainer is seen on this pottery vessel dating to the time of the Phoenicians. The scene may depict an early circus.*

The domestication of the horse gave mobility to the people of central Europe and southwest Asia. Tribes that otherwise could not have survived became nomadic, following their cattle and sheep and goats as the animals grazed. Food on the hoof that eluded them fell prey to a rider with a spear or bow and arrow. Horses also were used as pack animals and trade goods, while mare's milk was a staple. A horse and a woman were traded at equal value. Horses shared the tents of their owners, and as man and horse became interdependent, the animal was not eaten. He became a slave, often a friend. He also became an object for admiration. Because of his speed and beauty, his usefulness and adaptability, his virtues were celebrated in legend and in art.

*Horseman and rider are seen in Japanese Haniwa
figurines of the fifth century. Prehistoric China had similar art.*

*Buddha's farewell to his favorite horse Kanthaka:*
*"Truly a horse has the strength and swiftness of a god."*

In India, Prince Siddhartha, who was to become the Buddha, took great pride in his magnificent stallion Kanthaka. When he left his home, he called for the noble animal and spoke to him as a friend: "Today I go forth to seek supreme beatitude; lend me your help, O Kanthaka! Companions in arms or in pleasure are not hard to find, and we never want for friends when we set out to acquire wealth, but companions and friends desert us when it is the path of holiness we would take. Yet of this am I certain: he who helps another to do good or to do evil shares in that good or in that evil. Know then, O Kanthaka, that it is a virtuous impulse that moves me. Lend me your strength and your speed. The world's salvation and your own is at stake."

*Member of the Emperor's Guard in Kamakura period
(1185-1333) in Japan tries to control his Oriental stallion.*

*Some Roman invaders reached Iberia by horseback, but most horses pulled war chariots. Bridle is second century B.C.*

*Mounted on steed showing Arabian traits, Moslem spears a Christian knight. Painting is in Alhambra in Spain.*

By the time the Moslems invaded Iberia in A.D. 711, they had raised the breeding of horses to a fine art. Earlier, before the time of the prophet Mohammed, Arabic poets had celebrated the character of the horse of the desert. Mohammed himself said the greatest happiness results when a man is enjoying a woman, training his horses, or hunting wild animals. In Egypt, horse drawings and stone engravings had appeared as early as 1400 B.C. By the eleventh century —three hundred years after the Moslems on Arabian mounts had subdued the Visigoths—the fame of the "Spanish horse" had spread throughout Europe.

En · X · bng · comte
e mardis · de · bardslo
apoderador despanya

*Spanish knight rides down foot soldier during time of
El Cid, when Christians fought each other as well as Moors.*

*With delicate muzzles, triangular heads, and arched necks,
multi-hued horses carry Alfonso VII's court to 1126 coronation.*

*Spectators crowd rail to watch match race. Such events were popular in Japan during Momoyama period (1568-1600).*

As early as 1543, only fifty years after the first European horses reached the Americas, Portuguese explorers brought Arabian or "Spanish" horses to the islands of Japan. There they found horseracing was already well known. The Japanese had been importing, racing, and breeding the shaggy Mongolian horses for hundreds of years. Infusion of different horse blood followed as the Spanish, English, and Dutch came to the island kingdom. Though the Japanese resisted the foreigners' customs, they bred their steeds with the foreign horses and eventually imported Thoroughbreds. In recent times, since 1930, Thoroughbred racing, at modern courses that rival any in the world, has become — after baseball — the most popular spectator sport in Japan.

*Before adopting light horses of the Moors, knights fought from heavy breeds often carrying three hundred pounds or more.*

The armored knight, all four hundred and fifty pounds of man and metal, was the battering ram of medieval warfare. But when he fought in the Holy Land during the Crusades he soon found himself outflanked by unarmored enemies. This was a foe mounted on lighter horses which were bred for speed and stamina rather than weight-carrying. Even the English crossbowmen on foot at the battle of Agincourt outmaneuvered the ponderous and slow-moving French armor. The horses of the Mediterranean and Red Sea regions had been bred for speed and endurance and adaptability. The word quickly spread. From Iberia, Germany, and the Low Countries to France, the knights intelligently began to discard their heavy armor and plodding mounts. They adopted the Barbary, Turkish, and Arabian horses to form a maneuverable cavalry. William the Conqueror imported many fine animals from Normandy, Flanders, and Spain — most of his success at Hastings was due to his light cavalry. Soon the nobility was not only riding the lighter horses victoriously into battle but was also using them for sport, in the hunt and in racing.

*Painting of battle between Spanish and Moslems in Morocco in 1860 shows both sides mounted on spirited Arab horses.*

*Crude Indian painting of sixteenth century shows mounted conquistadores, carrying halberds, arriving in Michoacán.*

*Cavalryman's equipment is labeled in this Mexican painting of about 1650. Soldiers rode only stallions.*

46

*Painted horses were common among South Dakota tribes.*
*An Indian artist painted this colorful gathering on a deer skin.*

*Pawnee warriors fight with bows and arrows, rifles and*
*pistols in battle painted on buffalo hide in late 19th century.*

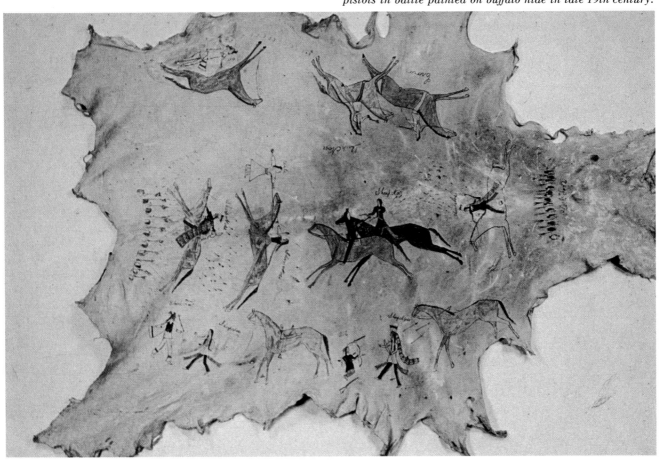

# The Przewalski Horse

*Last of true wild horses are Przewalskis, which have erect mane, dark dorsal stripe. Mongolia has a few herds.*

*Foaled at the San Diego Zoo, this Przewalski filly is one of few born in U.S. She will turn reddish brown later.*

*In the high country of Montana, many horses of stock
that once was domesticated have reverted to the wild state.*

# WILD HORSES OF THE WEST

Wild horse herds still exist in the Southwestern United States, Mexico, and South America but they have diminished in recent years. Since they are all descended from domesticated horses, they are not wild in the scientific sense. They have, however, reverted to a feral or wild state and are completely independent of man, who still is their enemy. Only on one range in the Americas are they protected from hunters who gather them for hides, meat, and, less often, for rodeo or ranch use. Other enemies are the predators, bears and mountain lions—but for generations they have defended themselves against these mammals. The horses shown on these pages are part of some three hundred which live in the Pryor Mountains. Even though deep snows and bad droughts plague this high country, and although the forage is shared with antelope, bighorn sheep, and smaller creatures, the horses have survived and grown even more resourceful. They fight among themselves; they breed; they bear young and live out their life spans just as their ancestors did before the dawn of man.

*Forefeet off ground, agile wild mare takes off down rocky cliffside. This wild country is in the Big Horn Mountains.*

*Still racing away from the men she has spotted, wild mare makes sure-footed dash to safety on sharp sliding rocks.*

*Mare with foal at side leads way to safety as stallion stands his ground. Stallion will attack a man when cornered.*

*One powerful and possessive stallion heads this large herd, which includes foals, weanlings, yearlings, and mares.*

*Led by an experienced mare, a wild herd streaks through the buffalo grass. Herds number four to twelve animals.*

In summer, wild herds grow sleek and fat. During the long winters their coats grow shaggy, their bodies spare.

(Overleaf) Mustangs keep to their own range, stallions avoid other herds. At right a stallion brings up the rear.

*Young stallion forced from herd by his sire might join stray mare; when older he may attempt to increase his herd.*

*A roan stallion stands protectively beside his mare.*
*Some wild horses have striped hoofs like the Appaloosas.*

*Catching up with the herd, a young stallion shows speed and style. Once hunted by mustangers, who sold them to rodeos as bucking horses, and by Indians for food, horses in Wyoming-Montana Pryor Mountain range are protected.*

*An older stallion when forced out of the herd by one of his sons lives out a lonely life in the high wild country.*

*Once captured, wild or feral horses soon become domesticated, especially when allowed to fraternize with tame animals.*

*Reminiscent of the early West, Jesse Redheart, champion
rider and breeder of Appaloosas, rides along a river in Idaho.*

# THE ARABIAN

In the hilly low country near Santa Maria, California, lies a typical Arabian horse farm of the West. It is a ranch owned and operated by one of the West's great horsewomen, Miss Sheila Varian. Ever since her early teens Miss Varian has shown, trained, and bred fine Arabians. To her they are like children, unruly sometimes, occasionally disobedient, but playful, intelligent, and good humored.

She likes to tell stories about her horses, about Bay-Abi, for instance, a horse that can untie any knot she can fashion. His memory, she will tell you, is extraordinary. Once on an endurance ride across country he was offered water just as the venture was starting. He did not realize water would not be available again during the next eight or nine hours, and he refused to drink. Bay-Abi never forgot those uncomfortably dry hours. Now whenever he comes to the smallest stream or passes a water trough he invariably stops for a drink whether he needs it or not. "You should see him opening gates," continues Miss Varian. "He is so adept that he can open a gate, let me through and, even if cows are crowding to get in, close it before they push through."

Conformation, appearance, breeding ability—while all important to the Arabian fancier—are not the things Miss Varian talks about. Her horses are part of her family. She knows how easily they learn voice commands, and she thinks they understand whole sentences. When I watched a mare push a foal away from her and give it a light kick, Sheila Varian told me about Arabian mothers. "There are good ones and bad ones, or modern mothers and the old-fashioned kind. The modern ones do not take the trouble to teach the foals proper manners but are satisfied to feed them and let them fend for themselves—the surest way to raise delinquents. The old-fashioned kind of dam cuffs the foals around if they nurse too hard or stray too far away—or play too rough. They learn to mind their mother as she teaches them good horse manners. When such a mother calls her foal, it comes a-running."

Arabians have lived so close to man for so many generations that it is probable certain characteristics are inbred. They have an attitude that can be described as friendly and polite; a well-handled horse looking alert and interested will come to the door of his stall to greet you. And whether in the show ring or in the pasture, they seem to take pride in their appearance. They move with grace and style. An Arabian never shuffles toward you with head hanging down and ears flopped back. They do not frighten easily and they have a tendency to resent unfair treatment. A good trainer encourages the horse to use his brain but never permits him to dominate. They learn very fast, and if you give them time to think they will work out a way to fool the trainer if they can. Arabians love to play tricks and games. You have to show a sensitive animal how to remove a loose scarf from your pocket only once. It is likely that each time you wear such a scarf he will reach in and take it out. But he will return it to you and let you put it back in your pocket so he can take it out again.

It would be an error, however, to say Arabians are always safe and gentle. This depends almost entirely upon their upbringing, and even a well-trained horse will sometimes bite or kick if he feels he is being mishandled. Not nearly so temperamental as Thoroughbreds, the Arabian can be handled with ease by women and children — again, if they have been properly trained. And training must start very early. They are not allowed to get too "high" or excited or too angry or, as trainers say, "too hot."

Training starts when the animal is a foal, and it continues through the weanling stage. By the time they are yearlings they have learned to live with people. Although the young horses are handled, talked to, and sometimes put on halters, they are not ridden until they are late two-year-olds or even three-year-olds. Then they are broken to harness and learn to carry a rider.

Well-trained Arabians give a soft springy ride. They respond quickly and easily to hand cues. Probably the most sensitive of all horses (with the possible exception of the Thoroughbred), the Arabian reacts to the lightest touch of the leg or the slightest movement of the bridle.

Breeding is not a major problem, for Arabian stallions are far easier to handle than most other studs. Many on California ranches are handled by women, who seem to have a special touch. Some stallions will stand quiet until a visual or vocal signal is given to mount the mare. A trainer gives such a signal by dropping a hand in which he holds a whip. But at California State Polytechnic College in Pomona some stallions are so competently trained that a voice signal is sufficient. Once trained properly, the stallions remain tractable during their lifetimes, and Arabian stallions continue to be potent very late in life. A number of stallions now standing in the West are in their thirties and are still fathering excellent foals.

Stud fees range between $500 and $1,000 with the guarantee of a live foal. It is, however, not easy to book one's mare to a leading stallion unless she belongs to a bloodline that breeds well with the stallion and unless the stallion's owner likes her conformation. But it is not always necessary to spend over $500 for use of a good Arabian stallion. Services of many, not the very top, can be acquired for $200 to $500 and occasionally their get turn out to be champions.

Because of the ease with which they can be trained and because they rarely forget their manners, Arabians make excellent family horses. They like people around them and constantly react to them. As show horses they are unexcelled, responding quickly to "quiet down," "show," or other commands. But the Arabian can be used in many ways. His endurance and smooth gait qualify him well for trail rides. His intelligence and quick reactions make for a fine cow horse. His innate dignity and gentleness make him good as a child's mount.

One of the best-known trainers of Arabians, Jim Alderson, gave me the following notes on proper behavior around Arabians, but his advice holds for all horses:

1. Make slow, deliberate moves when you approach or walk around the horse.

2. Never let yourself get into a position where

the horse can kick or step on you. You are safer standing right against the horse rather than a foot away. He can only push you away if you are against him, but he can kick you if you are not.

3. Stay close to the horse's head rather than his rear but never give him an opportunity to bite. Do not walk under his neck when he is tied. This causes the horse to jerk his head up and he may come down and bite.

4. Most horses seem to be more gentle when handled from the left side.

5. If you must pet your horse (and this is not advised) pet him between the eyes, under the chin, or on the shoulders or the withers. Never, never reach for his nose. It is the most sensitive part of the animal and he cannot help resent its being stroked. The horse's ears are very sensitive, too, and must be touched with care, if at all.

6. All horses learn by memory—by doing the same thing repeatedly. Never bribe a horse. If you want him to learn something, you have to teach him to be afraid of not doing what you want him to do. That is, teach him that he will be safer or happier if he performs in a certain manner than if he does not.

As racehorses the Arabians cannot compete with Thoroughbreds even though they contributed the original bloodlines for that breed. That is, they cannot win in the presently popular short races for Thoroughbreds. Yet all-Arabian racing is becoming more common in the United States, and competitions are held regularly with pari-mutuel betting at the Phoenix, Arizona, track, Turf Paradise, the only racecourse in the West to schedule events featuring Arabian horses. Because of the beauty of these animals, their speed and staying power, Arabian racing has proven very popular with racing fans generally. Some of the races in Arizona feature horses with riders in Arabian regalia, an exciting and unique event. But most Arabians race under the colors of their owners as Thoroughbreds do. The major difference is that they usually carry more weight and that races are longer, most

of them being one and one-half miles or over.

Two of the important runners are Orzel, who stands at stud at Scottsdale, Arizona, and Kontiki, another Western stallion who in 1969 held the American record for Arabians at one and one-half miles. He carried 142 pounds and ran the distance in 2 minutes, 47 3/5 seconds. Comparing this time to Thoroughbred records is not entirely fair. Arabian racing and breeding for racing are very new in the United States, whereas for more than three hundred years Thoroughbreds have been bred exclusively for running. Today a champion Thoroughbred should be able to beat the Arabian in a mile and one-half race by as much as a quarter of a mile. The Arabians do get off to fast starts, however. Gladys Brown Edwards, one of the truly great writers and judges of Arabians, points out that for the first quarter mile the Arabian time is very close to that of the champion Thoroughbreds. It should also be noted that not only do the Arabian racers carry more weight, but they are in almost every instance smaller than the Thoroughbred, which means they have more steps to take to cover the same distance with their heavier loads.

Thus far few Arabians are trained for racing, and purses are not high. Their racing future depends largely upon how many Arabian breeders— and more are joining the racing ranks every day— decide to concentrate on breeding for speed rather than for pleasure or show-ring horses. A great problem is that the Arabians, because racing them is so new in this country, are not evenly matched. Therefore, considerable distances often separate horses as they approach the finish. Not even proportioning weight is enough to take care of this until more horses in the same general speed class are bred.

But although the Arabians have not been trained and usually carry heavier weights, this does not mean that any Arabian horse now living could be prepared to compete with the Thoroughbred even at the longer distances. Mrs. Edwards points out in one of her definitive articles that Thoroughbreds can go farther in less time than Arabians have shown thus far, especially in steeplechases. This does not say Arabians do not have more endurance in marathon races or on trail rides. But at a full run the Thoroughbred has demonstrated both more speed and staying power. Yet the Thoroughbred does tire more easily than the Arabian when the going is over many miles and difficult terrain.

Western horsemen interested in Arabian racing have been shipping their horses to Evangeline Downs, deep in the Louisiana bayou country, to the town of Lafayette, where purses as high as $12,000 are offered. The most important race is known as the Arabian Classic, and more Arabian breeders each year are readying horses for this significant test.

In Poland, where the Arabian has been bred intensively for many generations, regular racing is popular. There is a derby for four-year-old pure-blooded Arabian horses, and in some of these races the entries carry as much as 154 pounds and run 3,000 meters (1.864 miles).

Before leaving Arabian racing, it is well to reiterate that from this strain came the Thoroughbred, and that many of the fastest Thoroughbreds show Arabian characteristics: head conformation, croup level, and the way some Thoroughbreds carry their tails out from their bodies. These are strong indications that with proper breeding and training for racing, the Arabians can be a real threat, in time, to the Thoroughbred. It must also be remembered that if so-called "new" Thoroughbred blood were introduced into Arabian breeding in the United States, it would be a matter of returning to the original strain rather than crossing the two lines.

High jumping is another salient attribute of the Arabian, with some of the great jumpers in the world coming from this breed. They are of course unexcelled as parade horses because of dignified manner, well-designed head, and naturally high tail carriage. Few horses can equal him in appearance when he is ridden in the costume class. Outfitted in the superbly colorful caparison dating to the desert sheiks and mounted by a rider attired in matching exotic dress, the Arabian has a breathtaking effect on the show audience.

While Arabians are bred for conformation, they are bred almost equally for disposition. If a yearling develops a foul attitude and continues to be mean when fully grown, his owner probably will send him to the gelding barn. Although he may be a highly valuable animal, most breeders would rather geld him than risk acquiring the bad-tempered progeny he might father. Trainers such as Jim Alderson, Watt Clements, and Sheila Varian claim the Arabian learns faster than other breeds. Because of this, he must never be allowed to learn bad habits. For once he has them they are difficult to eradicate. Like a child, if he does not feel his treatment is fair, he is quick to resent it and to show his displeasure.

Life is never prosaic around an Arabian ranch, and the things the trainers will tell you make it sound like they are actually talking about their children. One trainer told me a story about a pleasure-loving foal. During a fly epidemic one summer, the trainer noticed that this foal was being attacked by insects and was scratching itself against the front gate. The trainer purchased a fly repellent and every time she saw the foal scratching she would go out and massage the repellent into its coat. After the flies had left and the foal was in perfect condition, it nevertheless continued to go to the gate and scratch whenever it saw the trainer, hoping she would again massage it.

A famous Arabian breeder and trainer, "Frisco" Mari, sat with me one pleasant afternoon on his front porch near Riverside, California, and as we dawdled over our bourbon and branch water he began talking about a granddaughter of his. I had met three of his young and pretty daughters (Clara, Dorothy, and Rose) who handled the Arabians on his farm and I was sure none was married. It was not until he happened to mention how fast his granddaughter could run that I realized he was talking about a horse, not a child.

Arabians are not only friendly to people; they are usually friendly to each other. Sheila Varian tells a story of two fillies, Farlotta and Ronteza. They became inseparable on the ranch, spending almost all of their time with one another. Ronteza was then entered in the pleasure class in one of the Western Arabian shows. She was three years old. Ronteza performed well, winning a second-place award. But while she was away Farlotta went off her feed, fell ill, and died. When Ronteza returned and could not find her friend, she went into shock and became inconsolable. Miss Varian nursed her along and two months later bought a new mare. When the newcomer arrived, Ronteza nearly broke down the fences to make friends with her. She soon developed a relationship as close as the one she had enjoyed with Farlotta.

Like dogs, Arabians seem to enjoy submission to man. They quickly gain real attachments to their owners. Soon, unlike other animals (excepting the dog), the Arabian becomes a yielding friend. Yet each horse retains a distinct personality. Without sacrificing any of his independent spirit he accepts man as both companion and master. Such a bond between a horse and a man, woman, or child can last throughout the lifetime of the animal.

It is important to remember that the relationship between the Arabian breed and man extends deep into ancient history. It is not a rapport that has grown up in recent years but may well have started before the time of Christ when the nomadic people of the Middle East began not only to domesticate the horse but literally to live with him. These people, as we pointed out earlier, were not the first to domesticate the horse. But over the past three thousand years, through selective breeding, they developed the outstanding, swift-running, intelligent, enduring modern Arabian horse.

The words Arabian and Barbary in a geographic sense once covered a tremendously large territory, for Barbary in ancient times included much of the Middle East from Turkey through Syria, Iraq, and Iran south to Arabia. It was a general designation that also took in the desert and semi-desert of the entire peninsula now known as Saudi Arabia which stretches from the Red Sea to the Persian Gulf. But Barbary and the Barbary Coast did not stop there. It took in Egypt and much of the North African coast as well. The two kinds of horses that came from this extensive domain are known historically as the Barb and the Arabian. But in many cases the two words have been interchangeable, for they describe types rather than breeds. Both animals belong to what is now generally known as the Arabian.

Pursuing the history of Arabian horse breeding leads the researcher into mythology, legend, and — undercoating both of those enticements — facts. One day in the time of Ibrahim (Abraham of the Jews and Christians), an era which has been estimated to be two thousand years before Christ, Ibrahim's son, who was called Ishmael, was hunting. Within easy arrow shot, a graceful animal, which he thought to be an unusual type of antelope, appeared. Legend relates that the angel Jabrail (Gabriel) stopped him, saying he should spare the life of this elegant creature, which would become a great treasure and was indeed a gift from Allah to the Arabic people whom Ishmael would father. Ishmael spared the wild mare and captured her. He called her Kuhaylah, which in Arabic means painted antelope.

When the mare foaled, the newborn was placed in a saddlebag to be carried on a camel's back as the nomadic tribe moved across the desert. While the camel was jogging, the colt's spine was twisted. When the youngster was removed from the saddlebag, Ishmael saw how hunched its back was, and considered destroying the colt. But the angel again stayed his arm. The ancient legend says this is why Arabian horses have fewer vertebrae in their spines and tails than do other horses.

When Ishmael's colt matured, it was bred back to its mother. And many Arab peoples still believe that from this legendary and incestuous union all Arabian horses have descended. Although the legend lacks scientific foundation, two facts emerge. Wild horses were probably found in the lower Mesopotamian Valley between the Tigris and the Euphrates Rivers, the traditional home of Ishmael and of Ibrahim, four thousand years ago. Many Arabians have fewer vertebrae than other horses.

The mythology of Arabia records horses with wings. The wings, it is said, were taken from the horses by the will of Allah so the animals would become docile, thereby enabling them to draw the chariots of ancient kings and warriors.

While other nations in the Mesopotamian Valley, as well as north and south of it, domesticated the horse for uses that were almost exclusively to pull such chariots for war and to race, the Arabs bred their horses for more personal use. Man and rider became as an entity. The Arabian horse literally lived with his master. He bore him throughout the day and shared his tent at night. Before the Arab ate, the horse was fed, usually sharing the camel's milk that provided sustenance for both of them. In the desert, there is little that horses can eat. Camels forage closer to the ground and will eat foods that horses refuse. So a large herd of camels was kept not only for carrying burdens but to provide milk for the horses. It took the yield of five to seven camels to provide the eight quarts of milk necessary daily to sustain a horse, for camels give very little milk. Even today in the desert, stallions and mares are given this rich liquid as an important part of their diet.

Desert life was always difficult and usually hazardous, for tribal warfare was continuous. A man's safety depended entirely upon the training and conditioning of his horse. Stamina was almost as important as speed and intelligence, because water holes were often long distances apart, and the ride to camp often was more than a day's journey. Out of necessity the Arabs became the greatest horse breeders the world has ever known. Pride in their mounts was equaled by arrogance in themselves.

Mares always were the preferred mounts of the Arabs, even though stallions occasionally were ridden and of course were essential for breeding. In addition to being just as swift as stallions, the mares are less temperamental. And, more important, mares never neigh to give the alarm when approaching an enemy camp. According to an ancient and oft-told tale, this characteristic made possible the stealing of one of the fastest mares ever known in the desert.

This singular mare was noted for her speed, stamina, and intelligence. Clearly, she was the paragon of all the animals in the region. With reason, she was the pride of her owner, who was the ruling sheik. The fame of this wonderful animal became so widespread throughout other tribal areas that time after time attempts were made to capture her in battle or steal her from camp. But she always carried the sheik away from his pursuers. And during the night he kept her tethered next to him within his tent while he slept.

But a brave and clever enemy made elaborate plans. He first disguised himself in some of the sheik's cast-off garments so the scent would not disturb the animal. Before dawn he burrowed his way stealthily under the sheik's tent. Inside, he untethered the mare, which remained quiet, then silently mounted her and rode swiftly through the tent flaps. The sheik awoke, gave the alarm to his tribesmen and, mounting a swift sister of his stolen favorite, set out after her. Because he knew the trails, and because the thief was a heavier man, the sheik gained ground. But when he was within one hundred yards and when it seemed as though he would certainly overtake them, the sheik leaned along his mount's mane and shouted ahead to the thief: "Whisper 'Allah be praised' into her ear and press your right heel into her ribs." The thief did as he was told. And the mare responded by increasing her stride and leaving the sheik and his tribesmen far behind. As they rode back to camp, one of his lieutenants asked why he had given the secret signal to the robber when he could so easily have caught him. "Because," replied the sheik,

*In his native Arabia, noted stallion \*Haleb is admired by Bedouins before being shipped to U. S. by Davenport in 1906. This* *sire and 26 other* asil *(purebred) stallions and mares provided much of the stock for proliferation of the Arabian horse in U. S.*

"I could not have her pride hurt by having her outrun, nor could I live with myself had I allowed her to be outrun."

From these swift horses bred in the desert came the lightweight cavalry and racing stock transported to Europe when the Arabs invaded Iberia. In the generations that followed, the mounts that became known as Spanish horses, all from original

Arabian or Barbary bloodlines, found their way into northern Europe. As early as the eleventh century, William the Conqueror is known to have ridden a Spanish horse. And, even before him, Ethelstan, the Saxon king who united England between 924 and 939, is known to have imported horses from southern Europe.

After invasion by the Moors, Spain became the

diffusion center for Arabian horses for all Europe. They were valued highly throughout the Mediterranean countries, and trading for them extended throughout Europe and into Asia. Up to the end of the fifteenth century, the caliphs in Spain continued to breed for intelligence, speed, and endurance. At regular intervals fresh blood from desert stock was transported over the narrow Strait of Gibraltar. Then in 1492, Christian Spain, led by Fernando and Isabel, reconquered the last territory held by the Moors. Defeat and expulsion of the Moslems came in the same year that Christopher Columbus, Admiral of the Ocean Sea, sailed for the Indies.

Just one year later, after discovering a new world, Columbus set about selecting breeding stock for his second voyage. In 1494 the first stallions and mares were successfully landed on the island of Santo Domingo, and the earliest breeding farm in the New World had been founded. So from Hispaniola, the Santo Domingo of Columbus, horses of direct Arabian ancestry were transported to Cuba and Jamaica and finally to the North and South American continents.

Yet none of the blood of this early stock flows in the veins of today's Western Arabians. For, while a certain amount of selective breeding continued, Indians stole much of the original stock for their means of transportation and food gathering; others escaped into high country to revert to the feral state; and others became the ancestors of the mustang, or cow pony.

Although the records get rather misty, there is reason to believe that the first pure-blooded Arabian to arrive in the United States came to this country in 1765. His name was *Ranger, also known as *Lindsay's Arabian. (Imported horses are always indicated by an asterisk.) A light gray with excellent conformation, he stood at stud in Connecticut, "stamping his get" with his own characteristics including his light gray coat. Horses sired by this famous stallion were in great demand by the Connecticut militia. This cavalry troop, largely mount-

ed on *Ranger's descendants, became so famous that Commander George Washington sent General Light Horse Harry Lee (father of Robert E. Lee) to look them over. Lee, in turn, sent Captain Lindsay up to a village in Connecticut, where *Ranger stood. He must have been authorized to purchase the horse, for the records show that the sales price was 125 hogsheads of tobacco, which would have been worth some $3,000 in cash. The horse was moved to Lindsay's Mill in Virginia, where he stood in 1779 and 1780. A handbill of the time describes him as "the most beautiful and justly celebrated imported Arabian...whose form almost exceeds description, which is sufficiently evinced by the extraordinary figure of his colts."

In addition to being the first Arabian horse to come to the United States, *Ranger has an additional claim to honors. He sired Washington's stallion Magnolio, foaled in June, 1780. This favorite of Washington was the only horse he ever raced. And in a match against one of Thomas Jefferson's finest, Magnolio was defeated. He appears at the top of the list of horses on Washington's own stock inventory made in 1785. The record in Washington's handwriting reads in part:

"Magnolio—an Arabian
"Nelson—riding horse
"Blewskin—ditto."

Sixteen other horses, their height and age noted, follow on the list.

But because no Arabian mares were brought over, *Ranger could not sire a pure line.

The history of the Western Hemisphere's purebred Arabians begins much later. One attempt to start it occurred when Abraham Lincoln's Secretary of State, William Henry Seward, shortly after joining the Cabinet traveled to Syria on a diplomatic mission. After completing his business, he received three fine horses—a blood-bay stallion, a mare, and a chestnut colt—from his diplomatic counterpart, Ayoub Bey Trabulsky. U.S. Treasury records show that the shipping fee from Beirut to New York was $10,000. Unfortunately, the mare died during the voyage. With her loss, a pure Arabian line could not be founded. Even so, Seward had hoped the stallions would be bred to the best possible mares to improve American horseflesh generally. But even in this desire he was thwarted. He first offered the two stallions to the New York State Agricultural Society—but with strings attached. He hoped to get back the $10,000 sea freight for the government. But in view of the impending Civil War, the society turned him down.

The magnificent stallions were fast becoming a heavy and awkward liability to the government, rather than an asset. Seward finally found a way out by presenting them to a pair of horse fanciers in upper New York State. But as the Civil War ran its course the stallions had little chance to show their procreative abilities, although the younger won a medal at the New York State Fair in Rochester, where he was proclaimed "handsomest." But shortly thereafter he was sold to a stud farm in Ohio, dying there with a heritage of only two fillies. The older stallion died, it was said, of neglect, and without producing any recorded progeny. Yet these two stallions through their limited get nonetheless contributed to the total amount of Arabian blood that found its way into early American harness and Saddlebred stock. Such horses as Justin Morgan, from which the famous Morgan line has sprung, exhibit in their conformation unmistakable Arabian characteristics, as do the hunters and jumpers of the time as shown in contemporary drawings and paintings.

In the aftermath of the Civil War, former President Ulysses S. Grant, who had become an international hero, traveled around the world. While in Turkey, Sultan Abdul Hamid II gave Grant an outstanding pair of Arabian stallions. Grant and the sultan got along famously, both being excellent horsemen and breeders. Grant of course had spent much of the Civil War on horseback. So each rightfully considered himself an expert judge of horseflesh. As Grant strolled through the sultan's spacious stables, he admired a stallion called *Leopard. Unhesitantly the sultan gave Grant that prize. But, insisting he was at least as good a judge of horses as Grant, the sultan selected and gave to Grant another outstanding stud, later known as *Linden Tree. The horses were delivered by a Turkish ship, and this time there was no freight charge. However, the sultan might have possessed a latent motive for making those gifts and providing that gratis voyage: The ship docked at New Haven, Connecticut, which happened to be the home of Winchester Arms and the United States center of the munitions industry. The return to Turkey was made with a cargo of guns and ammunition, a deal that required government approval. That armament may have been used against the same desert tribes that had supplied the sultan's stables.

Like Secretary Seward, General Grant had little time for the horses once they arrived in the United States. In the stables of General E. F. Beale at Washington, D.C., the two magnificent stallions attracted horse lovers from throughout the region. One of those admirers, the sportsman Randolph Huntington of Long Island, New York, was an important raiser of harness horses. He bred his finest mares to the Grant stallions. Because his mares were not pure Arabian, his purpose—like Seward's—was not to develop the Arabian breed in the United States but to produce an improved American breed of horses utilizing fine Arabian and domestic stock. Unfortunately, financial reverses ended his breeding experiment.

Huntington, however, in addition to being interested in breeding, was also a scholar. He traced the lines of Secretary Seward's horses as well as some Arabians imported by A. Ken Richards and by President James K. Polk. His studies indicated that in 1880 no Arabian mares were available for breeding in the United States. He therefore imported *Naomi, a pure-blooded mare from England, and bred her to *Leopard, General Grant's stallion. Their only offspring, a handsome chestnut stallion named Anazeh, was bred back to his mother, and with her and other mares Anazeh sired several pure

Arabian foals. The founding stallion, therefore, and the first Arabian later registered with the Arabian Horse Club of America, was General Grant's stallion *Leopard. And the founding mare was *Naomi, a direct descendant of two desert-bred Arabs. So *Leopard and *Naomi are the Adam and Eve of United States Arabians.

There is a historic and rare handbill General Beale issued indicating where the horses first stood for service and at what fees. Unlike the Seward horses, *Leopard and *Linden Tree were popular with the masses as well as with breeders. Ten thousand dollars was refused for a half-breed son of *Leopard called after the sultan, Abdul Hamid II. This horse became a gold-medal winner and an important addition to a well-known Philadelphia stud farm. A granddaughter of *Leopard called Larissa brought $3,500 at an auction in New York in 1901. Earlier a grandson Fez and a granddaughter Keturah each won gold medals at the World's Columbian Exposition in Chicago. This event, popularly called the Chicago Fair, was staged from May through November of 1893, although the site was dedicated October 12, 1892.

Perhaps the most terrible disaster to befall a large contingent of Arabian horses occurred during that same Chicago Fair. The Turkish government shipped forty-five purebreds to the fair and it was understood that all of these horses would be returned to the desert. Accompanying them were 120 men, women, and boys, including some of the finest Bedouin riders. The trip, on a chartered Cunard liner, must have been the greatest voyage since that of Noah's Ark. On deck were the forty-five Arabian horses, twelve camels, several donkeys, some fat-tailed sheep for barbecuing, and most of the supplies the party felt it would need on the heathen shores of the United States. These included cracked wheat, soap, oil, butter, cheese, 2,000 pounds of horseshoes, trunks of Oriental wearing apparel, elaborate trappings for the horses, and six huge boxes. The boxes, almost unbelievably, contained one and one-half million admission tick-

ets to the Arabian exhibition—and each ticket was designed to sell for $1 in United States currency. It is recorded that the unfortunate Turks, after having been taken by some of the Chicago sharks, wound up having to burn their tickets to keep warm.

When they arrived in Chicago the entire contingent had headed for the Turkish consulate to pay respects. In that impromptu parade were wild-eyed horsemen wielding scimitars that flashed in the sun above the proud Arabian mounts. There were Turkish and Chicago entrepreneurs in open carriages, while numerous donkeys trailed them all, And everyone was shouting. A riot almost ensued. According to a witness, one newsboy was trampled, three milk wagons were upset, and a considerable number of Chicago citizens were mentally unhinged by the fantastic march.

The company had raised $112,000 in Turkey, a large part of it going to charter the ship and to get the horses and men, women, and children, together with all those necessary supplies, to Chicago. A considerable amount of money had gone to U.S. Customs, which levied a duty on each horse even though the few spokesmen who knew English insisted that all horses would be taken back. But the Turks did not understand the Americans and the Americans certainly could not communicate with the Turks. Within weeks the entire spread was bankrupt, and Chicago loan sharks soon possessed mortgages on everything—horses, donkeys, tents, and even clothing. Although the Bedouins from Syria have long had reputations for shrewd dealing, they were overmatched against Chicago's experts. The show finally got started on the Fourth of July.

The exhibition received some good reviews. But the tickets did not sell. A fire of incendiary origin killed seven of the best horses, Chicago creditors took over others, and ultimately the balance of them had to be auctioned. It would be pleasant to report that most of these purebreds could be traced today. However, few appear in the Arabian Registry, for reputable breeders acquired only a small number. So ended the first large-scale import of Arabians to the United States. There is no question that some of the finest blood from the desert arrived—but only a little of it flows through the early history of the Arabian horse in this country.

The breeding of Arabians did not become important in the United States until Spencer Borden imported purebred stallions and mares in 1905 and 1910. When Homer Davenport, a well-known cartoonist and caricaturist for the *New York Evening Mail,* became an *aficionado* of the Arabian horse, he also helped promote it. His father had been an Indian agent in the West, and over the years the younger Davenport had developed a passion to explore the Arabian desert and bring to America some of those magnificent steeds. He had the assistance of Theodore Roosevelt, then President, whose influence was felt throughout the world.

Davenport was accompanied by Peter B. Bradley, wealthy owner of the Hingham Stock Farm in Massachusetts. When Davenport approached him, Bradley put up the money to finance the expedition. A third member of the party, Charles Arthur Moore, Jr., went as photographer. His excellent pictures added considerable dramatic value to the book *My Quest of the Arabian Horse,* which Homer Davenport wrote upon his return from the desert regions.

The three young men traveled extensively in Turkey, Syria, and the northern Arabian deserts. They selected some of the finest blooded horses from various desert tribes, including sixteen animals of the Anazah type from the Fidan and Saba tribes and five from the Shammar. One outstanding stallion, a descendant of Bedouin horses, came from Aleppo. It was an adventurous journey made by a man dedicated to the cause of Arabian breeding. His importations were preceded by those of Spencer Borden and Randolph Huntington, but because Homer Davenport actually went into the desert for his stock and because he imported twenty-seven stallions and mares, his effect on the horse world is much greater. Other Davenport imports came from the Crabbet Stud in England.

Even though Davenport's horses did not arrive in the United States until 1906, it is possible that one of his previous imports from England, *Nedjran, was shown at the Lewis and Clark Exposition in 1905—one hundred years after the explorers had charted a course to the Northwest. The evidence is based on old-timers' verbal accounts and the fact that this stallion was on the West Coast around the time of the Exposition. It is probable, therefore, that a Davenport horse was the first purebred Arabian stallion in the West. That horse was followed a few years later by the English-bred *Ibn Mahruss, which Davenport had purchased from an importer and sold to "Lucky" Baldwin of Santa Anita fame. This outstanding stallion was owned by Baldwin's daughter Anita.

Davenport's interest in fine Arabians—an interest stressed by his outstanding imports—contributed tremendously to the present Western Arabian stock. Today the Arabian Registry lists hundreds of horses descended from Davenport's original imports. His Arabians are historically among the great horses brought to the United States. It will be of interest to all Arabian horse fanciers to read the translation of the pedigree of *Haleb, one of Davenport's more significant imports.

*"In the Name of the Most Merciful Allah: Praise be to Allah, the Lord of the Universe, and prayers and greetings upon our Master Muhammad, and upon all his family and his followers.*

*"God, the All-High, has said in his cherished Book: By those which run swiftly with a panting noise, and which strike fire, and which make an incursion in the morning, raising a cloud of dust and piercing the ranks of a host. 'Also, Ali, may God bathe his face with Glory, has said: Plenty is knotted to the horses' manes.' He has also said; '[On] Their backs are splendor and [in] their wombs are treasure.' And now: The pure brown stallion who is devoid of white and whose age is five years,*

*going on his sixth, is a* Manakhy Sabily. *His sire is a* Shuwaiman Sabbah, *who breeds pure and exclusive, and is consequently free of all defects. — And we have not testified except to what we have known, and we are incognizant of the unknown. — Written the 25th of* Hamada, *the last, 1324* (Hegira) *and the 15th of August, 1906 A.D.*

"(Signed) Ahmad Hafiz
"(Signed) Sheikh el-Bukhamis Ali Al-Rashid
"(Signed) Kaimakam Hagim Bey Menhad"

This magnificent stallion won first prize in the Justin Morgan class at the Rutland, Vermont, Horse Show in 1907. It was expected that he would be bred not only to Arabians but to Morgans; that his bloodline would be added to both breeds to the improvement of each. But it was not to be. A few days after his award-winning performance *Haleb died, having been in the United States less than a year. It was generally believed he was poisoned by a rival breeder.

Shortly after the Davenport group returned, a memorable meeting was held September 2, 1908, at the Hotel Belmont in New York City. There, the Arabian Horse Club of America was founded. At the end of the club's first year the U.S. Department of Agriculture, which recognizes only one registry for each breed, approved the Arabian Registry's studbook. Since then, well-bred Arabian stallions and mares have been registered with the Arabian Horse Club. In the beginning only seventy-one purebred Arabians were registered, and the club consisted of just twelve members. By 1969 there were 52,162 registered horses, 16,500 owners, and 4,500 members. Each year the number of registered horses increases approximately fifteen percent.

Homer Davenport must be considered an Eastern breeder of Arabians. It was not until W. K. Kellogg, "The Breakfast Food King" and a lover of all animals, established a foundation that the West obtained its first large Arabian ranch. Kellogg's love of animals and especially of horses began on a farm, where he lived as a child. And the idea of an outstanding Arabian breeding ranch can be traced to a favorite pony that young Kellogg loved. It was a Pinto without a pedigree. "Old Spot," however, was thought by young Kellogg to have Arabian blood, and at least to the growing boy he was an important animal of aristocratic breeding.

Herbert H. Reese, who was the first manager of the Kellogg Ranch in California, conjectured that Pintos and other dramatically spotted horses were used by most traveling circuses and that on posters they were almost always referred to as Arabians. Whether young Kellogg actually decided that "Old Spot" was an Arabian from attending circuses and seeing their posters we will never know. But we do know that when he began the Arabian Ranch he was very disappointed to find out that Arabians were never spotted as his old Pinto had been.

After being exposed to some of the purebred Arabians, Mr. Kellogg went ahead with his plans for the ranch even though he found that the prevailing colors for Arabians were bay, gray, and chestnut. Once his mind was made up he moved swiftly to acquire the finest breeding stock available, not only in the United States but in England, Poland, Syria, Arabia, Turkey, and Egypt. His agents searched throughout the world. No expense was spared, no stallion or mare was too far away to be examined by Kellogg's emissaries. As a result, W. K. Kellogg built a million-dollar monument to the Arabian horse.

The early days were difficult, for some undesirable bloodlines were inevitably picked up along with the good ones. Mr. Kellogg's romantic mental picture of regal, colorfully spotted animals was not at first reflected in the smaller, quiet-mannered Arabians. He thought of switching to Palominos, saddle-breds, or Morgans but after a time learned to love his Arabian stock, and he began a weeding-out process that finally resulted in horses of beauty, fire, stamina, and intelligence.

In the rolling hills of Pomona, California, 801 acres were acquired. The velvety grasslands were dotted with native walnut trees that provided oases of shade for the horses. Work began on the farm in 1925. A complete water system with extensive irrigation facilities was installed, roads were built, and magnificent stables in the Spanish style began to rise. The stables were built in a U shape, open at one end with Roman arches on three sides. Stalls were spacious, the grass in the center of the stable area was carefully manicured, and palm trees added a touch of the desert.

When the horses were first shown they performed in the small patio surrounded by the arches. But within a few years a large show ring was added. A grandstand seating hundreds of persons was provided and weekly public exhibitions were given free. All-Arabian shows were held in addition to the Sunday exhibitions. These exhibitions were not limited to showing the gaits of the horses but included liberty drills (with the horses free running in the ring) and stock horse routines in which even now a stallion called Farana is remembered for his fast spinning and backing as well as sliding stops that marked a large figure 11 in the turf as his back legs gouged into the ground. These maneuvers have become standard in all Western horse shows. Also demonstrated were a liberty jumping act, five-gaited and three-gaited routines, and "high school" acts such as "jumping rope" and "the Spanish walk." Certain horses showed ability for dancing steps. One horse performed by walking on hind legs around a ring. Another walked a narrow plank one foot above the ground—a very tricky balancing act.

But even though thousands of spectators applauded the horses each week and thousands more flocked to the ranch during the regular Arabian horse shows, it was the motion picture that brought lasting fame to a considerable number of Arabian stallions and mares. Shortly after the Kellogg Farm began its breeding and showing operations, the movie colony discovered it. Rarely did a pleasant Sunday afternoon go by without one or more movie stars showing up to be photographed with an Arabian beauty. Files at the Kellogg Ranch are filled with portraits of Tom Mix, Ronald Reagan, Gary Cooper, Victor McLaglen, Ramon Novarro, and many others. Among the glamorous women were Clara Bow, Lois Wilson, Olivia de Havilland, Loretta Young, and Lana Turner.

This brief list hardly scratches the surface. Literally hundreds of other stars and starlets flocked to the ranch. Jeanette MacDonald obtained horses from the ranch to start her own farm. So did Gene Raymond and Robert Taylor. Horses from the ranch participated in the Tournament of Roses and appeared at special exhibitions throughout the state.

The movie companies quickly learned that a lot of talent was to be had quite inexpensively, and some of the outstanding stallions and mares played important parts in such early successes as *The Son of the Sheik*, in which Rudolph Valentino rode the gray stallion Jadaan. A beautiful and well trained but fiery mount, Jadaan had come to the Kellogg Ranch from the Peter B. Bradley stables in the East. He was brought to California by Carl Raswan, an outstanding horseman who doubled for Valentino in scenes requiring fancy riding. Raswan, who was also a breeder and historian, collected eleven Davenport Arabians and sold them to the Kellogg Ranch.

Marlene Dietrich in the role of Catherine of Russia was mounted on the beautiful gray stallion, King John, in the film *The Scarlet Empress*. Other notable Arabian-studded films included *Under Two Flags* and *Lives of a Bengal Lancer*.

The picture has not changed perceptibly. Forty-four years later, in 1969, the motion-picture industry was still intensely interested in the trained stallions and mares available at the Kellogg Ranch, now a division of the California State Polytechnic College. How the Kellogg Ranch became a part of this college system is a fascinating story.

As Kellogg grew older he became more and more interested in having a greater number of people, especially young people, come into contact with the Arabian breed. In 1932 he donated the

*Arabian horses were mandatory in movies such as* The Son of
the Sheik. *Rudolph Valentino's mounts were borrowed from the*
*Kellogg Arabian Ranch near Pomona. The high saddle evolved*
*in Arabia to allow the rider to lean against it as he charged.*

ranch and its horses to the University of California.
The ranch became known as the W. K. Kellogg
Institute of Animal Husbandry. In World War II,
when the War Department indicated it needed a
remount station for the cavalry, the State of California with Mr. Kellogg's approval turned the ranch
over to the War Department. It became known as
the Pomona Quartermaster Depot (Remount). Then
a series of incredible events made possible the
rescue of one of the great Arabian stallions of all
time, and as a result the Kellogg Ranch gained
even more prestige.

The story begins in 1943 at the Janow Stud Farm in Poland. As the Germans attacked from the west and the Russians from the east, this home of some of the most valuable Arabian stallions was evacuated, and the prized horses were quartered at farms and homes throughout the region. When the Germans moved into Janow, they gathered from considerable distances all the purebred stallions and mares they could locate and, utilizing Polish trainers and handlers, continued breeding operations. The Germans with classical thoroughness then selected the best of the stallions and sent them to a newly organized stud farm in Hostau, Czechoslovakia. Several fine mares were also moved from Poland to this seemingly safe locale.

Toward the end of the war the Russians were attacking from the east, and the Americans led by General George S. (Blood and Guts) Patton from the west. The Germans were caught between the pincers. But the Russians concerned them most, for the Russian Army was hungry for any kind of meat, including horse. That these were the blue bloods of the horse world may not have been enough to ensure their survival. The German veterinarian in charge of the breeding farm was unable to live with the idea of the great Arabian royal family being delivered to the Russians. Even though he was in a battle area and in considerable danger, he contacted the United States Army and told how important his charges were.

He could have found no more sympathetic ear than that of the commander of the United States forces. A cavalryman most of his life, General Patton knew and loved good horses. While the area was still under fire, Patton arranged a daring rescue of the horses and transferred them first to northern Bavaria, then to Mosbach, to the coast by land, and by ship to the United States and safety. Their liberation meant that one of the great stallions of all time was spared and would go on to breed many of the grandest champions in today's Arabian show ring. He was *Witez II, and he with eighteen other purebred Arabians was shipped to the United

States. It should be mentioned that sixty-three Thoroughbreds were with the Arabians. And perhaps an even better-known story is about the nine Lippizaners which were liberated from Czechoslovakia. These also were shipped to the United States.

*Witez II and others of the Arabians were sent to the Remount Depot, better known as the Kellogg Ranch in California. With these additions and other breeding stock loaned by Arabian owners, the Kellogg Ranch became the most important Arabian breeding center in the country.

*Witez II added new blood to Arabian lines throughout the United States. His grandfather Kuhailan-Haifi had been brought from Arabia to Poland by Prince Roman Sanguskco at a critical time in the Polish Arabian breeding program. Some of their most important stallions were quite old, but the Poles did have an extraordinarily fine lot of brood mares. *Witez II, therefore, came from recently generated desert blood. He was foaled at Janow, Poland, the year before the Germans invaded that country. The story of his almost miraculous escape we have told, but his history after arriving at the Kellogg Ranch is almost equally dramatic, although short.

By the time World War II ended, the horse cavalry had almost disappeared and had been replaced by motorized cavalry. The War Department transferred the Arabian breeding operation to the Department of Agriculture. When this department decided to close the ranch and disperse the finest breeding stock ever concentrated in one place, and when they actually began to auction the animals, Arabian horse lovers throughout the West rallied to its defense. They enlisted a great many important figures who, if they did not know much about Arabians, did know that the government's plan was unpopular and badly conceived. Among them was young Richard M. Nixon, then a Representative to Washington from California. Nixon protested the sale to Secretary of Agriculture Brannon. Quickly, Senators William F. Knowland and Sheridan Downey joined Nixon in his objections.

But in the first stages of discussions they did not seem to make progress. Then hundreds of letters began cascading in on President Truman's desk, objecting to the auctioning of 120 of the finest Arabians in the United States and the closing of the great institution established and contributed by Kellogg. Kellogg himself, who was then eighty-eight years old and blind, added a protest. Also, the mayor of Pomona, James B. Pettit, went to Washington to plead with President Truman.

But perhaps the most important voice, and the man ultimately responsible for forcing the Department of Agriculture to abandon its plan to dispose of the ranch and horses, was Cecil L. Edwards, well-known Pomona horseman, who used all of the influential friends the Arabian cause could rally. On Friday, December 17, 1948, Cecil Edwards was able to report "mission accomplished." The government had backed down. The famed Kellogg Ranch would continue as a part of the California State College system. The horses would remain on the rolling hills near Pomona.

But before the government's incredible plan had been stopped, *Witez II had been shipped to Fort Reno, Oklahoma, for sale at public auction. The man who later was to become the first president of the newly organized International Arabian Horse Association, E. E. Hurlbutt, acted immediately. Hurlbutt boarded a plane and arrived at the auction in time to bid in *Witez II for $8,100.

*Witez II had rarely been shown, despite his prestige and popularity at the Kellogg Ranch. Nonetheless he won almost every important award he was entered for. In his first appearance, which was the Southern California All-Arabian Show at Pomona in 1950, he was grand champion. Two years later he repeated his performance for Mr. Hurlbutt and became grand champion for the second time. That year he also won the Pacific Coast stallion championship. And not only was he an outstanding champion, but he had the rare ability to pass along the qualities that made him great. Two of his sons, Zitez and Natez, were also grand champions, and

Natez became grand champion twice just as his sire had. The mares among his get were no less famous. His daughter Fertezza was a reserve Canadian national champion, and Ronteza (the same Ronteza we talked of earlier) became grand champion reined cow horse at the Cow Palace in San Francisco, defeating the Quarter Horses at their own business. Others of his get have won awards as Cutting Horses, racers, and hunters.

So *Witez II, connived away from the dinner tables of Russian troops, became a unique personality in the Arabian horse world. In 1964 he was signally honored when Poland issued a postage stamp of him. On the occasion a Polish diplomat called *Witez II one of Poland's most important ambassadors to the United States. In 1965 *Witez II died at Mr. Hurlbutt's estate in the San Fernando Valley near Los Angeles. He was twenty-seven years old and was still begetting potential champions. *Witez II truly was one of the most exalted Arabian stallions of all time. His bloodline runs in championship stock throughout the United States. Even now where *Witez II first stood in the West, two mares that are direct descendants still carry on his great characteristics. They are at the institution Kellogg started and which after World War II was named the California State Polytechnic College, as it is known today.

Courses in animal husbandry became an important part of the curriculum there, and students were able to work with some of the finest Arabian breeding stock in the world. Today over seven thousand students are enrolled, some one thousand of them in the School of Agriculture. A select group of those take the Horse Production course, and surprisingly enough about fifty percent of the enrollment are women.

Each Sunday, just as W. K. Kellogg originally planned it, an exhibition with highly trained Arabian horses is given for the public. Students who have become expert riders show off the magnificent animals. Wild-looking Bedouins — students in desert costumes — ride impetuously around the show track. And great stallions that are contributing to the important Arabian blood stock exhibit routines they have learned from student trainers.

With the rolling hills surrounding the horse farm, and the colorful Spanish-style buildings rising from a knoll in the center, the Kellogg campus is as pleasant a spot to study as can be imagined. From the classrooms, the office, the show ring, and the patio you can look down on the green pastures with paddocks for stallions and free-running areas for mares and foals. It is no wonder the four courses in horse production are oversubscribed. First-year college enrollees are accepted in the course called Elements of Horse Production, which introduces the students to the various breeds and types of horses and takes up such important subjects as feeding, diseases, and judging.

This can be followed by a course in Advanced Horse Production. Here the students are concerned with the management of stallion and mare during breeding and spend considerable time on conformation, bloodlines, fertility and sterility diagnosis, and the handling of mares during pregnancy. This course also includes office procedures and the keeping of records. Only students who have completed the previous course can take it.

When attending these classes, students are given field work. Both men and women learn to handle foaling problems with the vet in attendance, and Cal Poly has invented a unique way of informing the students of the birth of each foal. Whenever a Cal Poly mare foals, a red flag is run up on a special pole so dormitory students upon awakening in the morning can learn the news and dash to the foaling barn to welcome the newcomer. Because pregnant mares are kept in a pasture adjacent to the classrooms, students can observe the mares as they approach foaling time. But if mares are moved during the night, a quick glance over the classroom area tells a student why the mare is not in the paddock the next day.

All the courses, including Basic Horse Training Techniques — which comprises driving on long lines, breaking foals to lead, grooming, fitting, and teaching horses to show — are attended by both men and women. In fact, the three just-mentioned courses and the most popular of all, Basic Equitation, have a higher percentage of coeds than men.

The women become competent very quickly in handling the Arabians, and it is common to see one coed handling a mare and another the stallion in the breeding barn during this important procedure.

In the Basic Equitation class, which is especially designed for students interested in training to ride and handle horses, participants learn grooming, saddling, bridling, care of equipment, and riding techniques.

A fifth class has a considerably smaller percentage of women — fifteen percent — and this is Horseshoeing. Under the supervision of a professor with a master of science degree in horseshoeing, students learn the anatomy and physiology of the horse's foot, pastern, and leg. They learn how to trim the feet properly and fit the shoes. The professor teaches not only normal horseshoeing but corrective horseshoeing, which is necessary to remedy some walking or running faults in certain animals.

In three of the classes — Horseshoeing, Elements of Horse Production, and Advanced Horse Production — enrollment normally is fifty to sixty students. But for Basic Horse Training Techniques and Basic Equitation, enrollment is limited to twenty because each student is assigned a different horse to care for, and the number of animals available for this purpose is limited.

Emphasis is on observation by and personal participation of students. As special projects, students set up their study programs with a view toward understanding horses. By observing individual behavior patterns, by watching details of how the animals move, and by studying hereditary traits, a student at graduation time possesses a solid education about horses.

Among recent student findings it was noted in

observing fillies in a paddock that they spent considerable time chewing on a wooden pole within the enclosure. Colts in a nearby paddock with the same type of pole did not chew on it. When a pole was not available for the fillies to chew on, they pulled each other's manes and tails. Other observations revealed that fillies frighten more easily than colts but that colts have a tendency to snap, rear, and play more than the fillies.

One senior student, Carl Winslow, spent a twenty-four-hour period watching mares and geldings grazing. He found that the horses grazed for four to five periods in each twenty-four hours. The most intense grazing occurred shortly before sunrise, during midmorning, in the early afternoon, and just before sunset. In his wrap-up Carl wrote:

"Each animal moves slowly across the pasture while keeping its muzzle close to the ground, and at the same time the horse will bite and tear off mouthfuls of grass. The grass is usually swallowed without a great deal of chewing. As the horse eats the preferred grass directly under his muzzle he will shift slightly to the right, left, or forward to choose the next mouthful. By grazing in this manner a horse will graze a path equal to approximately twice its body width while moving through the pasture.

"In the process of grazing, horses cover a large area and seldom take more than three mouthfuls before moving a step or two. The upper lip of the horse is sensitive, strong, and quite movable, and while grazing it is used to push the grass between the incisor teeth, which cut the forage. Small bits of loose grass and other feed are gathered in by the lips and tongue."

Some students are engaged in rate-of-growth studies. At the time of birth fillies were found to weigh eighty-nine pounds, almost two pounds more than the colt foals, which weighed 87.2 pounds. Their statistics show that the lighter-weight foals at birth doubled their poundage in the first thirty days but the heavier ones had considerably slower growth rates. The fillies continued to weigh more up until one year of age, when the colts overtook them.

It was found generally that weight at birth, or even height at birth, had no significance in the ultimate worth of the horse. The tallest that was registered at birth turned out to be only the tenth tallest of the control group at the end of one year. Height at birth was found to be thirty-six to thirty-nine inches, and the horse gained in height as much in the first three months as he did in the next nine. Norman K. Dunn, who heads the Arabian Horse Department, believes, however, that careful observation of a foal at from one to three months will give a very good idea of his ultimate value. The way his ears and tail are carried does not change much; and the trot, presence, and animation of a three-month-old can help immeasurably in the projected evaluation of a three-year-old.

Dunn also believes that at one year a colt can be well evaluated as a potential breeding stallion. He and the students look for the Arabian style, balance, muscle and skeletal structure, manner of traveling, Arabian conformation — and then his pedigree.

Some important information has been collected concerning the weaning of foals. Because several techniques have been tried, the experiments at Cal Poly used control groups and experimented with the two basic principles: the first of abrupt separation, the second a gradual separation becoming permanent after seven days.

Results were dramatic. Those foals abruptly separated from their mothers showed dangerous weight losses. One filly lost twenty pounds the first twenty-four hours and two others lost thirty-five pounds each. The one which lost twenty pounds took twelve days to regain it. The others, even though weight loss was greater, regained it in seven days. Of three test colts, each lost approximately twenty-five pounds. It took them four, eight, and twelve days respectively to regain it. Both the mares and foals were restless and nervously walked their fences and whinnied almost continuously for from three to four days.

With the other group the foals were separated only four hours, from 8 A.M. to noon, and only on the first two days. Even when they were separated it was merely by chain link fence so they could be completely aware of and visible to each other. On the third day, nursing was halted, although the mares were still in the adjoining paddock. After five days of this situation, the mares were led quietly to a distant pasture. The results were almost diametrically opposite. Five of the seven foals actually gained weight during the two days of partial separation and they stayed the same during the next five days. One lost five pounds but regained it on the sixth day. At the end of eight days four of the colts had gained twenty pounds, two had gained ten pounds, and one had gained fifteen pounds. In contrast to the shocking weight losses which occurred when mare and foal had been abruptly separated, weight gains were steady. There was little nervous fence walking. Even though the process takes a bit longer, it is the only way weaning will be done in the future with the Arabians at California State Polytechnic.

Not all of the research is done on foals. Mares, stallions, and geldings receive equal attention, but the rate-of-growth program has been of basic importance, for Arabians acquire eighty percent of their height in the first six months and gain forty-four percent of their weight. The average foal at birth in the test group at Cal Poly weighed 87.9 pounds. At six months it weighed 453.8 pounds and at one year 663.9 pounds.

In an attempt to find out about feeding patterns, students observed one mare and foal for thirty-six hours and two other such pairs for twenty-three and twenty-two hours. The first colt nursed an average of 3.4 times per hour and nursed for approximately two minutes each time. Once every 1.2 hours he lay down for an average of thirteen minutes. The other foals fit generally into the same pattern. Such observation has been valuable in

feeding orphaned foals, for it is now known that obtaining small amounts of feed at frequent intervals follows the natural tendencies of the youngsters.

The great mares, or "producers," at Cal Poly are just as carefully observed and just as gently handled as any of their foals. Norman Dunn has described a great mare as a distinctive horse with a genetic and physical potential to produce quality offspring when crossed with a variety of outstanding stallions. A number of mares such as Gamyla, Almaza, and Coulyfa have proven to be such great producers.

Because Arabian horses respond readily yet gently to humans, the courses in Horse Production at Cal Poly utilizing these purebred animals attract students who might find it difficult to handle less tractable stock. A unique example is sophomore Janet Christine Johnson. In her first year she finished Basic Horse Production and became enthusiastic over contact with the horses. She followed this in 1969 with Advanced Horse Production. In addition to her required time, she spent many free hours learning the physical characteristics of the horses. Then she started Horse Training and Equitation. This may not seem unusual even though Janet was only eighteen, but it did seem remarkable for a girl blind since infancy.

Janet's life at Cal Poly revolves around the horses, which with their riders make up an intimate circle of friends. She knows the horses by touch, their riders by their voices. Janet makes no concessions to her blindness. She has learned the terrain, and even though she often finds herself suddenly running into a fence or sliding down a hill, she moves about freely as though she could see. It is a tribute to the intelligence and gentleness of Arabian horses that she feels secure with them.

Of special interest to Arabian owners and breeders (and to all breeders) is research now going on at the University of California at Davis. Here Yoshiko Suzuki and Dr. Clyde Stormont of the

Department of Veterinary Microbiology have established a considerable number of horse blood-type combinations. While the number of blood types may be infinite because of minor differences, certain basic patterns have emerged.

The immediate application of their findings is of prime importance to all horse breeders. For it is now possible by determining a foal's blood type to rule out certain stallions (which may have covered the same mare) as his possible sire. As with humans, while it is not always possible to determine parentage, it is possible to disprove it.

Of almost equal importance is research on hemolytic disease. This in humans is well-known as the Rh factor. It soon will be possible to tell whether the blood types of mare and stallion are compatible or whether antibodies present could hamper the ability of the mare to nourish the foal properly. If the hemolytic factors are known, it would be possible to predict a problem foal and to give the mare corrective treatment which would enable her to feed the foal normally.

In the field of blood transfusion, after the first transfusion in which it would seem blood typing is not a vital factor, it does become important—if continuous transfusions are given—that the blood type be known. This precludes creation of certain antibodies that would be harmful.

It must be pointed out that although this research has been going on for a decade, only limited time, money, and personnel have been available. The blood types of certain breeds have not been thoroughly analyzed. And blood specimens have not been available from Clydesdales, Przewalskis, and other breeds.

Perhaps the most extraordinary discovery thus far has concerned the relationship between Arabians and Thoroughbreds. For unlike other breeds so far analyzed neither the Thoroughbred nor the Arabian possesses a certain D factor present in the other breeds. The absence of this factor indicates the direct relationship between these two breeds, an involvement which, although known historically, had not been proven scientifically.

This leads the writer into the field of conjecture. It is entirely possible that continuing research that identifies various blood types might be used in the future to tell whether certain blood types pass on such characteristics as running ability, conformation, and even disposition. It is possible even now to rule out certain horses as purebred Arabians or Thoroughbreds. Who knows how far the future can take us in this field?

Research into blood types is new. But many other characteristics illustrate the differences between a purebred Arabian and other breeds. It would be possible without blood typing for anyone truly familiar with Arabian conformation to recognize him as a distinct subspecies of horse. His relationship to the primitive, desert-bred horses of ancient Arabia remains visible. Here is a head-to-toe, withers-to-hoof description:

There is no mistaking the distinctive Arabian head. Its triangular shape which diminishes to a small and delicate muzzle likens him somewhat to the antelope. Remember in the legendary account of Ishmael's first sight of Kuhaylah, considered the first Arabian horse, that he mistook her for an antelope and almost killed her. The tender muzzle is no bigger than the palm of the hand. The Arabian's lips are narrow and smooth. But it is the long, curled nostrils that also give the Arabian his special look. When he is running or excited, these nostrils dilate to give a bold, sharp, and vigorous expression. The cheekbones of the Arabian are chiseled sharply and the face is slightly curved, or dished, below the eyes. His eyes are set wide apart and usually are large and soft when the horse is quiet, but become fiery and penetrating when he is aroused.

The Arabs prize a slight protrusion that in some strains occurs over the forehead and extends to just below the eyes. It is called the *jibbah*. This protuberance is considered by some experts to indicate an even larger brain capacity than is apparent by the spacious forehead. Because the cheekbones

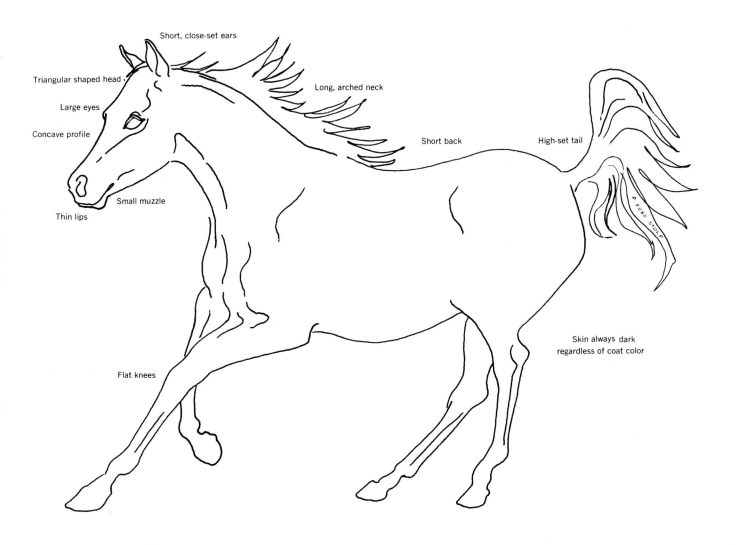

Short, close-set ears

Triangular shaped head

Large eyes

Concave profile

Thin lips

Small muzzle

Long, arched neck

Short back

High-set tail

Skin always dark
regardless of coat color

Flat knees

Average height: 14.2 hands to 15.2 hands.

Average weight: 800 to 1,000 pounds

*Distinguishing Characteristics of the Arabian*

spread wide at the throat, the muzzle can be drawn in without compressing the windpipe. This allows the Arabian to breathe without distress while running.

Most stallions have comparatively small ears. Those of mares are slightly larger but both are pointed and evenly set in upright positions. They have great flexibility. The overall effect of the Arabian head should be finely drawn and clearly etched, giving the impression of intelligence and energy.

The distinctive head of the Arabian is set upon an equally unique neck structure, which is long, arched, set high, and runs well back into the withers. The arch of the neck, caused partly by the way the head is set at an angle slightly more oblique than in breeds other than the Thoroughbred, imparts to the horse a somewhat swanlike grace. The Arabs give their word *mitbah* to the way the head sits on the neck in a slight line before the neck curves.

Arabians are rarely large horses, the average height being from 14.2 hands to 15.2 hands; or, measuring four inches to the hand, from 56.8 inches to 60.8 inches. There have been exceptions to this rule including the famous Jadaan, previously mentioned, which was over sixteen hands high.

Before considering the torso of the horse, we should mention his skeleton, which differs in several particulars from that of other breeds. For in addition to relative shortness of skull and a decided slenderness in the lower jaw many specimens show a larger brain cavity and fewer vertebrae in the back and tail. This latter detail is believed to give the Arabian a greater weight-carrying ability and is also responsible for his high tail carriage. Unlike many breeds, the Arabian exhibits few callosities on the hind legs and small ones on the forelegs.

Building on this strong practical skeletal structure, the Arabian has heavily muscled high withers set well back. The shoulders are long, deep, and broad at the base but the points of the shoulders are light. Arms are long, oblique, and muscular with the forearm broad at the elbow. Square, deep, and unusually large knees give the Arabian a solid base. His shank or cannon bone is short, flat, and clean with strong, heavy tendons. The fetlock joint is larger than in most breeds and he has pasterns that are long, sloping, strong, and elastic. The hoof created from generations of pounding desert sands is hard, large, round, and wide, and at the heel it is low. His legs are set parallel in front, straight from the side. They toe squarely ahead.

The lung capacity and food-storing ability of the Arabian are shown by his large rib cage, which runs to great depth beneath the chest. Seen from direct front or rear, the ribs bow out and protrude beyond the quarters. They are close-coupled to the point of the hipbone. As we mentioned, the back is generally short due to the absence of one lumbar vertebra and to the unique angle of the Arabian shoulder.

From the middle of the horse we go to the important hindquarters and find that the croup is even with the withers in height. The loins are broad and the haunch is long in proportion to the body. An often-remarked and well-known feature of the Arabian is a tail set on high. In the animal's first motion the tail is arched up and carried like a flag in the air. The quarters are well muscled, narrow, and long. The hams are well-filled out. Of almost abnormal size are the hocks, which give great leverage to the tendons at the gaskins. Again the shank bone is flat, clean, and short with large tendons. Like the front legs, the hind legs are placed vertically and squarely under the hindquarters and parallel to the body.

All of these structural points refer to what the ideal Arabian should be, and although there are many badly bred or less-well-formed specimens, the great majority of the purebreds conform. But even in those animals without perfect conformation, lungs and chest are almost always well developed. Few Arabians have heaves. Roaring is rare because of the size and position of the windpipe.

Because of his generations of desert breeding, his stomach is smaller than in most breeds, and therefore the feed required to keep him in good condition is considerably less. It is estimated that for weight carried the Arabian can subsist on about one-half the feed of the average European horse.

He weighs from eight hundred to one thousand pounds, with some larger animals exceeding this. For his weight and height he is able to handle heavier loads for longer distances than other breeds.

In the natural gaits and the gallop the Arabian moves smoothly because of the elasticity of his hind parts and his long pasterns. The trot is not natural to the Arabian but he can learn it. His natural action is long and low because for generations he was bred not only for speed but for covering long distances. As a jumper the Arabian has both dexterity and boldness and he handles his forefeet with the grace of a boxer. His reflexes are so quick that he has been known to strike a bird or butterfly in midair.

Grays are much prized but they do not constitute the highest percentage of Arabians. Fifty percent are bays, thirty percent gray, and the remaining twenty percent chestnut or brown. Rarely there is a pure white or black. Common markings include blaze faces, stars, stripes, and snip noses. White feet —maybe only one—or white stockings are often seen. A certain amount of speckling, often a red variety on the rump, is fairly common. But there are no duns, piebalds, yellows, or parti-colored horses among the Arabians.

Registration of purebred Arabian horses is strictly governed by the Arabian Horse Club Registry of America. Generally speaking, the organization automatically accepts any foal born in the United States, Canada, or Mexico if sire and dam are listed with it. If born in Mexico the foal, sire, and dam are also registered with the Mexico Jockey Club. A horse may be registered if while in foal his dam is imported into the United States, Canada, or Mexico providing dam and sire are named in the same foreign registry—and if the dam is registered

in the United States, Canada, or Mexico. Also, an unbroken pedigree of both bloodlines must trace to the Arabian desert countries or to a studbook approved by the registry.

Under certain other conditions, a horse may be imported into the United States, Canada, or Mexico from Arabian desert countries or from a country maintaining a studbook approved by the registry: If he has papers establishing purity of breeding and if he has an unbroken authenticated pedigree tracing each bloodline to the approved studbook of the country of exportation or to Arabian desert countries. In addition, after inspection abroad or on arrival and after payment of fees and expenses, an outstanding Arabian selected from desert stock may also be accepted.

The naming of Arabian horses is fascinating and intricate. Most breeders try to use names indicating desert origin. They also attempt to identify offspring of outstanding sires and dams with at least a portion of their names. But no horse will be registered by any name which is a duplicate of one already listed. Neither will directors allow a horse to be a junior or a senior. It is prohibited, for instance, to place a I, II, or III after the name of an animal of a given line. Nor may horses be registered if the name contains punctuation, such as a comma or apostrophe, or diacritical markings, such as a tilde, circumflex, or macron. To make it even harder no name may be composed of more than three parts or a total of seventeen letters and spaces.

Because all Arabian horses imported are imported for improvement of the breed, the Arabian Horse Club Registry has made up a list of faults that would exclude a horse from the registry. They include a parrot mouth, lop ears, small deep-set or off-color eyes, straight shoulder, low withers, a low back, a high, short, or too-sloping croup, a short thick neck or a U neck, a crooked tail carriage, or an off-color horse.

Legs are especially important, and these faults can keep a horse from being accepted: Toes out splay-footed or toes in pigeon-toed, knock-knees, bowlegs, a too-narrow or too-wide base, bench knees, or too-short and straight pasterns. They continue with sickle hock, which means the foot is set too far under the horse; or cow hock, which means that when viewed from behind the hocks are closer together than any other part of the leg. Types of feet that are disliked are pony or small feet, contracted feet, or mule feet. When it comes to action, the disqualifying faults are paddling, winging, overreaching, pacing, or a mixed gait.

Anyone can learn to observe the faults and virtues of an Arabian's actions. It is most important to observe one thing at a time. A good judge will concentrate on the right knee only for a few strides, then the right fetlock joint, then the right front foot as the horse runs or jogs in a straight line. It is possible then to add all three observations to see whether knee, fetlock, and foot move straight forward or whether they deviate. After getting a clear picture of the right leg, he then observes the left front leg, then one hind leg and the other. For a beginner, it is necessary to have the horse walked and jogged several times, but an experienced judge can make an analysis of his motion the first time around the ring.

The front-leg action can be best observed when the horse moves toward the observer. The hind-leg action is best observed when the horse moves away from the observer. His length of stride, his ability to move, and his lightness of foot (it has been said that his feet should fall upon the turf like rain upon the pasture) can best be judged when the horse moves briskly across the field of vision of the observer.

When viewing a horse from behind, try to imagine parallel lines dropping from the points of the buttocks through the hock and fetlock joints. These should remain approximately straight and parallel as the horse walks or jogs away.

Because Arabians adapt to every kind of climate, they have spread throughout the world. Purebred breeding is as popular in Russia as it is in Poland, the United States, Australia, or South America. Differences in climate range from extreme cold to tropical. The Arabian endures both and thrives. But in the Western United States he seems to have found a home that agrees with his natural characteristics and temperament. Moreover, he has found hundreds of *aficionados* to whom the Arabian with his aristocratic "way of going" has become a way of life.

*Neck extended, mane flying, head held high, ears alert, stallion Fadjeyn has desirable classic Arabian profile.*

# ARABIAN HORSES IN THE MODERN WEST

A legendary horse, origins lost in time, the modern Arabian can nonetheless be traced back over two thousand years. All light horses of Europe and the Americas are infused with his blood. He first came to the New World with the *conquistadores*. His descendants supplied mounts for the American Indians. In Europe he was the basis for the Thoroughbred, a breed which like the Arabian was spread throughout the modern world. In modern times original desert Arabians moved from Egypt, Syria, Saudi Arabia, Poland, and England across the United States to the West. Now on ranches, large and small, the Arabian has found a new home where he thrives and where he is bred to show and to race and to ride.

*Streaking gracefully across California hills, a band
of Arabian mares runs for sheer fun at Sheila Varian ranch.*

Grazing peacefully in the high country of California,
these Arabian mares become wary as they see photographer.

*A show champion as a three-year-old, Fadjeyn was sired by Fadjur, out of the \*Raseyn mare, Sur. (\*of foreign origin)*

## The Stallions

Perhaps because of the hundreds of years of unbroken association with man, the Arabian stallion is the easiest of all breeds to handle. Although like all stallions he becomes excited in the presence of a mare, he never forgets his human companion entirely. He rarely or never becomes dangerous. While he is bred for conformation and in some instances for speed, he most normally is bred for disposition. This is reflected in the total ease of handling during the breeding season. In this period, which lasts about one hundred days, an Arabian stallion will cover seventy or more mares, with a high percentage of the mares producing foals.

*Striking Arabian coloring is seen as many-times champion stallion Mikado sprints nimbly across his spacious paddock.*

*Speed and conformation, even in small paddock, are shown at Los Amigos Ranch by Karonek, an heir of famed *Raseyn.*

*Neck arched and showing excellent Arabian conformation, stallion rears up in his paddock.*

*Tail held high, imported Arabian stallion *Ibn Moniet El Nefous, opposite page, confidently paces toward camera.*

*Egyptian Arabian Fadjeyn is seen free-running at Green-gate Farm. Owner Jay Stream specializes in Egyptian stock.*

*Young Egyptian stallion *Ibn Moniet El Nefous, also shown on previous page, exercises in his California paddock.*

*In Arizona, multi-champion \*Bask shows off splendid form that long has made him a sire extensively sought after.*

*A daughter of \*Bask, called Fame, exhibits style and "way of going" of her sire on Lasma Ranch near Scottsdale.*

*One of the West's outstanding Arabian stallions is \*Gwalior. Like \*Bask and Fame, he is owned by Dr. Eugene E. LaCroix.*

*Breeder, trainer, rider, owner, Miss Sheila Varian talks quietly to well-disciplined Bay-Abi, one of her top studs.*

*Clara Mari leads Amerigo on La Puente, California, ranch of her father, "Frisco" Mari. She and her sister train horses.*

*With well-known trainer Jim Alderson up, Poly Royal,*
*show horse and breeding stallion, takes off in Western style.*

## Western Style

Western-style riding comes from the Arabs, the cavalry, the American Indians, and the Spanish. Its tack evolves from war horse and workhorse. Full days in the saddle made a broad, comfortable seat important, while use of the lariat called for development of the high saddle horn. Although size and shape of the basic Western saddles are almost as distinctive as the men who use them, there are Spanish, Texas, California, New Mexico, and Arizona styles, plus hundreds of local variations.

*Hoofs flying, Poly Royal skims hilly terrain at Cal Poly, where he is star performer in breeding shed or show arena.*

*Wearing a crash helmet which he has not yet needed, twelve-year-old Raymond LaCroix on Aanadra nears obstacle.*

*Midway over, boy and mare show form. LaCroix Arabians are breeding stock which have athletes showing in many classes.*

*Arabians are willing jumpers. But because they cannot be forced, it takes time and patience to train them properly.*

## Eastern Style

Eastern-style tack and riding techniques derive largely from European riding schools. Saddles are almost flat and must be well-fitted to horse and rider. Stirrups are shorter than in Western style. To keep the rider's weight over the horse's center of gravity, stirrup leathers are set forward. Show riding, shown on these pages, requires a double bridle — snaffle bit, reins, cheek straps, and crownpiece, and over this another crownpiece, more cheek straps, a lip strap, curb bit and reins, brow band, and throatlatch.

*The walk is a natural gait of Arabians. Riding Eastern style, student Judy Halleran of Cal Poly demonstrates.*

*Standing with legs well under her, ears up, tail relaxed, the horse waits patiently for a signal from student rider.*

*The trot is not natural but Arabians learn quickly.*
*Tail carriage must be high and natural, never set or rigid.*

*The canter is another natural gait of the Arabian.*
*From canter the Arabian moves easily into a smooth gallop.*

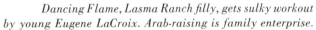

*Dancing Flame, Lasma Ranch filly, gets sulky workout*
*by young Eugene LaCroix. Arab-raising is family enterprise.*

*Mares and foals play on one side of the paddock fence as yearlings romp on the other near San Bernardino hills.*

## Mares and Foals

The desert Arabs prized mares over stallions. They admired their quiet manners, their speed, and stamina. Characteristically good mothers, most Arabians bear and rear healthy and well-behaved foals. For Arabians, as for all horses, the gestation period is approximately eleven months. Like Thoroughbreds, Arabians become one year old on the first of January no matter when they are born. For this reason breeders try to get the mare in foal during the early months of the year, so the foal will be well-grown on his first birthday. Foals are born in the position of a diver, front legs extended. They weigh approximately eighty-five pounds, and can stand and nurse within a few hours.

*Promising and confident, Arabian foal, six weeks old,
poses on well-tended Cal Poly lawn. Good traits show up early.*

*A good mother to her offspring, \*Naganka is shown here galloping across spacious pasture exercising a recent foal.*

*The foal is stretching every muscle and covering a lot of ground to keep up with pace set by prize-winning mother.*

*Although heavy with foal, one of great producers
at California State Polytechnic College flies across pasture.*

*Nuzzling against dam makes foal at left feel
secure. Below, he nurses. Foals feed three times per hour.*

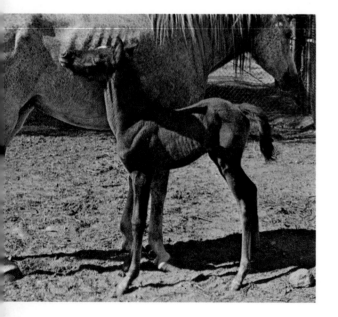

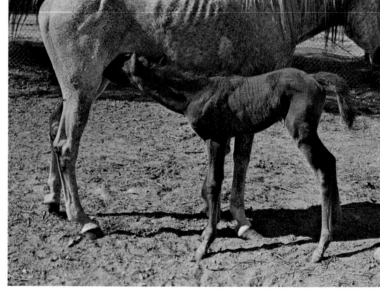

*Another great producer at Cal Poly keeps wary eye on her foal. Some mares are descendants of early Kellogg stock.*

*Students pose with mounts in Cal Poly patio.*
*For equitation course, each student is assigned a horse.*

*Built in the Spanish style in 1946 by W. K. Kellogg,*
*the Arabian headquarters is a southern California showplace.*

*The purebred Arabian head is easy to recognize by looking for scooped or "dished" nose, the large eyes, and delicate mouth.*

## California Polytechnic Institute

The fortunate students in the Horse Production courses at California State Polytechnic College in Pomona, California, study and work with some of the finest Arabian stock in the world. The atmosphere at this campus, where the Spanish-style stables and the spacious paddocks are located, combines the old and new West with echoes of the Moors in eighth-century Sevilla and Córdoba. In the well-equipped show arena, students stage an Arabian circus twice each Sunday from October through May. Attendance averages eight hundred spectators, with income going mostly for tack, arena and grandstand equipment, and some student wages. Most popular acts are the liberty horses, jumping events, cow-penning, and Western-style riding. The shows were started in the days of the Kellogg Ranch in 1925.

*Corrective horseshoes make difference in way some horses move. Ray Johnson shows class how to fit special shoes.*

*Daily weight check is necessary in breeding season when stallions lose pounds. Students weigh top sire Courier.*

*Although blind since infancy, Janet "Jan" Christine Johnson takes the regular Horse Production course at Cal Poly.*

*Jan regularly handles foals, mares, and stallions. She can easily recognize them by touch. Foal here almost got away.*

*With feet well-set, Jan holds foal steady. At two weeks, youngster weighs almost as much as does eighteen-year-old Jan.*

Trick horse Tedazi rocks a baby carriage, fires gun,
and ends act in difficult pose with student trainer Cindy Muns.

*Mighty stallion Poly Royal, his muscular form unfet-
tered, willingly obeys voice and hand signals during the show.*

*At end of his performance, Poly Royal makes a bow. Students say Arabian horses learn quickly and enjoy entertaining.*

# THE THOROUGHBRED

One of the most exciting examples of man's ability to observe and plan is shown in the creation of the Thoroughbred horse. This esthetic animal has been carefully bred for generations to put on the final burst of speed whether racing against time or rival horses. Every muscle has been observed, the speed of his forebears has been carefully weighed and analyzed. His conditioning is a major concern, and when the Thoroughbred is ready for the track he is a tribute not only to the beauty, speed, and stamina that are his heritage but also to the skillfulness of man.

And when you talk of Thoroughbreds you must talk of gambling. The two themes have always been synonymous. Men have found many ways to gamble. But when you consider the smoke-filled poker room, the roulette and blackjack casino, or two humans attempting to destroy each other's brains in a roped-off elevated square, none compares with horse racing for beauty and excitement, risk and judgment and suspense. This is gambling at its zenith. The scene is the limitless outdoors, and the animals you wager on bring a human element to the race. They are flesh and blood, muscle and bone, grace and beauty.

When a man wagers, he bets on a horse, not symbols representing mathematical formulas on a stock-exchange board. Nor is he betting on whether the price of cotton will go up or down, nor reaching into a deck to turn over a card. He is participating in the greatest and most satisfying of all the ways to gamble.

No one knows when men began racing horses against each other, although it can safely be conjectured that this occurred the first time the owners of two domesticated mounts met on some prehistoric afternoon. But more has been written about the Thoroughbred breed, fleetest of the racers, than of any other breed. This is because the Thoroughbred, as it is known throughout the world, began in comparatively recent years. At most it is less than three hundred years old.

To think of the Thoroughbred as a breed it is necessary to recall its Arabian ancestors. On the desert, horses were bred for speed and endurance and were used most effectively in cavalry. But in England, France and, indeed, most of Europe, the wars of the fifteenth, sixteenth, and even the seventeenth centuries required horses of great size and strength to carry men clothed in as much as two hundred pounds of armor. Add to this the armor for the horse and the weight of the man, and it was necessary for a horse to carry four hundred to five hundred pounds. But the kings and knights learned from bitter and bloody lessons that men without armor—warriors massed on foot, armed with only bows and arrows and usually clothed in leather jerkins—could annihilate the brave and well-protected paladins on their plodding horses. In the Crusades they saw for the first time what light cavalry could do, how it could outflank them or make swift and devastating raids into their camp and be gone before a man could even fasten on his breastplate.

So the Thoroughbred's ancestors developed as the cavalry of Europe became a light, flexible instrument of war. A good cavalry horse had to be responsive, fast running, yet own considerable staying power. So the Arabian horse was brought to England, and there he was used not only as a military mount but was raced by the nobility for pleasure and profit. It was rightly called a sport of kings.

In England, racing records date to a track which

121

was laid out in Doncaster in 1595. But nothing is written to show what kinds of horses raced there. That in Eng6and racing was considered a vice as early as 1654 is indicated, however, by a proclamation Oliver Cromwell issued that year forbidding racing for six months. But large-scale racing in England probably did not get under way until the reign of Charles II between 1660 and 1685.

Now, in a general way, we have indicated that three factors entered into the development of the Thoroughbred: the necessity for a more maneuverable cavalry; the need for a fast, competitive steed for pleasure racing; and that gambling seems to be as deeply a part of the human condition as running is of the horse's heritage.

We know that men do gamble, although no one is certain why, nor is anyone certain why one horse tries to outrun another. Some zoologists have conjectured that every horse wants to be in front because, during his long-time environment when he was vulnerable to predators (lions, wolves, tigers), horses realized that the one in front of the herd was least likely to be pulled down.

But no matter why, the early Arabian imports to England proved to be fleet runners on the track and, fortunately, written records were kept of the early imports so that it is possible today to trace every Thoroughbred in the world to three great Mediterranean sires. These three unique stallions may be classed generally as Arabians, although they came from the Barbary Coast and Turkey as well as Arabia. The first we have any record of is the Byerly Turk, which was identified by John Cheny, who in 1727 published the earliest account of racing in England. It was called a historical list or account of all the horse matches run and of all the plates and prizes competed for in England (of the value of ten pounds or upward). Cheny in this work mentions "Captain Byerly's charging horse" which was used in the Irish Wars. It is believed that he was foaled about 1679 and was standing at stud as late as 1698.

Next to appear on the racing scene was the Godolphin Arabian, which followed some fifty years after the Byerly Turk, around 1725. Several stories tell how he became the property of the Earl of Godolphin, famed English sportsman. How he got to England is not now known, but one story tells that the Emperor of Morocco gave him to Louis XIV of France. Another tale written by the French romantic novelist Eugène Sue relates that he was stolen from a royal stud in Morocco and taken to Paris where he pulled a milk wagon until he was rescued and taken to England. Regardless of the truth of these accounts, the Earl of Godolphin did have in his stud an outstanding Arabian sire (which may have had some Barb blood) that stood about fifteen hands high and became one of the three ancestors of all modern Thoroughbreds.

The story of the third of the great founding sires can be stipulated with some degree of accuracy. Called the Darley Arabian, he was purchased in northwest Syria, in the city of Aleppo, by a young man named Thomas Darley, who sent him as a gift to his father in England in 1704 when the horse was a four-year-old. Young Darley's letter to his father was dated in Aleppo, Syria, December 21, 1703:

". . . Since my Father expects I should send him a stallion, I esteem myself happy in a colt I bought about a year and a half agoe, with a desyne indeed to send him ye first good opportunity. He comes four the latter end of March or the beginning of Aprill next; his colour is Bay, and his near foot before with both his hind feet have white upon them; he has a blaze downe his face something of the largest. He is about 15 hands high, of the most esteemed race among the Arabs, both by Syre and Dam and the name of the said race is called Mannika . . . ."

According to the studbook records the Darley Arabian produced foals for almost thirty years.

Upon the hereditary traits of these three stallions the Thoroughbred line has been based. But modern pedigrees trace all Thoroughbreds not to these three sires but instead to their descendants. These are Herod, an outstanding stallion foaled in 1758; Matchem, foaled in 1748; and Eclipse, foaled in 1764. The Byerly Turk is the great-great-grandsire of Herod. The Godolphin Arabian is the grandsire of Matchem. The Darley Arabian is the great-great-grandsire of Eclipse. No other branches of the original male lines exist except these three. Every Thoroughbred in the world today traces directly to Herod, Matchem, or Eclipse.

But how accurate are the ancient records? Did any other bloodlines creep in? And what about the mares mated to the first Thoroughbred sires? Some authorities have questioned the increase in the size of the Thoroughbred based on the short span of time between the first Arabian arrivals in England and the present-day horse. Two possibilities are certainly conceivable. One, that matings with larger animals such as the coarser Barb horses were involved, or that some of the early mares may have belonged to the earlier heavy, large-boned animals used by the knights in armor. Another ingenious theory has been advanced by Mrs. Marguerite Farlee Baylis, one of the great writer-researchers on Thoroughbreds in the United States. She suggests that the progenitors of the Thoroughbred, both stallions and mares, may have belonged to a larger breed of Arabians which became lost or extinct in their native countries; that over the early years only Arabians of a particular larger, faster type were imported and that the finest stock moved to England, leaving almost none of these "special, of the blood," horses.

But of course if we accept the sizes as recorded in the early record books, it still does not seem entirely possible that Throughbreds could have grown four to five inches in two and one-half generations. No, it seems more likely that the key may lie in the direction of either imported Barbary mares or in mating to the heavier northern breeds.

This could account for some of the confusion and inaccuracies regarding what is known in pedigrees as the tail-female line. The original English studbooks list less than one hundred "tap root"

mares, and the great majority are unnamed and are only identified by the name of the owner or of the sire that bred them. For instance, the book will list as dam "Burton's Barb Mare" or "a royal mare" or "a mare by Gascoigne's foreign horse."

Actually, the fastest and best-bred stallions were mated to the best available mares. The daughters of such matings were bred to other imported stallions or fast-running sons of the earlier imports. The result was that after only a few generations the dominant imported strain obscured the characteristics of the native stock. A few of these founding mares do trace back to Mediterranean origins, but it is entirely possible that on the female side the Thoroughbreds may have draft horse, Scotch pony, Highland dun, and other minor mixtures. But in the main there can be no doubt that the most important blood in the Thoroughbred is Arabian. Even the name Thoroughbred is a rough translation of the Arabic *asil*, meaning purebred.

However, more than Arabian blood was required to create the present Thoroughbred. Selective breeding for over two hundred and fifty years has caused the Thoroughbred to be larger physically, with somewhat different conformation from his ancestors from the Barbary regions, and has given him greater speed. While the average Arabian has remained fourteen to fifteen hands high, the Thoroughbred has increased to an average height of almost sixteen hands.

The leap from the foundation Thoroughbreds to the Thoroughbred in the Western regions of the United States is a great one. But because records have been increasingly comprehensive it is possible today to trace to its homeland the modern racehorse of Santa Anita, Del Mar, Hollywood Park, and other famous tracks in the Western United States.

America started its Thoroughbred development later than England, but settlers of Virginia, Maryland, and other East Coast colonies brought with them not only a love for the sport of racing but also considerable experience in setting up racecourses and in breeding Thoroughbreds. Even before Thoroughbreds were imported, however, racing was conducted along the East Coast, possibly in New York, for we know a track was established on Long Island as early as 1665. Many of the races were over short courses of one-quarter mile. These sprint runners were later known as American quarter-running horses. Thoroughbreds did not get started until *Bulle Rock was imported in 1730.

Officially, Maryland must be recognized as the first state to begin racing between pedigreed horses in the English style. This occurred at Annapolis in 1745. The governor of the state, Samuel Ogle, was responsible for its introduction. This same Governor Ogle brought over the stallion *Spark and the famous mare *Queen Mab.

Other great Thoroughbreds imported between 1745 and 1760 include *Traveler, the racing mare *Selima, *Othello, *Janus, and *Fearnought.

As the horse carried the early colonists westward, the Thoroughbreds moved with them. By the time Daniel Boone moved on from Kentucky to Missouri, both Tennessee and Kentucky were liberally sprinkled with Thoroughbred breeding farms.

As a result of assistance received from France during the Revolutionary War, two Kentucky towns later famous for their Thoroughbreds were named Paris and Versailles. And the Marquis de la Fayette, a tireless traveler and a great horseman, contributed his name to Fayette County, also famous for Thoroughbreds. The Easterners who settled Kentucky were the ancestors of those adventurers who pushed on westward. It took over fifty years, but when gold was found in California in 1848, horse racing in the tradition of Kentucky and New England came to the Far West. In 1816 an early Kentucky historian, Mann Butler, had written, "Every young man I know has a horse, a gun, and a violin." In the West the violin was dropped, often in favor of a dark-eyed, brown-skinned beauty descended from California's Spanish or Mexican settlers.

Thoroughbreds were necessarily rare in the West before 1900. Yet a few were brought out by Eastern or Southern families after the Civil War, and regular racing was held in the fast-developing communities of Denver, Sacramento, and San Francisco. The Spanish settlers of southern California, Arizona, and New Mexico had long raced horses, but these, although of Arab descent, were not Thoroughbreds in the technical sense. Still, they added to the tradition of racing, and when the Thoroughbred did begin to come into the West, both for breeding and for sport, there was wide and popular acceptance of him as a breeding sire and the Thoroughbred improved the Western horse immeasurably.

A fine horse of Thoroughbred blood was prized over all possessions. He was handled with care and bred for speed, endurance, and beauty. Many a horse that outran Indians and outlaws mounted on less highly bred mustangs had some of the Thoroughbred blood brought from the East.

Because Thoroughbreds are nervous, sensitive, and temperamental, the first to come to the West were given special care whenever possible. They are likely to injure themselves in large pastures and so they were rarely used as cow horses. Many of the old-time ranchers were opposed to working cattle with horses of more than half Thoroughbred blood.

By definition the Thoroughbred is a running horse. As we mentioned, he is also a horse descended in all lines from ancestors bred and trained for racing for over two hundred and fifty years. That breeding stock was selected as a result of the horse's performance on the track. However, it is important to remember that to be a Thoroughbred the horse must without flaw trace through all of its breeding branches to animals that were registered in the *General Stud Book*. And the *General Stud Book* has been closed since 1827. No horses whose ancestors were not recorded therein before that date can be admitted.

Many persons are strongly critical of the English

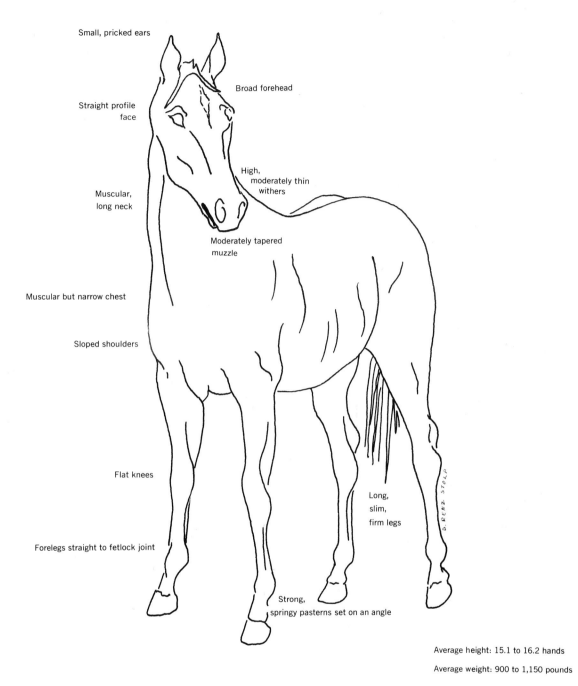

Small, pricked ears

Broad forehead

Straight profile
face

High,
moderately thin
withers

Muscular,
long neck

Moderately tapered
muzzle

Muscular but narrow chest

Sloped shoulders

Flat knees

Long,
slim,
firm legs

Forelegs straight to fetlock joint

Strong,
springy pasterns set on an angle

Average height: 15.1 to 16.2 hands

Average weight: 900 to 1,150 pounds

*Distinguishing Characteristics of the Thoroughbred*

*General Stud Book* and its rigid interpretation of Thoroughbred breeding. It has been said the book manages to accept a great many impurities but only if they occurred before 1913.

Thoroughbreds vary in size from small animals of only fourteen hands to very tall horses of seventeen hands. (Four inches equal a hand.) And they weigh anywhere from 850 to 1,350 pounds. Thoroughbreds come in a good many colors, but they most often are bays, chestnuts, or browns.

It is interesting that almost all gray Thoroughbreds trace to a gray stallion called Alcock's Arabian, which was imported into England around 1710. A gray horse must have at least one gray parent, and if the grays are followed carefully through complete pedigrees they usually lead to the Alcock Arabian. The few which do not can be traced, also in an unbroken line of grays, to another Arabian stud, this one called the Brownlow Turk.

So by the time the Thoroughbred came to the Western states, he had been a well-defined breed for more than two centuries. In the United States the records of sires and dams are probably more accurate than the early records in England, for by 1750 well-bred mares were available in the United States whereas one hundred years earlier in England there were very few that came from racing stock.

Breeding in the Western states followed a pattern similar to that of the East and of England. The best possible stallions were brought in and bred to the best mares available. The daughters of these were bred to the best stallions, often to their own sires, as had been done with the founding sires in England. But the final test was the racetrack. Only there was it possible to tell whether a horse was worthy of his breeding. Thoroughbreds have a natural gallop. They run with a long, straight, free movement. The action of their legs is easy but not high. Although similar examples can be found in almost every breed, Thoroughbreds are said to have great "heart" even when "bottom" is lacking. Fine horses have ruined themselves permanently by finishing races after being badly crippled. Generations of breeding have caused the muscles of Thoroughbreds to develop such strength that the fine joints, because they are not a heavy-boned animal, cannot stand the strain from the pull of the muscles and the pounding the delicate bones take at high speed. Some Thoroughbreds when raced too often go unsound from straining these tendons and joints.

The first Thoroughbred to arrive on the West Coast of the United States complete with a pedigree that went back to one of the three founding sires was a jet mare called *Black Swan, which arrived by sailing vessel in the mid-1800's. By piecing together bits of local history, we reach the conclusion that *Black Swan was shipped from Australia consigned to a buyer in San Francisco. From San Francisco she was walked, or perhaps ridden, down the coast along El Camino Real—the royal road—to Los Angeles, where she would be a principal in the most famous match race of early California history.

According to one account, *Black Swan made that long overland venture under an agreement between her owners, whose names have not come down to us, and the flamboyant Mexican, José Andrés Sepúlveda, to race in Sepúlveda's colors against the stallion Sarco, pride and boast of Pío Pico, who had been California's last Mexican governor, and of Pío's brother Andrés. Sarco was considered the fastest racer on the West Coast and was almost certainly of pure Arabian blood, bred from ancestors of those Arabians shipped from Spain to Mexico.

Sepúlveda and the brothers Pico were rivals in social life and in their prodigalities. For all of them, horse racing was a passion. Here were the wagers for this match race: $25,000 cash, five hundred horses, five hundred mares, five hundred heifers, five hundred calves, and five hundred sheep.

This was a nine-mile race in March, 1852, from where Seventh Street now crosses Alameda to a stake four and one-half miles distant, and back.

It generated tremendous excitement. A spectator, Thomas D. Mott, wrote:

"No preparations were made to put the track in condition, and not much of the race outside of start and finish was seen, as mustard on both sides of the road was ten feet high.

"The length of the course was nine miles, or more properly speaking, three Spanish leagues . . . Everybody in the country was present and the whole country as far north as San Luis Obispo and south to San Diego was depopulated. They all came to see the great race."

And that newcomer, that outsider—that first pedigreed Thoroughbred on the West Coast—defeated Sarco by seventy-five yards. The jubilant (and now somewhat wealthier) Sepúlveda then purchased *Black Swan and sent her to his Rancho San Joaquín, where he hoped to breed her and improve his stock. There, however, the great mare stepped on a nail, suffered lockjaw, and died.

Unfortunately, as much legend as fact seems to ride through this story. Yet there is no doubt that a Thoroughbred called *Black Swan was imported into California in the mid-nineteenth century. But there were no Thoroughbred stallions, and if this mare was bred to any of the Spanish horses no record remains.

Within two years, however, in 1854, the first Thoroughbred stallion was brought across the country. He was Belmont, which had been Eastern-bred, then moved to Ohio. The Williamson brothers, California's first recorded Thoroughbred breeders, rode over the plains and mountains to California with Belmont and two Thoroughbred mares. Although he never raced he became the sire of a number of California's first Thoroughbred stock.

Thoroughbreds remained rare for the next few years but it is reasonably certain there was a Thoroughbred race for two-year-olds in Sacramento in 1857. It was a match race between the filly Desdemona and a chestnut colt called Vigilance. Both were from the stallion Belmont's first crop of foals. The filly won.

Races were longer in the West in the old days than they are today and horses were bred not only for speed but for endurance. Courses ranged in length from two to four miles and occasionally more.

The early Thoroughbred picture emerges more clearly after the Civil War. A tycoon, Theodore Winters, a versatile gentleman, started breeding on a large scale. He seemed to have made money out of everything he touched and in Sacramento had been involved in trade and commerce as well as gold mining. The attractive small city of Winters on the west bank of the Sacramento River marks the spot where his first breeding farm was located.

The leading sire on the Winters farm was Norfolk, most famous son of the Kentucky-bred Lexington, still considered by most racing experts to be America's greatest Thoroughbred stallion. After Lexington had been retired from the track and was standing at stud at Woodburn Farm, owner Richard Ten Broeck, who was then racing in England, met up with a fellow Kentuckian, Richard A. Alexander. Alexander offered Ten Broeck $15,000 for Lexington. It was considered a phenomenal price because not only had Lexington been retired from the track, but his foals had not yet raced. Alexander made only one stipulation. It was that Lexington still be alive when he returned to America. And Alexander told Ten Broeck he thought Lexington was a great bargain, and he swore to him he would sell one of Lexington's foals for more money than he paid for the stallion. Norfolk was that foal. Alexander sold him to Theodore Winters for $15,001 just to prove that he could sell him for more than he had paid for his sire. Norfolk at that time was unbeaten. He had outrun all of the Thoroughbreds that had challenged him in the East, and at Passaic, New Jersey, had won the first "Derby" ever run in the United States.

Norfolk sired what is generally considered one of the West's outstanding runners, Emperor of Norfolk. He was known as the Western nonpareil or the California Wonder. Certainly he was the finest two-year-old and the most remarkable three-year-old of 1887 and 1888.

Emperor of Norfolk's lineage was not only outstanding on the male side but he was out of the superlative producing mare Marian. She was also the dam of what is usually considered the second fastest (and by some the fastest) Thoroughbred in the West, El Rio Rey. Indeed she should be considered the most important producer of California Thoroughbreds. For not only was she as great a racing champion as the just-mentioned horses, but she produced The Czar, Yo Tambien, Duke of Norfolk, and Rey del Rey. While all of her notable offspring with one exception were sired by Norfolk, the fleet Yo Tambien—which had an untouchable racing record of forty-four wins, eleven seconds, and nine third places in seventy-three starts—was sired by Joe Hooker.

But Emperor of Norfolk outshone them all. He became the property of the almost legendary E. J. "Lucky" Baldwin, and under Baldwin's aegis he won twenty-one of twenty-nine races against the best horses in America. He was out of the money only twice, and his earnings, although he raced only one year and two days, came to $72,290. That sum would be worth at least five times as much today—and "Lucky" Baldwin bought this majestic racer from Theodore Winters for only $2,500. Emperor of Norfolk was the first of a long line of great Western-bred horses.

San Francisco developed the first significant racetrack in the West. It was called the Pioneer Race Course and racing began on March 24, 1851. The course's front stretch was along present-day San Francisco's Twenty-fourth Street and its backstretch was along Twenty-sixth Street, with the turns touching Capp Street on the west and Florida Street on the east. The grandstand was located near Twenty-fourth and Shotwell Streets. But it was not long before other tracks sprung up to feature Thoroughbred races.

Senator George Hearst, father of publisher William Randolph Hearst, put up the money for the Bay View Course located on the shore of San Francisco Bay and opened in 1863. The action then moved out to Ocean View Park Course near Lake Merced until Leland Stanford financed the building of Bay District Track on Geary Boulevard. In the last twenty-five years of the nineteenth century, major tracks were built in all the Western states when gambling was allowed.

"The Richest Race in the World," or at least up until that time, was run at San Francisco's Ocean View Park Course on November 15, 1873, and the purse was $20,000 in gold. The field included several champions not only from the West but Thoroughbreds sent by rail from the East. Among them was Joe Daniels which the year before had won the Belmont Stakes worth only a paltry $4,500, and the Traverse, worth only $5,500. In the end (for it was run in three heats) a Western-bred horse, Thad Stevens, won. There was more racing in the East but no more enthusiasm, and stakes were often smaller. Big-time racing in the United States can be said to have originated in New York and California.

The importance of Theodore Winters and "Lucky" Baldwin as foundation breeders in California cannot be overemphasized. Baldwin, who developed an outstanding stud, got his nickname "Lucky" by a smile of fate that commenced when he left to hunt tigers in India and commissioned his broker in San Francisco to sell certain gold-mining shares after the stock had reached a specified price. But Baldwin forgot to give the broker the combination to his safe, as he had planned. During the year Baldwin was away, the locked-up shares went up and up in value, quickly passing Baldwin's stipulated selling price. By the time Baldwin returned they were worth millions of dollars instead of the thousands he had planned to sell them for.

Before leaving discussion of late nineteenth-century racing, I want to mention a wonderful California mare, Molly McCarthy, which also was raced by Baldwin. She was undefeated until she was shipped East, and it is generally believed she was in poor condition after her cross-country trip. Her race against the champion Ten Broeck in Lexington, Kentucky, on July 4, 1878, is considered one of the great competitions in the history of American racing. It was a $10,000 match—each owner putting up $5,000—winner take all. Molly McCarthy led for the first two and one-half miles but then fell back to lose to the Eastern champion by a considerable margin.

One of the outstanding California-bred horses was Rey del Carreras. After being shipped to England, where he was renamed Americus, he sired Americus Girl, the dam of Lady Josephine. Through this tail-female line some of the world's leading present-day bloodlines were founded, for such outstanding stallions as *Blenheim II, *Nasrullah, and Royal Charger trace their lineage to those mares.

California-owned horses from the Baldwin nursery won four American derbies. They were the Emperor of Norfolk, Volante, Silver Cloud, and Rey el Santa Anita. Baldwin was proud of his successful horses. To honor those who galloped away to the pastures of heaven, he placed a large Maltese cross in the horse graveyard at his ranch. Today that cross stands in the garden at Santa Anita Park —almost precisely where Baldwin's stable stood.

But if "Lucky" Baldwin had the most successful breeding farm in California, it was nowhere near the largest. Perhaps the greatest Thoroughbred farm ever known was that splendid operation developed by James Ben Ali Haggin. It covered almost fifty thousand acres, adjoining Sacramento on the north. James Ben Ali Haggin had one stirrup in the West and the other in the East. He had been born in Kentucky but was reared in the West, and there he began his vast breeding operation. His horse Tyrant won the Withers and the Belmont, and Ben Ali, a horse born in Kentucky and reared in California, won the Kentucky Derby in 1886. Others from this superb racing string included the outstanding mare Firenze, *Africander, and Rubio, which in 1938 became the first American-bred horse to win the Liverpool Grand National Steeple-

chase, one of Europe's most difficult courses.

Ben Ali's glory as a Kentucky Derby champion encouraged his owner to stand him at stud in California on the Haggin Farm, which might be the largest of all time. Haggin had 30 studs, 562 brood mares, and more than 1,300 yearlings, sucklings, and weanlings, making a total of almost 2,000 Thoroughbreds. Late in his breeding career Haggin sold out and returned to his home state of Kentucky, where he acquired Elmendorf Farm. The California stock went to New York to be auctioned, and Haggin bid in many of his own Thoroughbreds to stand at his Elmendorf stud.

Other great names in Thoroughbred racing in the West include Leland Stanford, who in addition to founding a university established a Thoroughbred farm at Palo Alto, and William O'B. MacDonough, who developed a stud farm at Menlo Park. He called it Ormondale after the undefeated English stallion *Ormonde, which stood there in 1893. MacDonough paid $150,000 for *Ormonde and an additional $25,000 to ship the horse to Menlo Park. This horse has the unique distinction of still standing, for his bones were disinterred in California and his skeleton was reassembled in England, where it is displayed at the National Museum. The reason for this unusual distinction is that before coming to California, *Ormonde sired the line of stallions that resulted in *Teddy, the great racer that established the *Sir Gallahad III-*Bull Dog-Bull Lea line so important today.

Senator George Hearst bred horses at his San Simeon ranch and raced them in New York and San Francisco. And Colonel Dan Bums and Clarence Waterhouse ran a unique two-thousand-acre breeding farm at Hopland, California. There they not only bred horses but operated a recuperation home for run-out, exhausted Thoroughbreds. Horses from their breeding farm led the field in the West from the turn of the century until 1910.

Because of bad management, bad publicity, and occasional dishonesty at the tracks, California passed a no-betting law in 1909. As a result, most tracks closed down immediately. This was true not only of California. Racing had developed a bad name in Illinois, Missouri, and Tennessee. As a result, the bottom dropped out of the Thoroughbred breeding business. However, there was some hope for a comeback. Markets were sought in Europe and Australia but American Thoroughbreds became impossible to sell. Some sold for as little as $25 a head and—incredible as it may seem to us now—some were turned out to join the wild herds of the West.

But between 1910 and 1933, when wagering again became legal, the Thoroughbred breeding industry did not die in spite of almost unbelievable hardships. It was kept alive by a few men who loved Thoroughbreds and who continued to breed even though their market was almost entirely outside the West. During the war years the colorful trainer-owner Charlie Boots stood such outstanding stallions as Palo Alto, Liberty Loan, *War Cry, and, after the war, *Brig O'Doon. It was partially through the efforts of Charlie Boots that the Thoroughbred industry was maintained in California. Yet he was also partially responsible for the adverse legislation which had stopped racing in the state. For it was his fight against practices and conditions he felt were detrimental that caused much of the publicity which ultimately resulted in the halt of legal wagering in California.

Up in the Jack London country of Napa Valley, another devotee of Thoroughbreds continued to build his stud during the nonracing years. This was Adolph Spreckels, who operated a magnificent facility called Napa Stock Farm. There he bred Runstar, Dr. Leggo, *Runnymede, *Solitaire II, and other outstanding runners.

But Spreckels' most impressive achievement, and perhaps his most notable horse, was Morvich, sired by *Runnymede. A brother of Morvich, Runstar, was foaled at approximately the same time in 1919. Runstar, with almost perfect conformation, was the favorite of Spreckels, who considered Morvich, a more stocky, less attractive colt, not

nearly as good. So Spreckels sold Morvich to Fred Berlew, who peddled him to Ben Block of New York.

Morvich became the sensation of the East. As a two-year-old he won more than $100,000, going unbeaten in such outstanding stakes events as the Saratoga Special and the Pimlico Futurity. But his greatest feat, and one that will never be forgotten in the West, was his victory in the Kentucky Derby in 1922, the first Western-bred horse to win this cherished event. Also, in one of those Eastern races he met his brother, Runstar. Morvich easily outdistanced him. And when Morvich retired he was the sixth leading money winner of all time. Only Man O'War, Exterminator, Domino, Sysonby, and Colin had exceeded his earnings of $172,909.

Even though Thoroughbreds were not being raced in California, the belief continued that California climate, California grass, space, and water, would produce good Thoroughbreds. At Rancho Wikiup, near Santa Rosa, John H. Rosseter built an outstanding Thoroughbred spread, and he continued to breed fine horses. But the market crash of 1929 destroyed this important farm. Miramonte Farm, also in Santa Clara County, was developed by A. K. and Dr. H. J. Macomber, brothers who imported the finest bloodlines from France and England. They raced them in the East and in Europe and brought some of the best brood mares and stallions to California.

Down south in San Diego County was Baron Long's Rancho Valle de las Viejas. There such stallions as Cherrytree, Blind Baggage, Runstar (remember, he was Morvich's brother who never amounted to too much), and Iron Crown stood. In 1930 the horses from this farm won 251 races on United States tracks.

There were many breeders and from these sportsmen came the founding of the California Thoroughbred Breeding Association. With its formation and the resumption of legalized betting (and therefore racing) in California came the new great era of the Western Thoroughbred.

Why do hundreds of thousands of men and

women go to the races? The reasons are myriad. The races take you outdoors. They allow you to see amid ideal conditions the most beautiful horses in the world. But more than this, they allow you to have a Thoroughbred of your own, if only briefly. First, it is possible by checking over the program carefully to learn who the ancestors of your horse are, who owns him, what weight he is likely to carry, and who will ride him. But even better than this is going into the outdoor paddock and selecting the horse you like the best. You watch the long-muscled, graceful Thoroughbreds move about. You see them saddled and decide whether they are skittish, overly temperamental or, in your opinion, ready to win. And then, at some mysterious moment, you decide this is your horse. In fact, you may even turn to someone with you and say, "I'm on Flashfire," and you are. When the jockey mounts him, you are mounting him too. You are on him for the duration of the race. He's your horse.

You watch very carefully to see what position he draws at the post, and your heart leaps as he bounds out of the starting gate. You have bet on him and now you are riding him around that track keeping up with his every move. Your heart is pounding with his hoofbeats as he comes into the stretch, and he is still your horse whether he wins or whether he loses. And you have owned a Thoroughbred for a short time for as little as $2. You will not have to feed him or train him. He will go back to his stall well attended. But for another $2 on another day he can be yours again.

Racing bettors have another great advantage: They can be certain they are receiving a fair shake for their money because a Frenchman named Joseph Oller, who did not like any bookmaker deciding the odds, developed the pari-mutuel betting system almost one hundred years ago. It means, in effect, betting among ourselves. His system finally resulted in the invention of the electric totalizator, which was first used in England in 1929 and adopted in the United States in 1933. In pari-mutuel wagering, all money is allocated to pools. Money bet on a horse to win, for instance, goes into a win pool for that runner. Second-place wagering is designated for the place pools of the horses bet on. All third-place wagers go into the individual show pools of the horses bet to finish third. On the tote board (or totalizator) in the track infield you can see those totals growing as fans put down their bets.

The amount each bettor receives depends on how many people wager on the horses that take the first three places and on how they bet them to finish. A show bet, for instance, on a horse that finishes among the first three will reward the bettor with a payoff from that horse's show pool — this payoff being determined by dividing the number of that horse's show bettors into the amount wagered on him to finish third. But a win bet on a horse finishing second or third results in a torn-up ticket.

The only funds deducted from the total are taxes due the state and in some cases a percentage that goes to the track and which is used to establish purses paid to owners of the front-running horses. Most tracks are largely supported by admission charges to spectators, parking and clubhouse fees, food and drink concessions, and sale of programs. Generally, not more than fifteen percent of the total bet is deducted for state and federal taxes and track percentage. This means that the bettor, if he selects one of the three front-running horses, gets a very fair return for his investment.

Betting is not a grand professional event in which seasoned and shrewd gamblers go to the tracks and bet large sums of money. Indeed, it is just the opposite. Surveys show that about one-third of money wagered is in $2 bets. The other two-thirds is made up primarily of $5 and $10 bets, with $20, $50, and $100 bets making up the smallest amount.

How honest is Thoroughbred racing? It is just as honest as the Thoroughbred Racing Protective Bureau, a leg of the Thoroughbred Racing Association, can make it. And that is very honest. The protective bureau has been operating since 1946. When the Thoroughbred Racing Association realized how necessary it was to keep racing honest, it tried to get J. Edgar Hoover to head the bureau. Hoover declined. But he suggested a former administrative assistant of his, Spencer Drayton, who had been manager of the FBI's special intelligence section. Drayton agreed, and he set up this unique, self-policing organization and headed it for more than twenty years. Drayton gathered around him numerous former FBI agents and set out to make the tracks honest. His first step was to insist that everyone involved, even in the smallest capacity, be fingerprinted and checked for police and FBI records. This includes stableboys, exercise boys, jockeys, cashiers, and in fact every employee you will meet at a Thoroughbred track. Just the knowledge that such a thorough checkup is made keeps many undesirables from trying to finds jobs at the racetracks.

Many of the operatives in the protective bureau are undercover men. Very few are known to the public or to the occasional gamblers who try to fix a race by bribing a jockey or by some other means.

In the bureau's early days, one popular type of chicanery—and a plague that already had irritated racing for many years—was the introduction of a ringer, or substitute, for a horse. It worked like this: A comparatively slow horse would be run in a series of races until the betting public and the so-called smart money did not feel this horse had a chance. Then the fixer, who had located an animal of almost exactly the same conformation and color —but an animal with speed—would switch the horses. Then the fixers would bet heavily at very high odds and obtain a killing. A number of colorful characters, one of whom was finally deported to England as an undesirable alien, could do a great job of painting or dyeing a horse so his markings looked exactly like the other's.

But ringers have been eliminated by a unique system which requires that every horse at the beginning of his racing career have a lip tattoo. On the inner surface of the upper lip of every Thoroughbred running today a letter is tattooed with an indelible dye that indicates the year of foaling. This is followed by the last four numbers on that animal's registration. At the time of the tattoo the inside of the upper lip is photographed so that today, even if the markings of two horses are exact, the tattoo—the letter and the numbers—is a giveaway. Ringing in a substitute horse is not even tried any more.

The central headquarters of the Thoroughbred Racing Protective Bureau is in New York City, with field offices in Baltimore, Chicago, and Los Angeles. Seasonal offices are in Boston, Miami, and New Orleans. This organization covers all member racetracks. The lip-tattoo identification record department at headquarters covers more than 155,000 Thoroughbreds. And there are 200,-000 sets of fingerprints and 45,000 cases that have been investigated.

And the long whip of the investigating group can reach out at any time to snap up an operator on any given track in order to help clear out racing's most colorful and pernicious character, the tout. Touts range from fairly rough criminal types to very suave operators who always stay within the law. A few are former jockeys who never made it big. But the great majority are simply confidence men who profess to have inside information on which horse is most likely to win. The tout as a rule does not ask for any money but suggests that in return for his inside information the bettor put a wager on the horse for him. This convinces a considerable number of gullible bettors, particularly since they do not know that the tout is likely to give a different horse to each of his contacts, thereby ensuring that at least one of his bets will be paid off.

By no means are these touts confined to the racetracks. In fact, their number at tracks is dwindling daily as the protective bureau picks them up and banishes them. Most touts operate around off-track bookmaking establishments (always an illegal operation), or they buy or select a list of bettors and send them telegrams or phone them their choice at a given track. Again, as in the case of the tout at the track, a different horse's name may be given to each "sucker." The gullibility of the sucker is almost unbelievable. Without any valid introduction and although a high percentage of the "inside" information turns out to be useless, he will nevertheless continue, sometimes over a period of many years, making bets for himself and the tout who supplies him with the "inside" information.

Most touts represent themselves as having a connection either with the owner, the jockey, or the stableboy. Such contacts almost never exist, although former trainers and former jockeys have been picked up and barred from tracks. The sooner the public learns there are almost no fixed races and no possible way that an owner, trainer, or jockey can tell definitely whether his horse will win, the sooner the tout will go out of business. No jockey or trainer would take the risk of losing his license permanently and being involved in criminal prosecution in many states.

Of course, for the gullible gambler, reading this will do no good. He will simply say, "That doesn't apply to my contact. He really knows racing and what he's talking about when he gives me a horse."

In addition to the track stewards, who are the final judges, two other important developments in recent years have kept racing honest. One is the motion-picture film patrol. Cameras mounted on platforms follow each race from beginning to end. Telephoto lenses are used so that it is possible to see every detail after the race. These films are picked up and processed immediately so that judges can review the entire race if any questions are raised. When he can avoid it, a jockey no longer takes a chance on jostling another horse, or even striking another horse or jockey with his whip, as was sometimes done in the old days. But it works both ways. Most jockeys feel more confident because they know that if they are fouled the dirty work will show up on the film.

Of course, the finish is always photographed electronically, and many a horse has won a race because the jockey lifted the horse's head a quarter of an inch so he could win by the tip of his nose.

With the electronic camera, dead heats, in which two or more horses finish at the same moment, are rare; yet they still happen and two such dead heats with three horses, noses on the wire, occurred during 1966.

The second important protective measure is the testing of saliva and urine taken from each winning horse and any other horse the stewards may select. The states have different rules in this regard. In some states, the horses that finish first, second, and third are tested. This means that it is almost impossible for a horse to be doped without detection. New tests are being developed constantly as new stimulating or depressing drugs become available.

But even if the public did not know how well it is protected they would still go to see the Thoroughbreds run. For there is no more thrilling sight than the view of Thoroughbreds going into the stretch and heading for that wire. They move as though they do not feel the ground under them.

A jockey now has a more serious distraction than ever before. In addition to keeping an eye on the other horses, he may pause to keep an eye on the attractive girl riding next to him. Male jockeys waged a hard fight against the licensing of female riders. They lost, and none too gracefully. Now women jockeys have not only become accepted on Thoroughbred and other tracks, but they are proving to be regular winners.

Male jockeys still contend it is no job for a girl, that the going is too tough, and that in a bind they are likely to lose their nerve and cause a pileup. But so far the facts have not borne this out. The danger is that a male jockey may overreact and get himself out on a limb either trying to show he is a better rider or trying to "show up" the girls and thereby getting himself penalized. Jockey talk, by the way, is admittedly not the sort of language you are likely to hear at Sunday school, and at least one of the girls has taken to stuffing her ears with cotton during her association with the boys.

Any objections to the way a race is run or any claims of foul can be made by jockeys, owners, or trainers, or else the stewards themselves can make an inquiry. In such a case, there is no payoff and no race is declared official until stewards have viewed the films and decided.

Popular horses on the track may be stallions, mares, or geldings, and they all win races. An ingenious student at California State Polytechnic College, which lies almost in the shadow of the Santa Anita track, decided to base his term paper on the winning percentages based on age, color, and sex of the Thoroughbreds. So for the racing season Joe Lifto spent his afternoons pleasantly enough watching them run at Santa Anita. He checked out every race on the basis of which sex, which color, and what age horse won most often. He correlated his findings after evaluating eighty-one contests.

He found that among male horses winning, 73.1 percent were geldings, 25.4 percent were colts, and 1.5 percent were ridgelings (colts with undescended testicles). In checking out the age group he found that 57.14 percent of the races were won by four-years-olds, and the second largest percentage was by five-year-olds. But the ratio of wins went down as the horses were older. The average age of the greatest number of winning animals was 5.19 years. Among the females the wins were divided equally between mares and fillies. There again the four-year-olds won the greatest number of races, followed by the five-year-olds, and only 16.7 percent of the races were won by six-year-olds. Among the females the average winning age was 4.24 years. In the color spectrum of the males that won races, 65.8 percent were bays, 24.5 percent were chestnut, 4.9 percent were gray, 3.2 percent were roan, and 1.6 percent were black. These findings were very similar among the mares and fillies.

At the close of Lifto's paper he remarked: "I would advise you to refrain from betting on Thoroughbred races. You would be much better off if you would sit back and watch top-running horses perform. However, if you feel you must bet, try your luck on the five-year-old bay geldings. The percentage is with you."

Stallions and mares are more valuable than geldings in the long run, because after their time on the track the stallions can be retired to stud to produce more racers, and the mares can be retired to bear them.

A stallion does not become a sire until his first crop of foals has been dropped. A mare, after dropping her first foal, becomes a dam, and if her progeny turn out well she is known as a producer. The final test of a stallion is a sire that begets winners. And of a great producer it is said that when she drops a foal it's off and running.

Most dramatic but becoming increasingly rare is the match race. It involves only two horses, and some of the most famous match races of all time have drawn great audiences and caused excitement throughout the racing world. One such competition was that between Molly McCarthy and Ten Broeck at Lexington, Kentucky, in 1878, an event we mentioned earlier.

The match race of this century probably was the big run between Seabiscuit and War Admiral for $15,000 on November 1, 1938, at Pimlico, Maryland. Easterners, because of their longer history of Thoroughbred raising and the vastness of this business in the East, have as a group frequently belittled Western racers. They had heard all about Seabiscuit, of course. Some had even seen him. But Seabiscuit was a Western horse. War Admiral, which was treated like a dandy, was the jewel of the East. George Woolf, the ill-fated, cold-nerved rider known as "The Ice Man," was on Seabiscuit. Charles Kurtsinger rode War Admiral. Both horses were sound. The excitement was electrifying. The West won by four lengths.

Earlier in 1938 Seabiscuit had run another celebrated match race. It was at Del Mar against *Ligaroti, a South American router owned by Bing Crosby, who also owned the track, and by Lin Howard. The 'Biscuit, owned by Howard's father, C. S., won by a nose. Woolf on Seabiscuit and Spec Richardson on *Ligaroti had ridden so roughly that both were penalized.

A more recent famed match race, and one which also generated the enthusiasm of the racing world, was a duel in 1955, also between West and East. This was that singular competition between a lovable California colt named Swaps and the temperamental Easterner, Nashua. The background for this confrontation also was singular. While Nashua was not a record-setter, he was a great runner. And he was a consistent winner. Also, he was from the East. When owner Rex Ellsworth and trainer Meshach Tenney brought Swaps out from Chino, California, for the Kentucky Derby in 1955, the smart money had only to say, "He's a Western horse." They could also point out that no fully Californian horse had ever won the roses at Louisville. The previous year, of course, Determine — in Ellsworth's colors — had won them. But Determine had been bred and foaled in Kentucky. Back in 1922, Morvich had won the Derby. But although Morvich had been bred in California, he won the roses while wearing Eastern colors.

So on that first Saturday in May of 1955, when Swaps won the Kentucky Derby, he was the first horse bred and foaled and developed in California — and still wearing a Westerner's colors — to break the Eastern string of domination in this event. Nashua in that Derby was second, one and one-half lengths behind Swaps. The match race was inevitable. Finally, for a $100,000 purse, it was arranged for August 31, 1955, at Chicago.

Swaps frequently had suffered with a misery in the frog of his right foreleg. But trainer Tenney had always been able to relieve the pain with a homemade patch. Of course he was hoping he would not have to repair him for this one. So the Swaps stable experienced compounded irritation and distress when a few days before the race Swaps suffered an enlarged ankle on the same leg.

Nelson Fisher, West Coast racing authority who saw the match, says:

"I got my hands on all the money I could and went to Chicago for the race. I knew how wonderful Swaps was. I was going to put it all on him. But I got there the morning of the race and found out — from men I knew I could trust — about Swaps' injury. It may or may not have been related to the frog trouble. But they told me he didn't have a chance.

"Still, the race had to go on. Too many people were counting on it. The second they were in the gate they were sent off. Eddie Arcaro got Nashua going instantly. When Bill Shoemaker and Swaps started, Swaps came down on his bad leg. It buckled, and he nearly fell. Nashua was 'way out. Swaps lost by six lengths. All of us felt pretty bad. The injury. The reputation of the Western horse and all that. It's strange too. I couldn't bet on Swaps knowing he was hurt. But with all that money in my pocket, I wouldn't bet on Nashua either."

Back East when you talk about Swaps and Nashua they will tell you that the Derby was at least close, "And look how badly Nashua beat him in the match race." You do not hear about the Californian's injury. But proof of Swaps' greatness was reiterated in 1956. Fully recuperated, Swaps set world records for the mile, mile and one-sixteenth, and mile and five-eighths. He even broke his own mile record. Then he was hurt again late in 1956 (a different leg injury this time) and was retired to stud and was sold. He stands now in Kentucky for the Darby Dan stable. A son of Swaps, Chateaugay, won the 1963 Kentucky Derby — a feat no Nashua get has been able to duplicate. In the East they now believe in the wonderful Westerner called Swaps.

It would be difficult to select the most dramatic true Thoroughbred horse story of all time. But the tale of Moifaa, a Thoroughbred raised in Australia, is a leading contender. When Moifaa was being shipped to England by steamer he was traveling in a padded stall on deck. About one hundred miles off the coast of Ireland the steamer sailed into the terror of a raging storm. The horse was swept overboard, and everyone assumed he was drowned.

But Moifaa was a marvelous animal that did not

know how to stop trying. He possessed in abundance, maybe even in excess, the magnificent Thoroughbred characteristic: heart. Although it seems impossible, the horse swam that one hundred miles through the cold and stormy Irish Sea, to be washed up on a deserted beach on Ireland's east coast. The year was 1904. It was midwinter and a local fisherman saw a strange object lying on the beach. He cared for the horse as well as he could and managed to lead him to his property where he kept him warm in a shed with blankets and fire.

Now this fisherman was a man of considerable knowledge. He also kept up with the newspapers and he was sure the horse he had found was the great Australian runner Moifaa. So he wrote the British Jockey Club telling all he could about the horse and asking that someone be dispatched to examine his find. The Jockey Club duly notified the horse's owner, Spencer Gollan, who immediately set out for Ireland. There he found that it was indeed his champion Thoroughbred, but he also found that the horse was in pitiful condition. He shipped him to Aintree near Liverpool to give him a chance to recover. Gollan planned on putting him out to stud because he thought the horse could never race again.

But they also had believed this remarkable animal could not possibly have swum one hundred miles in a violent sea, and as the date of the Grand National Steeplechase approached, the horse seemed to improve miraculously. Yet no one considered him being able to run in the world's most grueling race, which is four miles long and has thirty different jumps. But Moifaa long before had been entered in this race. He had never been scratched. When one of the stableboys told the owner he felt it would be "a rather jolly good thing" to give the horse a run—at least let him start and if he was doing badly they could always pull him up—Gollan listened sympathetically. Not only did the stableboy feel this would be an interesting test, so did the trainer. Gollan reluctantly agreed but

only as a gesture to a gallant creature. Moifaa nearly fell at the first jump. But he recovered and and went on to gallop away and to soar over each obstacle with ease. In the stretch he outran the front runners. And Moifaa won that 1904 Grand National.

But that is not quite the end of the story. The King of England was so impressed by the performance of this remarkable animal that he insisted upon purchasing Moifaa. After racing the horse only once again, King Edward VII retired him but honored him with personal use as his mount for ceremonial occasions. And when the king died six years later, it was Moifaa, with empty saddle, which paced behind the funeral cortege that took Edward VII to Westminster Abbey.

We have said very little about Thoroughbred jumpers but there is no question that they excel in that athletic sport of steeplechasing just as they do on the flat track. One of the most exciting and difficult jumping courses occurs at the Olympic Games, where the finest jumpers from every country in the world need almost perfect scores to win. The victor in the 1968 Olympic Games was a Thoroughbred racehorse which had almost always been out of the money. He was semi-retired, with tendons that threatened to give out. But according to Bill Steinkraus, he had the basic physical and gymnastic qualities with the plus-factor of an ideal temperament that combined courage and endurance.

Steinkraus spent four years riding and training this horse, Snowbound, for the Olympics. As the finals progressed Britain's entry and Steinkraus on his American mount were the only two with perfect scores. Then the British horse faltered on two jumps. Steinkraus had to handle six of the seven jumps to win. They made the first three hurdles perfectly, then the fourth. On the most difficult, the fifth, Snowbound's legs hit the bar. But he recovered and sailed in perfect form over the final two jumps to win the gold medal—the first ever won for the United States in that event.

*Separated by fence, well-developed Thoroughbred weanling and his dam are permanently parted. Both are reluctant.*

# THOROUGHBREDS IN THE MODERN WEST

The Thoroughbred is the aristocrat of the horse world, and he looks it. His ancestors were the fleetest desert-bred Arabian stallions that could be found. Englishmen—kings and commoners—bred him for sustained speed, for bottom, for conformation, and for heart. The *General Stud Book* of England dates from 1793, but it drew on earlier records. The Darley Arabian, the Byerly Turk, and the Godolphin Arabian, three great progenitors, passed on their traits. Their offspring were bred back to them; with each new crop of colts and fillies, the best were bred to the best. If he is not descended from one of those three, he is not a Thoroughbred. What then is a Thoroughbred? He is a horse whose recorded breeding has been based on his performance on the race track for more than 250 years.

New crop of foals comes along every spring. The curious, awkward youngsters must spread their long legs to graze.

Foaling barn is built in circle so observer can keep an eye on each mare. Note attendant watching through bars.

*Thoroughbred mares and foals happily surround hay rack
at El Peco Ranch of George Pope, Jr., near Madera, California.*

*Fillies exercise and play between water and trees.*
*Many will go to annual Del Mar, California, yearling sales.*

*Lineage is apparent in conformation and head shapes
of fillies at Granja Vista del Rio near Corona, California.*

*Almost lifting groom, proven Thoroughbred stallion Crazy Kid rears up in paddock at Rancho Santa Fe, California.*

*On Flag Is Up farm the young stallion Successor
streaks across paddock. Farm is new, one of best-equipped.*

*Coursing's records include getting high percentage
of his mares in foal. His yearlings brought $30,000 average.*

*One of West's historic Thoroughbred stallions
is Hillary at El Peco Ranch. His get includes stakes winners.*

*Among the great stallions of the West is Nashville, a son of famed \*Nasrullah. Owner is entertainer Desi Arnaz.*

*This is Flag Is Up, training, boarding, and breeding farm near Solvang, California. It has a horse medical center.*

*A major problem has been solved on Western ranches by use of mechanical walker to keep horses moving at easy pace.*

*Portable three-horse starting gate is used to train Thoroughbred racers to behave when they reach the big tracks.*

HIP NO. 5
NOW BID
22000

*Yearling goes to highest bidder at semi-annual yearling sale at Del Mar, California. This colt brought $25,000.*

The most colorful yearling sale, and one of the most important, is held in the summer at Del Mar Race Track, between Oceanside, California, and La Jolla. It is a social as well as a business event, with horsemen and women from the entire racing world in attendance. The program begins with a parade of the yearlings in the flower-be-decked paddock. It continues with a cocktail party and buffet dinner in the comfortable clubhouse. The main event is held in the huge Bing Crosby Hall. In two evening sessions of four hours each, some 150 sleek yearlings are auctioned as one and one-half million dollars changes hands. The bidding is as frisky as the colts and fillies.

*At Del Mar race meet*, aficionados *watch horses in outdoor paddock before race. Bing Crosby developed the track.*

*Located 20 miles north of San Diego and 100 miles south of Los Angeles, Del Mar has excellent turf, fine main track.*

*One of the great racetracks in nation, Santa Anita was once ranch-estate of "Lucky" Baldwin, its first operator.*

*The judges at Santa Anita, in Arcadia, California, are*
*picked up and taken to viewing posts by coach and horses.*

*As horses approach finish line, tote board, far right,*
*reflects odds and betting pools of the pari-mutuel system.*

151

*Santa Anita Derby, Western warm-up for Kentucky Derby, draws top three-year-old racers and crowds like this one.*

*Determine, Swaps, and Majestic Prince stood here in Santa Anita Derby triumphs — all later won the Kentucky Derby.*

# THE QUARTER HORSE

The story of the Quarter Horse is colorful and has many rare and entertaining facets. And although this horse does not date back as far as the Arabian or the Thoroughbred, he comes from excellent stock, and he was developed for an essential and specific purpose. Along the way, because he always has been raced as well as worked, he provided sport.

The history of the Quarter Horse begins in Mexico four and one-half centuries ago on the spacious ranches, those haciendas of the conquerors from Spain. It is generally taught that the primary economic endeavor of the Spaniards was the mining of gold and silver. Actually, by far the most important activity of the Spaniards after the conquest of Mexico was the development of huge cattle and horse ranches. This was in fact almost the only respectable business open to a Spanish gentleman.

Cortés was perhaps the first large ranch owner, for the Spanish Crown gave him the entire Valley of Oaxaca, which at that time included what is now the state of Chiapas and most of the country that later became Guatemala, which then was a piece of Mexico. He began a large cattle operation, stocking his ranch with Longhorns and with horses from the breeding farms of Cuba, Jamaica, Hispaniola, and Sevilla. He called his ranch Cuernavaca.

Of course the horses imported were various strains of Arabian blood. But the early ranchers in New Spain developed them as cattle horses. They bred for short bursts of speed and for the ability to cut an animal from the herd, which meant high

maneuverability. And because the horse's size was not a factor in his usefulness, he was not bred for height, as was the Thoroughbred in England. Consequently, Mexican cow horses became small, wiry, hardy, alert muscular athletes.

As noted earlier the Indians got their horses by liberating them from Spanish ranches. Because many of the animals escaped from both the ranches and the Indians, large herds ran wild. Inbreeding and the difficulty of finding food created in these mustangs a stamina which may have even exceeded that of their Arabian ancestors.

Racing was loved by the early Spanish settlers of Mexico and by those later settlers who contributed the first European culture to the Southwestern sectors of what is now the United States. Because of their great admiration for horses, their joy in watching them run, and their happiness at the risk-taking aspects of betting on one horse's ability to run faster than another, these early Spanish settlers raced their cow ponies at every opportunity. Indeed, racing became the primary spectator sport in Mexico and the Southwest. And although most of the races were informal affairs with spectators lining both sides of the track, it was not long before spectator stands were built and well-tended tracks came into being on some of the large haciendas.

While these fast cow ponies were evolving in New Spain, racing a quarter of a mile was becoming increasingly popular in the English settlements along the East Coast. Several theories have been advanced concerning the beginning of the Quarter

Horse line on the East Coast. One of the most popular has to do with Spanish horses similar to those brought into Mexico by Cortés. They were imported into Florida from the same basic stock.

It was over one hundred years before the Florida area was partly colonized by the Spanish. Then, like the Indians in the West, the Chickasaw Indians of Florida began acquiring Spanish horses. It is believed that these Indian ponies were traded north as far as Carolina and from there trickled into Virginia. The Chickasaw horses, like the cow horses of Mexico and the Southwestern United States, were small, agile, and muscular, for they too had been bred to work with cattle or as mounts for the Indians. There is certainly considerable historical evidence to support this theory of the beginning of the Quarter Horse on the East Coast. But it is not enough to account for all of the speedy little horses that were soon running short races in Virginia, Maryland, New York, and Connecticut.

At the same time that these Southern Indian ponies were infiltrating the Eastern states, the colonists were importing both ordinary and Thoroughbred stock from England. And in the early days, enough Thoroughbred mares certainly were not available to be bred to the few Thoroughbred stallions that were imported. Therefore infusion of Thoroughbred bloodlines from such stallions as *Monkey, *Jolly Roger, *Fearnought, and *Janus inevitably mixed with more ordinary stock including whatever Spanish mares that made their way north. *Janus, considered by most experts to have contributed greatly to the development of the American Quarter Horse, was foaled in 1746 and was imported into Virginia when he was six years old. He was said to be by Old Janus, which was sired by the great Godolphin Arabian.

*Janus is not listed in the English studbook but there are so many accounts of his parentage and of his undoubted quality that there is good reason to believe he was in fact a grandson of the Godolphin. *Janus sired literally hundreds of foals. Because he was comparatively small and because of the popularity of short distance races, he was bred to many prestigious Thoroughbred mares. There is no question that the get of *Janus were unusually swift runners at the quarter of a mile. He was given credit for passing on his characteristics to his progeny.

Several accounts describe this small wonder horse. Perhaps the most complete is by Sir Patrick Nisbett Edgar in the *American Race-Turf Register, Sportsmen's Herald, and General Stud Book.* He said *Janus was a chestnut horse *sui generis* of low stature, about fourteen hands and three-fourths of an inch high, bred by Mr. Swymmer, foaled in 1746, imported to Virginia about 1752.

"The stock of Old Janus in Virginia and the Southern states has been distinctly marked for the last 50 years as if he had been of a different species," Sir Patrick wrote. "For power, swiftness and durability, they have been equalled by no other breed of horses. [His son] *Janus had great bone and muscle; round, very compact, large quarters, and was very swift; all of which desirable qualities he imparted so perfectly to his progeny that many of them remain in the stock at this remote period, and great speed and muscular form are still found in many horses whose pedigrees reach him, if accurately traced through different branches; or when, after it is sometimes called, there is a 'double *Janus cross.' Nearly all of his immediate descendants were 'swift quarter Nags'; they never could run far. He was the sire of an immense number of short distance racers, brood mares and stallions."

This was written in 1833 but he was basing his information on statements made as early as 1757 by Mordecai Boothe, 1780 by Senator John Good, and 1781 by John Bilbo and other horsemen who knew this remarkable progenitor. When Sir Patrick produced his *General Stud Book* in 1833 he referred to the get of *Janus and other well-known racing horses as "American Quarter Running Horses."

In his studbook Sir Patrick listed over one hundred horses and mares that carried the blood of *Janus. Alongside them were the letters FAQR, which meant Famous American Quarter Racer.

It would seem that Sir Patrick, in setting up the *American Stud Book,* listed as Thoroughbreds *Janus' get that could run four miles or better in record time, while those which were adept only at the quarter mile were called American Quarter Running Horses. Of course it must be remembered that in the days of *Janus there was no English *General Stud Book* and therefore in a realistic sense no Thoroughbred line. Yet records had been kept in England with reasonable care ever since John Cheny's work in 1727 that listed an account of the horse matches run in England that year. Following Cheny a series of studbooks appeared, but it was 1793 before the first official volume was issued.

In the last half of the eighteenth century many turf writers commented on quarter racing in Virginia and Carolina during that period. Such races were usually matches between two horses on a straight track. These speedsters were generally regarded as faster than the Thoroughbred at a quarter of a mile. But the writers said the short-distance runners had "no bottom" when it came to the greater distances.

Dr. John B. Irving in *Turf in South Carolina* said, "Before the year 1754 the horses most regarded in South Carolina for the draft or the saddle were known as Chickasaw breed. This was a stock of horses originally introduced into Florida by the early Spanish. They were in general very well formed, active and easily kept, but small. The mares seldom exceeded 13 1/2 hands, but being remarkable for their muscular development and great endurance; when crossed with the imported Thoroughbred they produced animals of great beauty, strength and fleetness, improving thereby the stock of the country in a very great degree."

It would seem, as more and more Thoroughbred racing stock was imported to the United States, that at least among the wealthier class the little Quarter Horse became less important. Yet on the country tracks throughout the East, in towns and villages and even sparsely settled areas, match races over short distances continued to be run. As they too began dying out the Quarter Horse nevertheless continued to be the great everyday working horse of the pioneers. Ranches existed in Virginia and the Carolinas as well as in some of the Northern states, and it was the descendants of the earlier Quarter Horses that handled the cattle just as they were handling them in Mexico, California, and the Southwest at the same time.

There is one noticeable difference. The horses of the Southwest were not to have the infusion of so-called Thoroughbred blood until much later. The Quarter Horse continued to walk, gallop, and race his way across the United States. In the 1820's pioneer ranchers, farmers, and adventurers of all kinds were moving westward from as far north as Boston to the Louisiana Territory. In the South, Stephen Austin, after whom the city of Austin, Texas, was named, moved in from Louisiana and obtained a huge grant of land from Mexico with permission to colonize. With him came the Quarter Horse. So the same basic stock brought by the Arabs to Spain and by the Spanish to Mexico and to Florida met on opposing sides perhaps for the first time during the war between Texas and Mexico in 1836. A steady stream of Quarter Horses from the East continued to infiltrate the West to be bred to mustangs and Spanish jennets. The short race so popular in the East was reborn in the West.

Over the years this combination horse built up a following. He excelled as a cow pony and short-distance racer, and he was the most important means of transportation the West knew before the advent of the railroad and the automobile.

This mixture of Eastern and Western blood now went through one hundred years of natural selection. He was bred by various Indian tribes primarily for speed, although sometimes for color. Indian cavalry was mounted on the ancestors of the present Quarter Horse. He became as much a symbol of an aristocrat or gentleman as his Arabian ancestors had been to the Spanish, for a man without a horse in the early West did not have status. A

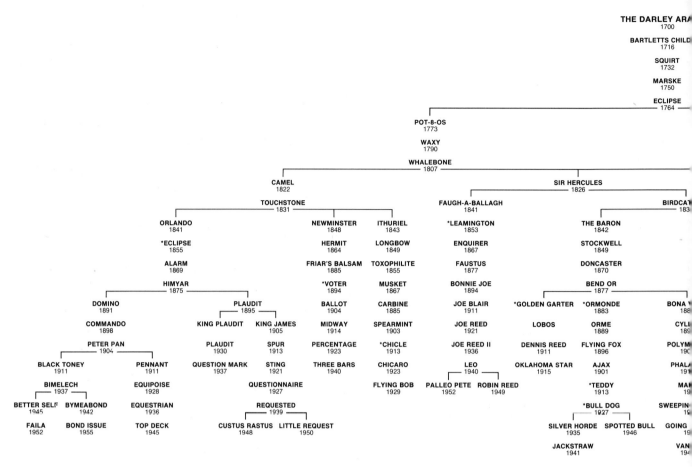

THE DARLEY ARA
1700

BARTLETTS CHILD
1716

SQUIRT
1732

MARSKE
1750

ECLIPSE
1764

POT-8-OS
1773

WAXY
1790

WHALEBONE
1807

CAMEL — 1822 / SIR HERCULES — 1826

TOUCHSTONE — 1831 / FAUGH-A-BALLAGH — 1841 / BIRDCAT 183

ORLANDO 1841 / NEWMINSTER 1848 / ITHURIEL 1843 / *LEAMINGTON 1853 / THE BARON 1842

*ECLIPSE 1855 / HERMIT 1864 / LONGBOW 1849 / ENQUIRER 1867 / STOCKWELL 1849

ALARM 1869 / FRIAR'S BALSAM 1885 / TOXOPHILITE 1855 / FAUSTUS 1877 / DONCASTER 1870

HIMYAR — 1875 / *VOTER 1894 / MUSKET 1867 / BONNIE JOE 1894 / BEND OR — 1877

DOMINO 1891 / PLAUDIT — 1895 / BALLOT 1904 / CARBINE 1885 / JOE BLAIR 1911 / *GOLDEN GARTER / *ORMONDE 1883 / BONA 188

COMMANDO 1898 / KING PLAUDIT / KING JAMES 1905 / MIDWAY 1914 / SPEARMINT 1903 / JOE REED 1921 / LOBOS / ORME 1889 / CYLI 189

PETER PAN — 1904 / PLAUDIT 1930 / SPUR 1913 / PERCENTAGE 1923 / *CHICLE 1913 / JOE REED II 1936 / DENNIS REED 1911 / FLYING FOX 1896 / POLYM 190

BLACK TONEY 1911 / PENNANT 1911 / QUESTION MARK 1937 / STING 1921 / THREE BARS 1940 / CHICARO 1923 / LEO — 1940 / OKLAHOMA STAR 1915 / AJAX 1901 / PHALA 19

BIMELECH — 1937 / EQUIPOISE 1928 / QUESTIONNAIRE 1927 / FLYING BOB 1929 / PALLEO PETE 1952 / ROBIN REED 1949 / *TEDDY 1913 / MAI 19

BETTER SELF 1945 / BYMEABOND 1942 / EQUESTRIAN 1936 / REQUESTED — 1939 / *BULL DOG — 1927 / SWEEPIN 19

FAILA 1952 / BOND ISSUE 1955 / TOP DECK 1945 / CUSTUS RASTUS 1948 / LITTLE REQUEST 1950 / SILVER HORDE 1935 / SPOTTED BULL 1946 / GOING 19

JACKSTRAW 1941 / VAN 194

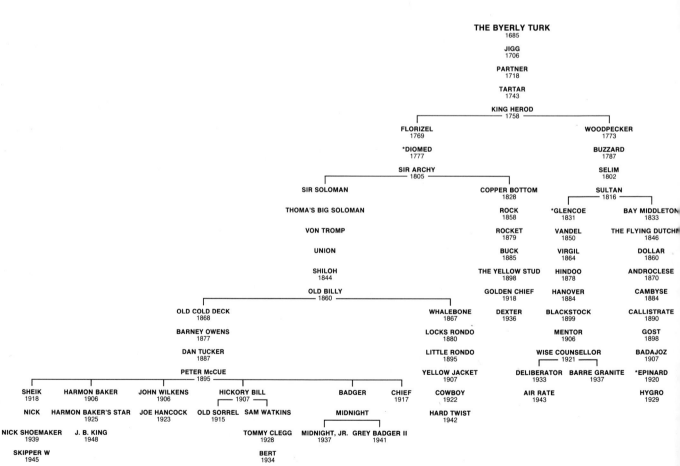

THE BYERLY TURK
1685

JIGG
1706

PARTNER
1718

TARTAR
1743

KING HEROD — 1758

FLORIZEL 1769 / WOODPECKER 1773

*DIOMED 1777 / BUZZARD 1787

SIR ARCHY — 1805 / SELIM 1802

SIR SOLOMAN / COPPER BOTTOM 1828 / SULTAN — 1816

THOMA'S BIG SOLOMAN / ROCK 1858 / *GLENCOE 1831 / BAY MIDDLETON 1833

VON TROMP / ROCKET 1879 / VANDEL 1850 / THE FLYING DUTCH 1846

UNION / BUCK 1885 / VIRGIL 1864 / DOLLAR 1860

SHILOH 1844 / THE YELLOW STUD 1898 / HINDOO 1878 / ANDROCLESE 1870

OLD BILLY — 1860 / GOLDEN CHIEF 1918 / HANOVER 1884 / CAMBYSE 1884

OLD COLD DECK 1868 / WHALEBONE 1867 / DEXTER 1936 / BLACKSTOCK 1899 / CALLISTRATE 1890

BARNEY OWENS 1877 / LOCKS RONDO 1880 / MENTOR 1906 / GOST 1898

DAN TUCKER 1887 / LITTLE RONDO 1895 / WISE COUNSELLOR — 1921 / BADAJOZ 1907

PETER McCUE — 1895 / YELLOW JACKET 1907 / DELIBERATOR 1933 / BARRE GRANITE 1937 / *EPINARD 1920

SHEIK 1918 / HARMON BAKER 1906 / JOHN WILKENS 1906 / HICKORY BILL — 1907 / BADGER / CHIEF 1917 / COWBOY 1922 / AIR RATE 1943 / HYGRO 1929

NICK / HARMON BAKER'S STAR 1925 / JOE HANCOCK 1923 / OLD SORREL 1915 / SAM WATKINS / MIDNIGHT / HARD TWIST 1942

NICK SHOEMAKER 1939 / J. B. KING 1948 / TOMMY CLEGG 1928 / MIDNIGHT, JR. 1937 / GREY BADGER II 1941

SKIPPER W 1945 / BERT 1934

156

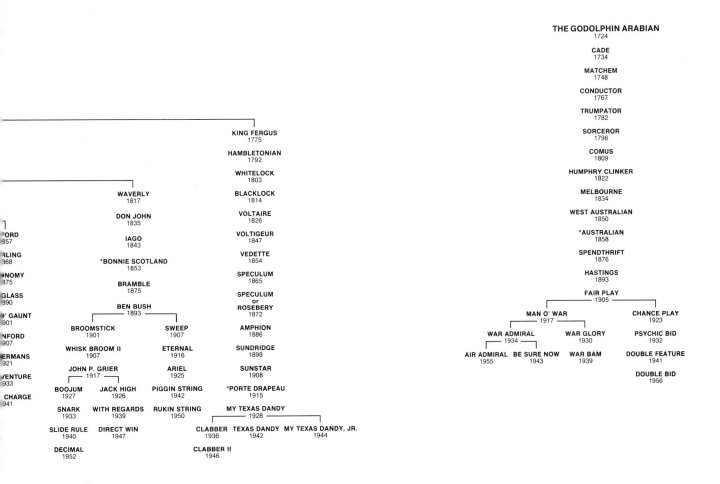

THE GODOLPHIN ARABIAN
1724

CADE
1734

MATCHEM
1748

CONDUCTOR
1767

TRUMPATOR
1782

SORCEROR
1796

COMUS
1809

HUMPHRY CLINKER
1822

MELBOURNE
1834

WEST AUSTRALIAN
1850

*AUSTRALIAN
1858

SPENDTHRIFT
1876

HASTINGS
1893

FAIR PLAY
1905

MAN O' WAR
1917

CHANCE PLAY
1923

WAR ADMIRAL
1934

WAR GLORY
1930

PSYCHIC BID
1932

AIR ADMIRAL
1955

BE SURE NOW
1943

WAR BAM
1939

DOUBLE FEATURE
1941

DOUBLE BID
1956

KING FERGUS
1775

HAMBLETONIAN
1792

WHITELOCK
1803

BLACKLOCK
1814

VOLTAIRE
1826

VOLTIGEUR
1847

VEDETTE
1854

SPECULUM
1865

SPECULUM
or
ROSEBERY
1872

AMPHION
1886

SUNDRIDGE
1898

SUNSTAR
1908

*PORTE DRAPEAU
1915

MY TEXAS DANDY
1928

CLABBER
1936

TEXAS DANDY
1942

MY TEXAS DANDY, JR.
1944

CLABBER II
1946

WAVERLY
1817

DON JOHN
1835

IAGO
1843

*BONNIE SCOTLAND
1853

BRAMBLE
1875

BEN BUSH
1893

BROOMSTICK
1901

SWEEP
1907

WHISK BROOM II
1907

ETERNAL
1916

JOHN P. GRIER
1917

ARIEL
1925

BOOJUM
1927

JACK HIGH
1926

PIGGIN STRING
1942

SNARK
1933

WITH REGARDS
1939

RUKIN STRING
1950

SLIDE RULE
1940

DIRECT WIN
1947

DECIMAL
1952

FORD
857

RLING
868

NOMY
875

GLASS
890

GAUNT
901

NFORD
907

ERMANS
921

VENTURE
933

CHARGE
941

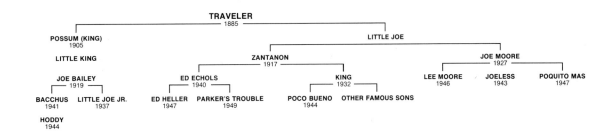

TRAVELER
1885

POSSUM (KING)
1905

LITTLE JOE

LITTLE KING

ZANTANON
1917

JOE MOORE
1927

JOE BAILEY
1919

ED ECHOLS
1940

KING
1932

LEE MOORE
1946

JOELESS
1943

POQUITO MAS
1947

BACCHUS
1941

LITTLE JOE JR.
1937

ED HELLER
1947

PARKER'S TROUBLE
1949

POCO BUENO
1944

OTHER FAMOUS SONS

HODDY
1944

*Any owner of a registered Quarter Horse can probably trace
the ancestry of his animal to one of the four founding sires
that head this chart. All Thoroughbreds trace to three of these
original stallions: the Darley Arabian, the Godolphin Arabian,
and the Byerly Turk. The genealogy of Traveler, a significant
Quarter Horse progenitor, would probably also lead to one of
the three if his blood lines could be traced. This important chart
was first published by the American Quarter Horse Association.*

man was often judged both in Indian and cowboy circles by the quality of the horseflesh he owned and rode.

The Western workhorse became inured to cold. His hoofs became hardened to the rocky, broken terrain and he developed a quality of patience, of seeming to conserve his strength until a special burst of energy was needed to run down a calf or a man. Food was often scarce, and horses of the old West learned to dig under the snow, beating down the crust with their forefeet to feed on the withered grass under the surface. Hardship made them rugged, wiry, and sturdy. Just as his remote ancestors had been bred amidst the hardships of the desert, the cow pony grew out of the hardships of the West.

His association with both Indian and cowboy was just as close as that of the early Arabian and his owner. This familiarity with man also contributed to the evolution of the Quarter Horse.

Soldiers from the East using imported cavalry mounts manned many of the forts of the West. These newcomers could not believe that the Indian pony, which is the same, of course, as the cow pony, could outrun their well-selected Eastern horses. But for a short distance the Western horses could almost always pull away from the larger, heavier military stock. An often told story in the West involves the officers of Fort Chadbourne, near the Texas border. Comanche Indians were encamped close by, and although the chief was reluctant he finally agreed to race one of his ponies against a much larger cavalry horse. The Indian horse when it appeared looked so bedraggled, small, and insignificant that the officers could hardly take the race seriously. Nevertheless, bets were laid and the horses were lined up to run a four-hundred-yard race. The Indian pony sprang into the lead and held it all the way to win, although by a very small margin. This led the Americans to bring out their best racehorse, a Thoroughbred Kentucky mare. The Indians made elaborate bets which included buffalo robes and cured horsehides, while the Army men put up such delicacies as sugar and tobacco. It is said that many of the men wagered a large part of their monthly pay, so sure were they of the outcome.

As the horses were lined up, the Indian pony was a ludicrous sight against the tall, well-shaped Thoroughbred. To be sure, he had heavily muscled hindquarters, a short straight back, and a well-balanced head. But he was much smaller and was ridden by a young brave who, to say the least, was somewhat dirty and unkempt compared to the cavalry officer astride the Thoroughbred.

As the pistol cracked for the start, the Indian pony shot into the lead. He increased it with every bound. Halfway down the course, the Indian swung around in the saddle and made derisive faces at the oncoming Thoroughbred and his well-dressed jockey. Incidents like this soon taught the soldiers stationed in the West respect for the Western-bred mustang.

There is no doubt that infusions of the blood of the Eastern horses brought out by the cavalry went into the Western cow pony. Indians did not limit their stealing of horses to Spanish settlements but often raided or stealthily removed the better mounts from the forts. George Bird Grinnell, the most important historian of the Indians and their horses, in relating how the Indians felt the horses belonged to them just as much as to the white man, tells the following tragic story:

One army camp had gone to great pains to build a corral that was almost Indian-proof. But one brave considered it a great challenge. Yet he became very annoyed working for hours to move the posts and untie the leather thongs that held the rails together. The longer he worked the more annoyed he became as he silently labored through the night. He said to himself, "I don't like to work like this and the white man shouldn't make me work so hard to get to the horses—so I'll get even with him for it." After releasing the desired horses and quietly taking them away, he returned to the camp, slipped stealthily into the tent of the leader, killed him with his long knife, and scalped him. "This is for making me work so hard," he said. "Next time he'll make it easier for me."

The term "mustang" which we have used and will use again in this book cannot be applied specifically to a single type of horse. It is usually used to refer to descendants of the Spanish horses which became wild. But it is also used, and quite justifiably, to describe the Indian pony and the cow pony that descended from the Spanish horses. While it is certain their origins go to the Spanish conquistadors' horses, and to the imports from Spain that followed them, they undoubtedly received some dilution from farm animals and military mounts brought to the West after 1840. Yet most of the mustangs retained some Arabian characteristics such as their small size, alert ears, and occasionally a concave profile. And while mustangs contributed greatly to the development of the present Quarter Horse, we must, as has been pointed out earlier, look to the Thoroughbred in combination with the Western horse for some of the characteristics of the Quarter Horse of today.

The modern history of the Quarter Horse begins with the birth of a foal with a dorsal stripe. He grew up to be about fifteen hands tall and to weigh about 1,200 pounds, and he was called Steel Dust. He traveled to the West as a yearling and arrived in Texas shortly before the Mexican War. He belonged to a log-cabin family that settled in a place justifiably named Hard Scrabble, later to be absorbed by Lancaster, Texas, which it was near. Steel Dust's sire Harry Bluff traced back to a stallion named Short Whip, but on the tail-female side Harry Bluff was said to be out of the Thoroughbred mare Big Nance who was by Timoleon by Sir Archy, one of the greatest racing sires of the Colonial period. The *Turf Register* for December, 1829, recorded, "He has done as much for the turf stock of this country as the Godolphin Arabian, King Herod or High Flyer for that of Great Britain. Most of the best stock at present in this country are either immediately from the loins of Sir Archy or

have been produced from his sons or daughters." Nothing is known of Steel Dust's dam. It is probable, however, that she was not a Thoroughbred because Steel Dust was not so registered.

In fact neither Steel Dust nor his sire was mentioned in Skinner's *American Stud Book* published in 1848, three years after the wonder horse was foaled. This did not make any difference, however, to Steel Dust, which went on to produce an incredible number of outstanding horses that carried his speed, maneuverability, and conformation. He stamped his get perhaps as thoroughly as any stallion since Justin Morgan.

He was said to resemble a compact, shorter version of the Thoroughbred. His progeny, which became generally known as Steeldusts, were closer to the ground and shorter in the neck and shoulders, with less forearm muscle than the Thoroughbred. Steel Dust was said to have a fairly coarse head. Some of his get were even known as the "big jaw" horses.

Bob Gray, well-known Texas horse historian, in his book *Great Horses of the Past* told how Steel Dust's fame rested not only on his ability to reproduce his characteristics but also on his speed as a short-distance runner.

Steel Dust was described as the fast horse that wrecked the economy of McKinney, Texas. Although he was already well known as a winner of most races that he entered, no one in McKinney believed he could beat their favorite racer, a big bay stallion called Monmouth, owned by a prominent citizen, Harry Stiff. The big difference between the horses was that Monmouth looked like a racehorse. He stood over sixteen hands. He was temperamental and had an excellent reputation for winning. Steel Dust was smaller and was anything but temperamental. In fact, his usual attitude could be described as lethargic. Besides, at the time of this race he was nearly twelve years old, which is usually considered over the hill for a racer. But his backers, which included the entire town of Lancaster, had no qualms about putting their money on his nose. He had beaten just about every other horse on the Texas frontier.

It was more than a match race. It was a spectacle. Mc Kinney, with a normal population of five hundred, managed to accommodate two thousand on the day of the race. Food of almost any kind was at a premium, and it was reliably reported that its one small hotel, the Foote House, which had only four rooms, put up thirty-two guests. The great majority of Steel Dust's fans camped out the night before the race, and wagering around the campfires went on into the night.

It must be remembered that with the exception of an occasional fistfight, shoot-out, or Indian raid, horse racing was just about the only entertainment available to Texans. It is no wonder they flocked into town from as far as one hundred miles away. This was a chance for men who felt that they knew horseflesh, and this included all Texans, to put their money where their opinions were.

The race was to start at 11 o'clock on Sunday morning over the protest of a few McKinney citizens whose hearts were unlikely to be able to cope with more excitement than the usual Sunday sermon. There is no record that the clergy put up any real opposition. It was a good-humored mob. They drank up all the whiskey at Whiteley's Saloon, where seven bartenders were kept busy pouring drinks as fast as they could handle the bottles. Because all of the interest was in being sober enough to see the horses run the next day, Sheriff James H. Lovejoy and his deputies had no problem handling the crowd. During that Saturday a large part of the crowd had watched Monmouth work out. His form seemed to justify the hopes of his McKinney backers.

On Sunday morning at 11 o'clock nothing happened. Buckboards, wagons, traps, surreys were still streaming into town. Wagering had become frantic. Everyone in McKinney wanted a little more time to dig up a little more security to bet on their favorite, which by this time they felt was a sure thing. The Lancaster contingent was ready to match

any bets. Some wagers took the form of livestock, saddles, wagons, bridles, tracts of land, and barrels of whiskey, in addition to a considerable amount of money.

By 1:30 everything was ready. The date was September 5, 1856. The crowd was perhaps the biggest until then to witness a race in the new state of Texas. The track was a mile long but the race was set for half a mile. This seems to have been a compromise because Monmouth usually raced the mile and Steel Dust the quarter mile. The riders were Bob Rudolph on Monmouth and a young Negro boy, Tom MacKnight, on Steel Dust. Captain Roy Hall, a historian from McKinney, quoted George A. Wilson, an eyewitness:

"There were not over five thousand people in Collin County but I believe twice that many were present. . . . Men, women and children, Negroes and Indians, and everybody had a bet up. We could see the starting point through the trees and saw Jim [J. W. Throckmorton, later governor of Texas] wave his black hat to start them off.

"They came down off the hill neck and neck and disappeared from sight in Williams Craw. People yelled, shouted, and women and boys started to climb trees to get a view of the horses — but before they got up the racers came up over the rise.

"Big Monmouth was taking gigantic strides but the little mousey horse was making two jumps to old Monmouth's one. They were not long strides but he was making them faster.

"Steel Dust was on the left with the little Negro boy lying squat down on his back. Bob [Rudolph] was thrashing Monmouth but I could not see that the Negro boy was doing anything to Steel Dust. Before we could think, they were at the finish line, Steel Dust three lengths in front. Steel Dust turned sharp off the track and plowed to a stop. Old Monmouth kept right on and ran into a thicket, sweeping Bob off his back [the riders rode bareback] and disappearing from view, crashing off down in the woods.

"I think everybody in the county lost something.

*In the spirit of the Steel Dust-Monmouth match race is this one photographed in 1912 as the horses sped down the main street of Ramona, California. Rider in foreground may be a judge. Note the boys perched atop the telephone pole.*

I was lucky. I only bet a pair of saddlebags. But John [possibly his friend, John Kincaid] lost a cow and a mule. There was a heap of cutting up in town that night, but mostly by the Dallas crowd. Most of us slunk off home, poorer but wiser."

Nobody knows just how much the town of Mc-Kinney lost but it was broke for a long time. All Sunday afternoon and Monday, McKinney cows, horses, saddles, bridles, wagons, and foodstuff found their way out of town on the dusty road to Lancaster. It is possible that never had so many lost so much in such a short time.

This may well have been the peak of Steel Dust's career. His owners, Middleton Perry and Jones Greene, continued to breed him and, as legend has it, to race him. But they did not keep much in the way of records and no one knows quite how many mares he covered in his long life, nor how many races he ran.

The pertinent facts, however, and the ones we have used here come from records compiled by Robert Denhardt, Helen Michaelis, and Wayne Gard. One thing is certain. Legends are not born and built without some facts to support them. There is no question that Steel Dust was the fastest horse in his part of Texas during his running years. He lost his last race by default, having reared against the side of his stall, injuring his shoulder. So he

was unable to go to the starting line against Shiloh, a horse about the same age as Steel Dust and with a pedigree that also went back to Sir Archy. Shiloh was taken to the starting line and galloped over the course alone to win.

But that Steel Dust was still alive and covering mares at the age of twenty is certain, for Jack Batchler, a friend of Steel Dust's owners, made a notation in his studbook in April, 1864, "Bred big filly to Stele [sic] Dust."

Fast as Steel Dust was, he was not the same mount by that name that Jesse James rode, even though in some parts of the United States the James steed was more renowned than the famed Quarter Horse progenitor. And although the horses' life spans overlapped, the Steel Dust of Quarter Horse-breeding prestige was foaled two years before Jesse James was born and therefore would have been too old for the daring young outlaw to use successfully during his lengthy career of banditry.

Besides, the famous sire was a racer. And it is unfortunate that the competition between Steel Dust and Shiloh did not occur, for along with Steel Dust, Shiloh was one of the great progenitors of the Quarter Horse. He was born earlier than Steel Dust and did not arrive in Texas until after Steel Dust had begun to make a reputation. He originated in Tennessee and was brought to Texas by the same

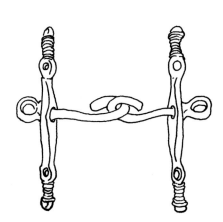

*Snaffle-type bit of Southern Russia dates from about the eighth century B.C. The origin of bits is not certain.*

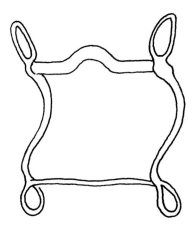

*Large ring on U.S. Cavalry bit of frontier days minimized pinching, curved shank made it almost impossible to lip.*

Jack Batchler who was one of the last breeders of Steel Dust. Shiloh was bred to Steel Dust mares, and this "nick" seems to have been a most successful one. For many years Texans have pointed with pride to either of these great stallions.

Even older than the Steel Dust and Shiloh families was the popular Copper Bottom line. This legendary family was established by 1832. Copper Bottom is said to have belonged to Sam Houston, later elected president of Texas. Copper Bottom was purchased by Houston in Lancaster, Pennsylvania, shipped to New Orleans and on to Galveston. Like Steel Dust and Shiloh, he too is said to be a descendant of Sir Archy. And it is quite possible, though unprovable, that all three of these families owe their speed to Sir Archy, the great son of the imported Thoroughbred stallion *Diomed.

But the older families that were not registered in a studbook tend to be forgotten, and Copper Bottom is not generally named as one of the three horses that were later to be considered forefathers of the Quarter Horse.

That honor falls to Peter McCue. This great racing sire was a son of the famous Dan Tucker who gave his name to one of the good minstrel-show songs around the turn of the century. But while old Dan Tucker was being celebrated in verse, his son Peter McCue was siring hundreds of mares and colts that spread his quality over the Southwest. Most experts agree that he and Steel Dust left more great horses behind them than any horses of their type. It was said of Peter McCue, "You could breed him to a boxcar and get a Quarter Horse." This presupposes a truly potent stallion.

Peter McCue was a big horse standing sixteen hands high and weighing more than 1,400 pounds. And he was a registered Thoroughbred with a bona-fide American Jockey Club number. His racing career is well documented. It shows he ran on recognized tracks and that in his early years he won more races than he lost. Of those early racers he is the only one said to have run a quarter of a mile in 21 seconds flat. As late as 1969 the record was 21.50 seconds. It is well to remember that in Peter McCue's day the times were occasionally measured from a running start and time measurements were nowhere nearly so accurate as the electric timers are today. Peter McCue was retired to stud early in his career. His great fame, like that of Steel Dust, lies in the ability he had to produce champions.

The *American Stud Book* shows twenty registered Thoroughbred mares sired by Peter McCue. Because much better records were kept in Peter McCue's day than in the days of Copper Bottom, Steel Dust, and Shiloh, it is possible to trace his get.

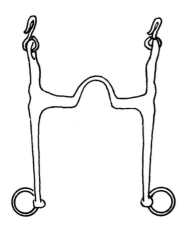

*Simple and rounded, the popular Tom Bass curb bit, sometimes called a Weymouth, is comfortable for the horse.*

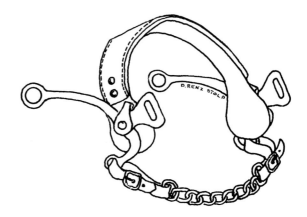

*Leather guard on this hackamore prevents chafing. Hackamore does not have a mouthpiece but uses leverage instead.*

163

His offspring, aside from founding their own type families, produced both running champions and arena champions. When the *Quarter Horse Journal* in 1957 produced male-line descent charts of the major Quarter Horse families, it showed Peter McCue leading in both the number of sires of American Quarter Horse champions (forty-three) and the number of brood mare dams of American Quarter Horse champions (also forty-three). It is probable that today some three-fourths of all the Quarter Horses registered, and probably those unregistered as well, can trace their ancestry to Peter McCue.

It would be of interest to *aficionados* of the Quarter Horse to have the great families between *Janus in 1752 and Joe Bailey in 1911 listed. Such a chart has been drawn up by Helen Michaelis, who was secretary of the American Quarter Horse Association. Her list follows:

*Janus, 1752 — Established by *Janus, 1746-80 by Old Janus — mare by Fox

Peacock, 1764 — Established by Old Peacock, 1760-86 by *Janus — *Old Spain

Mark Anthony, 1767 — Established by Lee's Mark Anthony, 1763-78

Babram, 1770 — Established by Goode's Babram, 1766-81 by *Janus — mare by *Janus

Bacchus, 1778 — Established by Old Bacchus, 1774-89 by Goode's Babram — mare by *Janus

Celer, 1780 — Established by Meade's Celer, 1776-1804 by *Janus — Brandon mare by *Aristotle

Twigg, 1782 — Established by Old Twigg, 1778-? by *Janus — Puckett's Switch mare by *Janus

Brimmer, 1787 — Established by Goode's Brimmer, 1766-86, by Harris' Eclipse — Poll Glaxen

Printer, 1804 — Established by Printer, 1780-1828 by *Janus

Whip, 1809 — Established by Blackburn's Whip, 1805-28 by *Whip — Speckleback by Randolph's Celer

Tiger, 1816 — Established by Tiger, 1812-32 by Blackburn's Whip — Jane Hunt

Copper Bottom, 1832 — Established by Copper Bottom, 1828-60 by Sir Archy — mare by Buzzard

Shiloh, 1848 — Established by Shiloh, 1844-69 by Union Shiloh

Steel Dust, 1849 — Established by Steel Dust, 1845-74 by Harry Bluff — mare unknown

Billy, 1866 — Established by Old Billy, 1860-86 by Shiloh — Ram Cat by Steel Dust

Cold Deck, 1872 — Established by Old Cold Deck, 1879-1901 by Old Billy — Maudy

Roan Dick, 1883 — Established by Roan Dick, 1879-1901 by Black Nick — mare by Greenstreet's Boanerges

| | |
|---|---|
| Rondo, 1884 | Established by Old Rondo, 1880-97 by Whalebone — Mittie Stephens |
| Traveler | Established by Traveler, 1885-1910; pedigree untraced |
| Sykes, 1891 | Established by Sykes Rondo, 1887-1907 by McCoy Billy — Grasshopper |
| Fred, 1897 | Established by Old Fred, 1893-1915 by Black Ball — mare by John Crowder |
| Peter McCue, 1899 | Established by Peter McCue, 1895-1923 by Dan Tucker — Nora M |
| Blake, 1900 | Established on Steel Dust, Shiloh, and Brimmer lines |
| Joe Bailey, 1911 | Established by Old Joe Bailey, 1907-34 by Eureka — Susie McQuirter |

It is difficult if not impossible to recognize specific characteristics still present in Quarter Horses that would allow us to trace them all the way back to these early families. It is also true that some of these progenitors had the ability to stamp their get more effectively than others.

To put in proper perspective the sires that helped create the modern Quarter Horse, let's sum up chronologically. The Eastern influences began with *Janus. He dominated the quarter-mile track during the Colonial era. The best description that places him in the proper historical perspective comes from *The Gentleman's New Pocket Farrier*, by Richard Mason, published in Richmond, Virginia, in 1814. Quarter Horse racing predates the foaling of *Janus. The colonists held match races from Virginia to Massachusetts from as early as 1674. It seems to have spread from Virginia and Maryland to the Carolinas and then north, and we know that two tracks were in Long Island before the Revolutionary War. All of these early tracks were straightaways. The circular track did not appear until after 1800, when longer races were run.

*Janus sired numerous important sons, all well-known sprinters. They include Old Peacock, Goode's Babram, Meade's Celer, and Old Twigg.

Robert Denhardt, the Quarter Horse historian, has divided the evolutionary period of the Quarter Horse into Colonial, until 1800; Transition, 1800-1850; Golden Age, 1850-1900, and Early Modern, 1900-1925. *Janus and his sons belong to Colonial. The Transition period marked the time when longer races became popular and a distinct cleavage occurred between the sprinters or Quarter Horses and the Thoroughbreds. At this point the quarter-mile racers were dropped from the Thoroughbred studbook and only in the appendix of the *American Stud Book* do some of the names of the great sprinters appear. By far the most important sire of the period was the Thoroughbred Sir Archy. He not only beat all of the racehorses of his day, but went on to add his bloodline to both Thoroughbred and Quarter Horse stock.

We noted before that either through the tail-male or tail-female line Steel Dust and Shiloh trace to Sir Archy. We will be meeting others, such as Cold Deck, Billy, and Copper Bottom, which trace to that same famous stud.

But in the Transition period another horse vastly influenced the developing Quarter Horse line. His name was Printer, and he was sired by *Janus. The *American Stud Book* states, "He was a Quarter Horse." Among his get was Boanerges, which sired the famous runner Monkey, named after the earlier imported *Monkey. His grandsons included such outstanding racers as Tiger, Bay Cold Deck, and a number of fast-running fillies that in turn produced many important sprinters. The experts will want to remember that there were two Printers. The first, which so influenced the Quarter Horse line, died in 1828. The second was out of a granddaughter of the original Printer and was foaled in 1872.

The next period, which Denhardt calls the Golden Age, includes those exalted horses Steel Dust and Shiloh, which seem to have dominated the picture and whose influence still is felt. One of Steel Dust's sons, Jack Traveler, sired numerous fast colts and fillies. In the appendix to the *American Stud Book*, Volume VII, the following items appear:

"Belle H., b.m., foaled 1887, bred and owned by James Owen, Berlin, Illinois. First dam b.m., foaled 1877 by Jack Traveler by Steel Dust." (page 1205)

"Mattie Luck, ch.m., foaled 1877, bred and owned by Thos. Watkins, Petersburg, Illinois... 2nd dam Crazy Jane by Harry Bluff (sire of Steel Dust) (by Short Whip and Big Nance of Timoleon)." (page 1223)

When we follow the lines from *Janus on down through Sir Archy, Shiloh, Steel Dust, Peter McCue, and others it is plain that without the Thoroughbred the Quarter Horse as we know him today would not exist.

In recent years, additional important Thoroughbred blood has been infused into the Quarter Horse strain. Owners have bred their best mares to such outstanding Thoroughbreds as Three Bars by Percentage-Myrtle Dee, by Luke McLuke; Top Deck by Equestrian-River Boat by Chicaro; Depth Charge by Bold Venture-Quickly by Haste; Little Request by Requested-Little Wichita by Royal Ford.

But this does not mean the Spanish horses that were the first mounts not only in the West but in the Americas did not make an important contribution. The Quarter Horse may have picked up some of his speed from the Eastern Thoroughbred line, but from the Spanish horses of the West (which were, after all, Arabians and Barbs) he inherited those same qualities that had for many years made them excellent cow horses. The Span-

ish horses, like their ancestors the desert-bred Arabians and Barbs, had lived with man, sharing his work and often his domicile for many more years than the Thoroughbred. They had what later cowboys called "cow savvy."

For it must be remembered that if the Quarter Horse had been only a quarter-mile racehorse he would never have had the important influence on the economy, the social life, and the traditions of the West. True, he could usually run a quarter of a mile faster than a Thoroughbred, but it was his relationship to the rapidly expanding cattle industry in the Western states — his ability and willingness to work with cows, calves, and men — that caused him to be bought by the thousands. For the Quarter Horse is a "use" horse. He is a working horse rather than an aristocrat like the Thoroughbred. He works equally hard at rounding up cattle, cutting out heifers, carrying schoolchildren who live in remote areas, furnishing short-haul transportation in most of the Western states, providing thrills at every major rodeo, and giving pleasure to over one hundred thousand Westerners who show their Quarter Horses in the smallest towns and villages to the International Horse Show in Los Angeles and other metropolitan centers. Other breeds have been taught to do almost all of the jobs the Quarter Horse can do. But none does them better. And none runs the quarter of a mile as fast.

Thoroughbred owners look disdainfully at Quarter Horses, usually describing them as squat, husky, muscle-bound creatures with a stride like a jackrabbit's. Quarter Horses, like Arabians and Appaloosas, no matter how fast they run or what their endurance records might be, are never allowed to race on a Thoroughbred track against Thoroughbreds. Even if they were, there is not much doubt that in distances of more than three-quarters of a mile the Thoroughbred would probably win. But it is one of the things that we will never find out, for the Thoroughbred book is closed. No matter how fast a horse can run he cannot get into the club unless his ancestors were members.

There is now considerable movement to close the Quarter Horse book and not allow entry of any horses regardless of speed or conformation unless they too have descended from one of the registered Quarter Horse lines.

Yet the Quarter Horse Registry is comparatively new. As late as 1935 there was no Quarter Horse association nor was the modern Quarter Horse even officially named as a breed. The honor of naming the horse goes to Bob Denhardt, who had written several articles for Western horse magazines tracing the lineage of the Billy Horses, Steeldusts, and descendants of Peter McCue, pointing out not only that they were related and could be traced back to early Eastern Quarter Horses but that they had gained their reputations on quarter-mile tracks. Against considerable opposition from the well-known horseman Jack Hutchins, who wanted to call the breed Billy Horse, and from prominent breeders Dan Casement and his son Jack—who as adamantly insisted it be called Steeldust—Denhardt prevailed. In the spring of 1940 the American Quarter Horse Association was formed, and Bob Denhardt was its first secretary.

But Denhardt was by no means the only founder. Long before the name Quarter Horse was officially adopted or the organization created, Billy Anson, usually known as "Uncle Billy," a unique Englishman who never lost his accent even though he lived most of his adult life as a Texas rancher, made numerous serious efforts toward getting a registry going. He had come to Texas to seek his fortune and he had found it. His knowledge of horses in England doubtless helped, but he soon developed a very high opinion of the Steeldusts, Billy Horses, and Peter McCues. A contract with the British government to supply cavalry horses gave him an opportunity to select some outstanding Quarter Horses for himself. An early student of the breed, he is well worth quoting:

"The breed has always been kept in a comparative state of purity. The occasional mixture was often mutual, being attributed to some stallions which showed Quarter Horse characteristics either of shape or speed. We accordingly find that they have been bred absolutely true to type and that they have a wonderful power of transmitting their shape and qualities to their offspring.

"The immense breast and chest, enormous fore-arm, loin and thighs and the heavy layers of muscle are not found in any other breed in the world in the same proportion. The desire for speed at short distances developed this type in distinction to that of the Thoroughbred, even as a [human] hundred-yard champion is generally thickset and heavily muscled in comparison to the miler.

"As a breed they rarely exceed 15 hands but attain great weight, many mature horses going as high as 1,200 pounds. In fact you can find 'more horse to the height,' to speak colloquially, among Quarter Horses than in any other breed. This in brief is a description of a breed of horses unique in the world, a pure American breed, and one which is destined to play quite a part in the future of Western ranches, a horse, be it noted, which does not dread the advent of the automobile."

It would be hard to find a better description. However, when at his ranch near Denton, Texas, I visited Rex Cauble, a present-day breeder and rider of outstanding Quarter Horses specializing in cutting cattle, he gave me a copy of his description of the Quarter Horse. It may not be quite as technical but is more poetic than "Uncle" Billy Anson's:

"He's half a ton of poised and controlled energy, held on an easy rein and a hair trigger. He's a workingman who can earn his keep on the range all week and be a handsome dandy at the track on Sunday afternoon. He's proud when he stands; looks lazy when he walks—but when he runs he can whip the tears from the corners of your eyes and plaster your hat brim against the crown. He's big in the haunches, supple in the withers, stout in the neck, and wide across the chest...to hold his great heart. He's cow-smart and brave—though sometimes a clown—and to the man with sky in his eye and mud on his boots, the Quarter Horse is a faithful hand. . . . And a friend!"

Another of the old-timers who influenced development of the Quarter Horse association was Dan Casement. He was active in Quarter Horse breeding and promotion up to his death, and his son Jack has carried on. It was Jack Casement, mentioned earlier, who wrote the first magazine article suggesting a studbook for Quarter Horses, although calling them Steeldusts.

In addition to the excellent pioneering research done by Bob Denhardt, the work of one woman stands out in Quarter Horse history. She was Helen Michaelis, a meticulous researcher and constant champion of the Quarter Horse. She was the second secretary of the American Quarter Horse Association.

It was at Fort Worth's Southwestern Exposition and Stock Show in 1939 that an informal meeting was held by men who outlined procedures that would be followed in forming the association. They included Denhardt, then a professor at Texas A & M University; R. L. Underwood, a Quarter Horse breeder of Wichita Falls, Texas; John Burns, manager of the famous Pitchfork Ranch; J. Goodwin Hall of the 6666 Ranches; Duwain Hughes of San Angelo, Texas; and Dean Marstellar, head of the School of Veterinary Medicine, and D. W. Williams, head of the Animal Husbandry Department, both of Texas A & M. A year later at the same show these people and seventy others held a jubilant dinner meeting. The American Quarter Horse Association was on its way. Its expressed aim was to "collect, record and preserve the pedigrees of Quarter Horses in America; to publish a studbook and registry and to stimulate any and all other matters such as may pertain to the history, breeding, exhibiting, publicity, sale or improvement of this breed in America."

Six years after the association had been formed, headquarters were moved from Fort Worth to Amarillo, Texas. In the first eight years the association registered fourteen thousand Quarter Horses. Now, nearly three-quarters of a million

are registered.

The fledgling days of the organization brought many problems. For instance, facilities were badly disrupted by World War II. But the biggest threat came from a rival Quarter Horse organization that called itself the National Quarter Horse Breeders Association. It too was made up of dedicated breeders, trainers, and owners whose aim was the registration and promotion of the Quarter Horse. To add to the complications, an American Quarter Racing Association was formed in Tucson, Arizona. It grew rapidly, establishing rules and regulations for timing, entering, and the many problems that arise at a track.

Until 1949 confusion was considerable. Some states recognized the American Quarter Racing Association, some the American Quarter Horse Association, others the National Quarter Horse Breeders Association. One thing was certain: if there was to be successful Quarter Horse racing, there must be a single studbook. The Thoroughbreds had proven that. In this emergency the American Quarter Horse Association suggested combining the existing registries. Because everyone's interest was basically the same, the amalgamation was successful. The three organizations merged into the American Quarter Horse Association, and today it operates the only official Quarter Horse Registry.

The association's modern plant is housed in its own air-conditioned building designed especially for its use. Batteries of computers line one wall, and more than 130 employees service the Quarter Horse industry. Every one of the 500,000 Quarter Horses has its own registry card, which includes its description, special markings, date of foaling, and every other activity of record until the horse's death. No human life span is as carefully analyzed and recorded.

Activities of the association range widely. It supervises 1,500 Quarter Horse shows each year in the United States and Canada. One cannot miss the long, low Spanish-style building that houses the association because next door is a somewhat ram-shackle Italian restaurant. It is called the Quarter of a Horse Restaurant. There is no connection between the two, but the restaurant serves excellent pizzas. A sense of humor has always been an essential element in Western tradition.

Because of the fantastic spread of Quarter Horse racing throughout the United States and especially in Western states, the association spends much of its time investigating and approving participants. Rules are just as stringent in Quarter Horse racing as in Thoroughbred racing, and every horse must be graded to qualify in the register of merit. To be placed at the top, which carries a Top AAA rating, a horse must be able to run the quarter-mile in 22.1 seconds. This means that if you get a cinder in your eye at a first-rate quarter-mile race, you are very likely to miss the race entirely. To earn a AAA rating, the quarter mile must be run between 22.11 and 22.5 seconds. To rate AA, a horse can run it as slowly as 22.9. An A classification runs from 22.91 to 23.3. This means that if you are even fourth on the list, your horse will have to run at a speed of approximately 45 miles an hour for one-quarter of a mile—and from a standing start, cowboy. The bottom, or D class, allows a horse to run the 440 yards in 24.11. Standard weight carried is 116 pounds.

Last year well over two million Quarter Horse racing fans paid admissions to eighty-six racetracks in twenty-six states. It is safe to estimate that ninety percent of them wagered money on their favorites. And the pari-mutuel handle was more than $82 million as more than nine thousand horses raced for purses totaling $7,283,615. One of the biggest Quarter Horse tracks, Los Alamitos, near Los Angeles, California, records in the neighborhood of $800,000 in bets each night of its operation. Like almost all Quarter Horse tracks, Los Alamitos uses the pari-mutuel system originated by Thoroughbred tracks. The organized race meet has effectively replaced the old-time Sunday races down a dusty course lined with spectators. Today's Quarter

Horse tracks are multimillion-dollar plants with every possible facility for efficiently handling the horses and their fans. The American Quarter Horse Association has seen to it that the tracks are competently run and well manned with knowledgeable horsemen, and above all they have kept Quarter Horse racing honest.

Some of the facilities and their operation should be of interest to people who like horses whether they attend race meets or not—but most Quarter Horse people do.

A major difference between requisites for a Quarter Horse track and a Thoroughbred track is expressed in the second of the basic requirements a track must comply with to have its races recognized by the American Quarter Horse Association. It reads simply:

"A sufficiently wide, relatively level straightaway of 440 yards or more, with a pull-up area of sufficient length to allow horses to ease before entering the turn, or a fenced and maintained pull-up area of at least 400 yards."

The Quarter Horse Association polices itself very much as the Thoroughbred Association does. Under definition number 18, the Rules and Regulations state:

"Fraudulent and/or corrupt turf practice shall mean any attempt to enrich oneself or associates or to gain an advantage, through unfair, unlawful or dishonest behavior in connection with the racing of horses."

A few other terms may be of interest to the novice racing fan. For instance, when referring to a horse generally it may be a filly (unbred female), mare, colt, or gelding. But when referring to sex specifically, an animal must be an entire male at least four years old before it is listed as a horse.

A breeder of a horse is the owner of its dam at the time of service.

Foul means any action by any jockey that tends to hinder another jockey or any horse in the running of the race.

Place in racing shall mean first, second, third,

and fourth and in that order is called win, place, show, and fourth. But only if the horse finishes in one of the first three positions is a man paid for a bet.

Handicap is a race in which weights to be carried by the horses are adjusted by a handicapper or board of handicappers to equalize their respective chances of winning.

Match is a race between two or more horses, the property of different owners, on terms agreed upon by the owners, to which no money or other prize is added.

A purse race is a run for money or any other prize to which the owners of the horses engaged do not contribute an entry fee of more than $50.

A claiming race is an event in which any horse entered may be claimed, based upon the amount of money the owner declares he is worth before the race.

A stakes is a race in which the stakes are to be posted by the owners of the horses. It remains a stakes race when money or other prize is added.

Entries must close more than seventy-two hours before the first race of the day such stakes are to be run.

A walkover occurs when only one owner is represented at the post. In a stakes race, unless otherwise specified in prerace conditions, the entry which appears may walk over the course and be declared the winner—and is entitled to the entire stakes and the winning percentage of the purse.

Scratch means withdrawing a horse after the closing of overnight entries.

A horse becomes a starter when the stall doors of the starting gate open in front of it at the time the official in charge dispatches the horses.

Racing has many additional intricate rules designed to protect the betting public, because should the bettors lose faith it would become impossible to continue race meets. One of the safeguards includes the weighing in and out of all jockeys. This is done by the clerk of the scales. He posts all overweights immediately after weighing and notifies the trainer concerned if any jockey is overweight. He does not allow any jockey to ride with more than two pounds of overweight until the trainer accepts the excess.

No race is declared official until the clerk of the scales has notified stewards that the final weights of the jockeys are within limits. Because weight-carrying is of such importance, jockeys are weighed in as well as out. It would be impossible therefore for a jockey to carry more weight when he weighed in and dispose of it before mounting the horse, thereby letting the animal run with less poundage. For at the end of the race the weighing takes place immediately, and that weight can be no more than before the race, nor no more than one pound less than before—the riders being allowed that small weight loss during the competition. Weighing is without whip or bridle. The bridle used in races must never exceed two pounds or a whip one pound. As a safety regulation every jockey must wear a crash helmet approved by the racing association.

In case some people might think jockeys may know too much about what is going to happen in a race, it is interesting to note that no jockey is allowed to have a personal attendant. He may make arrangements with the track operator for an attendant, but these aides (if allowed) must be paid by the operator, and no jockey may have the same attendant for more than two days nor may the attendant make a bet for himself or for anyone on any horse. If he is found to have done this he is immediately ruled off the track. No attendant may touch any part of the horse except the bridle.

The jockey must unsaddle his own horse after the race. Should a jockey touch any person or thing other than his equipment, his horse may be disqualified and the rider may be fined or suspended. No jockey is ever allowed to bet on any horse except the one he is riding. And he cannot even place that bet except through the owner. If a jockey should have any interest in any entry other than the one he is riding, or should he bet on some other horse—or should he even be known to receive presents from someone other than the owner he is riding for—his license can be revoked. He is not even allowed to train a horse unless he rides only that horse in a race.

To even the odds, that is, to give each horse a more or less equal chance to win, handicap races are run. In these events, horses which have shown more speed than others are given more weight to carry.

There are some major differences between Quarter Horse rules and other racing rules. For instance, all horses must qualify by being timed. Standard distances for qualification for the register of merit are two hundred and twenty, two hundred and fifty, three hundred, three hundred and thirty, three hundred and fifty, four hundred, and four hundred and forty yards. The elapsed time is measured from the instant the starting gates open until the horse's nose reaches the finish line. Times are measured in seconds and hundredths of a second. An electrical timing camera is used and a strip print is filed with the report of the race. This photo-finish strip has the times printed across it in hundredths.

Every Quarter Horse track must have a wind gauge, because if a tail wind is blowing at more than eight miles an hour the race time cannot be accepted for a record. However, if the tail wind is more than seven miles an hour but less than twenty miles an hour the horse can be admitted to the racing register of merit but he will be awarded a grade below the grade he would have received had not the stronger wind been blowing. The wind gauge should be situated at the eighth pole, at the height of a horse's withers.

It is important for Quarter Horse stallions and their get to earn points in the Quarter Horse register of merit, for this indicates their performance in any given year. One register-of-merit point is given for each race run in AA time, three points for each race run in AAA time, and five points for each race run in Top AAA time.

To keep racing controlled, no horses may be entered on a Quarter Horse track unless they are registered with the American Quarter Horse Association. Only records set by horses registered with the AQHA are recognized.

You may like to know what the requirements generally are for participating in an official race meet. For instance, if you are involved in book-making, you are out. This is also true if you have been convicted or found guilty of a felony, or if you have been habitually intoxicated at the track. They go even farther in this direction, for no one is allowed to participate who is engaged in any activity or practice which is undesirable or detrimental to the best interests of the public and the sport of horse racing. An application as an official, trainer, jockey, or groom must be approved and must show ability and integrity. Track officials and state racing commissioners are notified whenever an application is refused.

Perhaps the busiest man at a race meet is the veterinarian. It is his job to examine each horse as it enters the paddock to be saddled. And he has the authority to order any horse scratched that he feels is unsafe to be raced or which seems to be in such bad condition it would be inhumane to race it. He can and sometimes does suspend any horse which is unsound or unfit, and until the horse is in racing condition it cannot be entered. The veterinarian is also responsible for taking the necessary urine and saliva or other specimen tests from the winner of every race and from any other horses the stewards may designate. And if tests indicate presence of forbidden drugs or medication, that is considered evidence that such has been administered to the horse internally or externally. Urine tests are the most important, saliva tests the next most significant, and blood tests occasionally are taken. It is necessary for the owner or the trainer to be present when such tests are taken.

The most important man, however, and one who certainly is almost as busy as the veterinarian, is the racing secretary. He is the man who writes the conditions of all the races. He draws up the races and posts an overnight listing of horses that will be running. He also is the handicapper, so that he is responsible for assigning a weight to each entry according to his judgment. He also is expected (though he can have an assistant) to keep a complete record of all races and of all violations of racing rules. In addition to being known as racing secretary, he is known as clerk of the course. In this capacity he receives all stakes, forfeits, entrance monies, fines, and fees, as well as purchase money in claim races. He does not make any of the purses available to winning owners until the saliva, urine, or other tests have been cleared.

Until recent years Quarter Horse race riding was strictly for the boys. In fact, until 1967 the Quarter Horse Racing Association had a rule that read: "Jockeys must be male, 16 years of age or older." But on some of the small, bush-league tracks women jockeys began to get a leg up. Their weight was right, they handled their mounts well, and although the boys objected the girls managed to hang on. Slowly they raced their way onto the official Quarter Horse tracks. Now that rule reads only that jockeys must be sixteen years of age or older.

After the entries have been ordered to go to the starting post and the stewards direct the gates to be reopened, no one except racing officials is allowed on the course. All horses must parade and will be disqualified should the jockey dismount or fall off or if the horse loses any equipment. If a horse should misbehave either before he gets to the starting gate or in it, he may be excused, but he will be penalized by being put on the list of horses that have to go back to school.

Once a horse starts he may be just as responsible as the jockey for a foul on another horse or horses. In Quarter Horse races where running is on a straightaway every horse is expected to stay as nearly as possible in the lane in which he starts. Should he drift out or be driven out of his lane, either he or the jockey has committed a foul and the offending horse may be disqualified. This is true whether the foul was caused by the horse or the rider and whether it was avoidable or not. How-

ever, if stewards rule that the foul was caused by the horse rather than the jockey, no blame is attached to the rider and he is not penalized. Should the jockey be at fault, he may be fined or suspended or both. A jockey can even be fined for allowing his horse to get out of the lane too far even though no horse is fouled. And stewards consider chain reactions. If a horse crosses in front of another so as to block him or cause him to shorten his stride, he may be disqualified, depending on whether he crossed over by being forced to by another horse or jockey. Although it seems a bit unfair, if a horse is disqualified—especially if a foul seems to have been willfully committed by a jockey—every horse in that race that belongs wholly or in part to the same owner may be disqualified.

A good many of these regulations may be summed up by Rule 183 of the American Quarter Horse Association code:

"Any act of the owner, trainer, handlers or jockey of a horse which would tend to prevent the horse from running his best and winning if possible shall mean suspension of all persons found guilty of complicity."

But suppose two horses finish at the same instant, their noses touching the photo-finish line. In the old days such a dead heat would have been run off. Not so today in Quarter Horse competition, for when two horses run a dead heat for first place, for instance, all the prize money to which the first and second horses would have been entitled is divided equally between them, and each horse is considered a winner. In this case there would be no second horse, for the next horse following the winners would be in third place.

The basic official staff at a track consists of a presiding steward and two associate stewards. In some states stewards are appointed by the state racing commission. In addition there are placing judges, patrol judges, a clerk of the scale, a starter, a timer, a paddock judge, a veterinarian, and often, in addition to the racing secretary who sometimes acts in that capacity, a handicapper. One inflexible rule states that no racing official may in any capacity serve in any race in which is entered a horse owned by him or in which he has a financial interest or which is owned by a member of his family.

The placing judges are responsible for determining the order of finish of each race. But they are restricted in that the order must be determined exclusively by the horse's nose. In other words, should a horse's head be back or turned and his hoof reach the finish line first, the position of his nose must be the deciding factor. A horse cannot win a race by anything but a nose, a neck, half a length, or more.

Leading tracks are Los Alamitos, California; Ruidoso Downs, Ruidoso, New Mexico; Centennial Track, Littleton, Colorado; Evangeline Downs, Lafayette, Louisiana; La Mesa Park, Raton, New Mexico; and Portland Meadows, Portland, Oregon.

For sheer split-second excitement with a long build-up and a short but intense climax, probably no competition equals the richest horse race in the world. Prize money for the annual All-American Futurity in 1968 was nearly four times greater than the Kentucky Derby purse. It came to $615,000. The race is run on Labor Day in New Mexico at a village called Ruidoso, seventy-five miles west of Roswell. The name in Spanish means "noisy," and during the meet at Ruidoso Downs the population increases twenty times. The village is noisy. When the races are not on, finding Ruidoso is not easy. But when the races are on or approaching, the town becomes a colorful and significant site. Yet through the expert efforts of Walt Wiggins, vice-president of the track and director of public relations, publicity, and advertising, and track president A. B. Green — plus the cooperation of the fastest sprinters bred in the United States — Ruidoso Downs has become famous throughout the horse-racing world.

To be present at the All-American Futurity is like going to a colorful country fair, a beautiful modern racecourse, and a Western scenic para-dise. For Ruidoso Downs is set against a backdrop of the Sacramento Mountains, and they are beautiful mountains. Even in midsummer temperatures are in the low 70's. This is the real West. It is Billy the Kid country, and the track is close by the Mescalero Apache Indian Reservation. In the immediate neighborhood are Carlsbad Caverns National Park, Bottomless Lakes State Park, and a new recreation area called Sierra Blanca, where before or after the races you can take the gondola ski lift for a breathtaking view of the countryside.

Unlike at the exclusive Thoroughbred tracks, you get to see the great Quarter Horses in action as well as the distance runners, for Thoroughbreds also compete there. But basically it is a Quarter Horse crowd. This is emphasized on the day the All-American Futurity is run.

The track is big enough to accommodate well over the ten thousand enthusiasts who find their way there. Stables are large and modern and it is possible for all fans to see their favorite horses being saddled in the paddock.

Only ten of the speediest Quarter Horses compete in the big race. Qualifying events weed out the others. The distance is four hundred yards and all starters carry 119 pounds. All of the horses in the 1968 Futurity had run the distance in at least 20.22 seconds. The fastest, a brown colt called Three Oh's, by Three Chicks out of Oh My Oh, had streaked through the qualifying trial at 20.03 seconds and went on to win the race in 20.06.

The Futurity record is 19.09. It was set by Double Bid in 1957 and equaled by Savannah Dandy in 1967. To own a horse that can win over $8,000 a second for twenty seconds (plus almost as much in his qualifying trial) is like owning a running gold mine.

At the end of the race the atmosphere is more like that of a college football game combined with a huge family reunion. The owners of Three Oh's had risked $12,500 when they bought the colt as a one-year-old. He was, however, an excellent risk, for his dam, Oh My Oh, was one of the great quarter-mile race mares of all time. After Mr. and Mrs. Donald Strole got through the crowd to be photographed with their champion, it was the turn of jockey Jerry Nicodemas, who posed in the infield with his blonde wife and their daughter Shelley. By this time a considerable crowd had found their way to the infield to stand near the triumphant jockey and horse. The Nicodemas family was in tears, Mrs. Strole began crying too, and relatives and well-wishers numbering in the dozens patted them and each other on the back until track officials encouraged them to return to the grandstand.

An event of almost equal importance to the All-American Futurity is the All-American Futurity Sale, which is held in a specially built convention center. It takes up the evening before Labor Day as well as Labor Day night. Some one hundred and fifty yearlings by the outstanding Quarter Horse sires are auctioned. Young hopefuls are bid in for as much as $30,000 even though these yearlings have never won a race. All the yearlings on sale are eligible for the next year's All-American Futurity—if they can qualify.

So every important Quarter Horse breeder, owner, and trainer plans his visit to Ruidoso Downs to attend the race and sale. Two highly vocal auctioneers handle the sale while three assistants facing the audience relay the bidding and pass signals to the auctioneers on the platform. The chant of the agent resembles that of the tobacco auctioneer, and it takes a while to understand how the bidding goes. One man on the microphone extols the characteristics of the animal being shown and describes his ancestry in detail. The other repeats the last bid in a chant and encourages the buyers.

The tension of ten thousand excited people on a warm summer afternoon can be felt in the atmosphere just before the starting gates spring open for the All-American Futurity. Then ten highly trained, muscular four-legged athletes spring onto the straightaway like tigers pouncing or like jackrabbits jumping. The roar of the crowd is a deep rumble somewhat like nearby thunder. The con-

centration is intense for the next twenty seconds while the spectators follow the flow of the flying horses as sinewy legs churn furiously and every nerve and muscle and bone are extended. The pounding hoofs can be heard above the noise of the people, who now are literally holding their breaths. It is probable that during this twenty-second interval fewer eyes blink among the spectators at Ruidoso Downs than in any comparable period at any other event in the world. Tension is greater than that generated by a ball spinning in a roulette wheel, or by a gambler drawing one card to fill a straight, or by a victim awaiting a murderer in a Hitchcock film.

It is not the money that creates this mood. It is the spectacle of ten of the world's fastest horses sprinting along that track and each trying to shove his nose ahead of the others. The finishes are always close, usually only a few hundredths of a second separating the lead horses. If a horse finishes a quarter of a second behind the winner, he may finish last.

After they have crossed the finish line, you can almost hear everyone take long deep breaths as though the entire grandstand has just gone down a steep ski run and reached the bottom.

Some critics have suggested that the race is so short there really is no time to watch the horses running. I suggest that the quarter-mile fans, knowing exactly what to watch for, can concentrate so completely that no movement of the horses from start to finish is missed. As one breeder told me: "You look six times harder at a quarter race than you do at a mile and a half race—so you come out even."

The explosion in Quarter Horse racing is reflected not only in the increased number of tracks and spectators but also in the popularity of certain proven stallions and producing mares. Great stallions are often syndicated, and the financial history of one of them, Go Man Go, indicates how a knowledgeable Quarter Horse man with money and vision can select the right stallion and come up with a million-dollar property.

As an eight-year-old and a big money winner on the track, Go Man Go was sold by Johnny Ferguson to A. B. Green, well-known breeder and owner of Green Pastures Farm near Purcell, Oklahoma. Green paid $40,000 for the potentially great stallion. He sold him to E. L. Gosselin for an undisclosed amount. Gosselin undoubtedly made a huge profit, however, when he sold the horse to Frank Vessels of Los Alamitos, California, racing fame and William Peckham, a breeder from Richmond, Texas, for $125,000.

Vessels held on to his half of Go Man Go, and that portion continued to yield a profit. But after two years Vessels sold his fifty percent to Melvin Hatley of Briarwood Farms at Purcell, Oklahoma, for $300,000. This is certainly the largest price that half a horse has brought in the history of racing. Now the horse is owned by Hatley and Peckham. Hatley leases Peckham's half for an astronomical annual fee and stands the horse on his Briarwood Farm.

But not even these figures give any idea of Go Man Go's true value. For since artificial insemination was introduced in Quarter Horse breeding his worth has multiplied phenomenally.

Because it is possible to split a single ejaculate several ways Go Man Go is now serving from five to ten times as many mares as he could service directly. The American Quarter Horse Association, unlike the cattle industry and a few other registries, allows artificial insemination only when the mare and the stallion are on the same premises. There is a distinct possibility, however, that as frozen semen gains more acceptance and its distribution proves to be completely controllable that this provision could change. But even with the present-day artificial insemination techniques—and Go Man Go's owner receives $3,500 per service—it is easy to see how such a stallion has become possibly the greatest moneymaker in horse-breeding history.

The man who owned Go Man Go for two years,

Frank Vessels, who by the way was a founder of the important Los Alamitos Race Track, now stands the nearest horse he could find to Go Man Go. This is Duplicate Copy, one of the best sons of Go Man Go. Duplicate Copy is out of Triple Lady, twice world champion mare, and is exactly the same color and has the same markings as his distinguished sire.

But by no means are all the top stallions in Oklahoma and California. Perhaps the greatest concentration of them is in Texas on such large spreads as the 6666 Ranch, part of the Burnett Estates operation; the Pitchfork Ranch; and perhaps the best known of all, the fabulous King Ranch at Kingsville, Texas, north of Corpus Christi. Quarter Horse breeding has been developed there into a fine art.

Robert J. "Bob" Kleberg, Jr., along with others of the Kleberg family, contributed mightily to modern Quarter Horse evolution by developing the Old Sorrel line. The Klebergs' interest was primarily in breeding fine cow horses for their ranch empire. Old Sorrel, the foundation stud, dates to 1917. He was sired by Quarter Horse Hickory Bill out of a Thoroughbred mare. Old Sorrel sired a considerable number of excellent horses but his most important contribution was made after he was thirty years old when the best of his get, Hired Hand, was foaled. One outstanding example of the Old Sorrel line was the Quarter Horse Wimpy, a double grandson of Old Sorrel. This horse was sired by Solis which was by Old Sorrel. Wimpy was out of the dam Panda, also by Old Sorrel.

In contrast to the artificial insemination program practiced at Briarwood Farm in Oklahoma, the King Ranch breeding technique is to put the stallion and numerous mares into a large paddock, perhaps one covering twelve acres. The stallion becomes familiar with the twenty to thirty mares and then the paddock area is increased. However, as with wild herds, the stallion stakes out a territory and keeps his mares within a controllable area. Stallions and mares are turned out in the early spring around the first of March, and the stallions are returned to their paddocks about mid-June. By this time most of his mares are in foal. This technique has been going on at the King Ranch ever since I lived in Karnes City, Texas, in 1922. At this time Karnes City was a typical small Texas cow town. I remember what a great thrill it was to hear tales about and occasionally visit the even then legendary King Ranch.

It is difficult to stipulate the states that have the largest number of outstanding Quarter Horse stallions, for the leading sires tend to be moved around as they change owners. Perhaps the greatest of all modern sires of Quarter Horses switched from the West Coast to Texas. He was Three Bars, a Thoroughbred whose get until his recent death had earned well over $3 million. Three Bars commanded a $5,000 stud fee.

While the champion running stallions are bred to produce more champion running stallions, they are also bred to mares with special abilities in other fields. Within recent years, for instance, highly selective breeding has continuously improved the Cutting Horse.

The Cutting Horse goes back to the time when the first cow, probably one from the Longhorn herd that Cortés brought to Mexico, was singled out to supply food for the *vaqueros*. He has been essential in cattle handling ever since cattle were imported to the West at about the same time horses were. The cowboys soon found that not just any horse was a Cutting Horse. He had to be a horse with a feeling for working with cows—one that stockmen had always referred to as having "cow sense." So these horses, often the most agile in the *remuda*, were selected for this special and necessary job.

Even in the very early days of ranching in Texas, New Mexico, and California, "cutting" for sport or entertainment was popular. Opportunities for sport in those early days on the range were rare. A man who felt he had a good Cutting Horse would show how easily and effectively he could remove an animal from the herd and play it for a considerable length of time before allowing it to rejoin its group.

From this kind of informal beginning came the first recorded contest: A Cutting Horse event was included in the 1898 cowboy reunion at Haskell, Texas. Ten years later the first indoor Cutting Horse contest helped entertain the crowd at the Southwest Exposition and Fat Stock Show in Fort Worth. From then on it became a regular event in most rodeos, and in more recent years spread to Western horse shows generally.

The man who in recent years has had the greatest influence on development of the Cutting Horse is Marion Flynt, one of the three or four great Cutting Horse men in the world and president of the National Cutting Horse Association. A tall, spare Western type, he looks as hard muscled as the horses he rides. It was back in 1953 that Flynt and a bright-eyed, nimble, acute mare hit the Cutting Horse circuit with plans to win the championship. They took along, in addition to bedroll and tack, Flynt's friend and the mare's trainer, Buster Welch. It took them a year to get started, but by the end of 1953 Marion's Girl was in hair-trigger condition to outtwist, outjump, and outthink the fastest yearlings in the West. She proved it too. For in 1954 after only one year out, Marion Flynt had realized his dream. Marion's Girl was the world's Cutting Horse champion.

Now that is about all one should expect from a Quarter Horse mare, but Flynt expected more. They took it easy for a year, but in 1956 Marion's Girl returned to competition and became the only mare ever to win the national Cutting Horse championship twice.

"I was lucky," Flynt said, "to have a horse that could think for itself. She proved this to me one time as I was about to go into the arena in San Francisco. Only minutes before the event, I suffered an eye injury that left me for the moment almost totally blind. But the event had been called and I had a lot of confidence in my girl. Besides, I expected to be able to see any minute. Well, it didn't work out that way. I found I couldn't even tell the color of the cow; it was just a great big dark shadow. I certainly couldn't give the horse much help but she seemed to feel it and she knew just what to do. She quietly cut the cow out of the herd and worked it for the allotted two and a half minutes while I just moved with her. The difference between a good worker and an undependable Cutting Horse has a lot to do with its disposition. Marion's Girl liked cow work and she worked well when she was off her feed or even if she was crippled up. She could stand all night in a trailer and be ready to come out fresh and spry for the contest."

Flynt told me a Cutting Horse must have — in addition to speed and action — insight. "You need a horse that can read a cow's mind long before a man has any idea what the horse will do."

Marion's Girl might have gone on to win additional titles, but unfortunately she became ill suddenly and died while in foal to one of the King Ranch stallions. However, the death of his favorite mount did not diminish Flynt's interest in Cutting Horses. He became president of the National Cutting Horse Association and helped set many of the standards that now govern that widespread organization.

The association had been formed at Fort Worth in 1946. Over the next ten years it gathered many members and extended its influence over the Western states. It now has its own headquarters building in Fort Worth, publishes a monthly magazine, has 2,500 paid-up members, supervises over a half-million dollars annually in purses, and has 70 affiliated national and regional groups all over the United States using its rules and standards. The association, which approves 800 Cutting Horse shows annually, favors open events. In one of its open or championship contests, horses can be entered regardless of breed, age, sex, color, conformation, appearance, or previous performance. This is one event in the horse world where an animal is judged solely on what he can do rather than how he looks. But registered Quarter Horses dominate.

In the National Cutting Horse Futurity more than two hundred three-year-olds compete for purses totaling around $100,000. As all good cutting horsemen know, the most important thing a rider can do is select and judge the cow that is cut out of the herd. Some cows will not permit a horse to show off his skills. Others may be too small or too large. In a contest the rider should enter the herd quietly. The true Cutting Horse eases into the cattle, fully concentrating on his job. It is important that he make no movements that might trouble or unsettle the herd. The rider should remain in charge but not push his mount until the animal is separated. Then he should leave his horse alone, giving him enough slack in the reins so that it is obvious to the judges that the horse has taken charge of the cow. A good Cutting Horse will have complete control of the cow from this time on. He should show interest in handling the cow but not animosity toward it. Even if the cow manages to get a considerable distance away, the horse's movements should be counter to the cow's.

Ideally, the Cutting Horse will bring the cow quite a way from the herd toward the center of the arena. This keeps the herd from being disturbed. With every movement of the cow, no matter how slight, the horse should act faster so he will hold the cow tightly and not run her unduly from wall to wall and not need excess help from the two turn-back riders, who should stay effectively out of the action.

Each horse is given two and one-half minutes to perform. This time starts when the horse's name is announced. The rider then goes to the herd and works as many cattle within this period as he sees fit.

Official events have two judges. They evaluate how hard and fully the horse is challenged by the cow and how he responds to those challenges. They total penalty points for mistakes the horse makes, subtracting them from points scored. The judge's scores are then added together. The winner is the horse with the highest score.

Unfortunately it seems a lot easier to select a horse's mistakes than see what he does well, and the errors a horse is penalized for are numerous. For instance the entry loses points if the cow has to be turned back by the rear fence rather than by the horse, or if the horse scatters the herd while he is cutting, or if he is visibly cued or reined in any manner during his performance. He should never go past the animal so far that he loses his working advantage, and if—heaven forbid—he turns the wrong way with his tail toward the cow, he is disqualified. These are by no means all the rules but they give some idea of the proficiency and independence a horse must demonstrate to be a champion.

If a man's home is his castle, the Quarter Horse castle is the luxurious and efficient structure built at Denton, Texas, by Rex Cauble, stockman, oil man, sportsman, and horseman. Cauble, who has been interested in Quarter Horses for a long time, was the last owner of Wimpy P-1, the first horse to be recorded in the American Quarter Horse Association studbook. Out on the flat prairie five miles north of Denton, the Cutter Bill Championship Arena, which Cauble created, rises out of the mesquite. Established in honor of Cutter Bill, outstanding Quarter Horse cutting stallion, it is probably the largest edifice ever built to house a horse. Of course there are other horses occupying the twenty-nine stalls, but the structure was planned and constructed with world champion Cutter Bill in mind.

A museum forms the entrance to the arena. In it are priceless mementos of great horsemen of the past, including the saddle and bridle of the famous old-time Western actor William S. Hart. On the right just past the museum displays is Rex Cauble's large office, with swinging doors. On the other side of those doors is a replica of an ancient saloon which Cauble calls The Long Branch. The rinky-dink player piano is likely to be going full blast,

and the elaborate bar is completely equipped as a modern soda fountain.

The arena is 360 feet long and 160 feet wide, and music is piped throughout. In a place of honor is a magnificent painting by the well-known Western artist Orren Mixer of Cutter Bill at work. The arena's ideal training and working floor is formed of sand over a hard clay base. The sand is from Texas' Red River, and the arena is maintained in prime working condition. One new twist in the horses' stalls is a small, electrically operated, insecticide aerosol spray unit. This releases a fly eradicator every few minutes all day—and all night.

A wide, elevated ramp permits spectators to walk from one side to the other without interfering with the activities. This walkway is the ideal vantage point for watching the Cutting Horses during the various events staged there. Under the walkway are the calf pens. All of this is a great monument to a horse. But as a breeding stallion Cutter Bill has proven worth it. He will doubtless pay for his arena.

To quote Marion Flynt once more, "You have to teach a man how to ride and how to judge cows, but a good Cutting Horse has his cow sense inbred."

Rodeoing has become a big business for horsemen and horses. While there are no restrictions on what kinds of horses are used in rodeos, a very high percentage of those ridden in roping and cutting—in fact most of the events that require horse and man cooperation—are Quarter Horses. Because rodeos range from those of the traditional huge Pendleton Roundup, Cheyenne Frontier Days, and Madison Square Garden to the Sunday afternoon competitions where only local ranchers compete with each other and at which spectators often sit on the hillsides around a natural flat arena, thousands of horses of different kinds are used.

The average four-day rodeo, of which literally hundreds are held in the Western states every year, requires sixty-five to seventy bucking horses, ten to twelve parade horses, forty calves, thirty-five bulldogging steers, and twenty-eight to thirty bulls. To this must be added contestants who supply their own horses. Unlike most show-business performers these men have to pay an entry fee, and they do not take home any money unless they win.

Bucking horses come from a number of sources. Occasionally a Quarter Horse that is unbreakable will turn out to be a great rodeo bronc. Rodeo producers such as Jim Shoulders of Henryetta, Oklahoma, scout all over the West to find them. Every bucking horse has to be judged as an individual. Some will eat out of a man's hand while in the paddock and turn into a tornado when a man mounts him in the rodeo arena.

Some bucking horses behave like professionals — they do not go into their act until they are on the stage. Some are extremely well traveled, going to San Francisco, San Antonio, Houston, New York, and even Tokyo and Brussels. They come in all ages and sizes. Some of the best are well over twelve years old, while occasionally one four or five years old will win the national bucking-horse finals. A problem rodeo stockmen have is finding a good bucking horse that will buck with a very experienced rider. They will throw an amateur off quickly, but after an experienced rider shows the horse he knows what is going on, some horses will quit and start running around.

Although it looks like a tough life for these horses during the few minutes they perform at the rodeo, they actually have it pretty easy most of the time. Lots of good bucking horses live to be thirty years old which is about the equivalent of a man being ninety.

When a rancher finds he has a horse that is an "outlaw" he knows that even if he could break him to the saddle, he will not be of any use on the ranch in the long run. For horses are like people — some of them you just cannot trust. The truly ornery horse will kick, bite, or look for an opportunity to step on your foot when you least expect it. If he cannot buck you off his back he will fall and make an attempt to pin you under him. One of the most

revealing names ever given to a great bucking horse was "Sunbeam." Now this sounds like a gentle name but it was given to this horseflesh tornado because the sun was said to shine almost as much on his belly as it did on his back, what with all the twists, turns, jumps, and falls he did whenever he was mounted.

At the Oklahoma ranch of Jim Shoulders, this former all-time great rodeo cowboy runs an interesting school, giving instruction in bareback riding and saddle bronc and bull riding. School takes up four times a year and each session lasts six days. The enrollees, usually teen-age boys, apply from all over the United States, including Hawaii, and from Canada. More potential rodeo pros apply than can be accommodated. Almost all are ranch-bred boys who want to pick up the fine points so that they can spend a little time seeing the country and rodeoing.

The Quarter Horse association is not directly involved in the rodeo business, which is operated by the Rodeo Cowboys Association. Every year the RCA puts on six hundred rodeos in the United States.

But outpulling the rodeo in attendance are the more than 3,000 horse shows or gymkhanas in which young people participate. Some 1,800 of these events are association-approved or sponsored youth shows. The production of such shows requires that they be open to all Quarter Horse owners eighteen years of age and under. There may be classes for horses other than Quarter Horses, however, in shows approved by the AQHA. The organization tries to keep shows separated and nonconflicting by withholding approval of shows held on the same day if the two are located within 150 miles of each other. They have attempted to improve judging standards by insisting that a judge must be selected from the AQHA-approved list.

The age rule has an interesting aspect, for the age of a youth on January 1 becomes his age for the entire year. For example, if a youngster is still eighteen on the first of January, he remains that

*In Texas and Arizona during the peak years of cattle raising, working saddles resembled this one with its high wooden horn and high cantle. John Rockfellow, early day Arizona rancher, had this saddle made around 1880, apparently in Tucson.*

age for show purposes until the end of the year, no matter when his nineteenth birthday falls.

Events approved for a youth show include showmanship with the horse at halter, cutting, barrel racing, calf roping, working cow horse, jumping, working hunter, and reining. These are considered full-point classes. Half-points are given in Western pleasure, Western riding, trail class, stakes race, Western horsemanship, breakaway riding, and pole bending. Some of these are especially popular, and all are carefully selected so that even the novice rider or the very young one

has a chance to show off his or her skills as well as that of the horse.

The trail-horse class measures the horse's ability to handle himself and his rider on a trail ride. Various obstacles such as logs, gates, and wooden bridges are placed along the course. Barrel racing is a fine test of speed, agility, and horsemanship. The contestants race against time, making turns as tightly as possible around the barrels. Western pleasure is an event designed to show the walk, trot, and canter and how well a horse responds in changing gaits. Here the disposition of both

*This modern all-around saddle is a flatter, sturdier, more comfortable refinement on earlier saddlery of the Southwest.*

*Hand-tooled, silver-studded, and with a silver horn, it was designed by Matlock Rose, a champion rider of Cutting Horses.*

horse and rider is important. Somewhat like Western pleasure, Western riding is conducted over a planned course. It tests the all-around disposition of the horse and the ability of horse and rider. It is a competition in performance—neither a stunt nor a race.

Pole bending does not mean the poles bend but rather that horse and rider do the bending back and forth as they weave through a line of upright poles at top speed without touching any or knocking any down. In recent years this has become one of the two or three most popular events.

Reining is especially popular in shows throughout the West. This shows the rider's delicate control. The course over which the horse performs requires him to change leads, turn, stop, and back up. The horse must keep his feet well under him while performing the various patterns of the contest. He must rein easily, always cooperating with his rider. There are few more exciting events in any Western show, be it for youths or for adults.

Other events include steer roping, calf roping, cutting, jumping, and working cow horse. This last event combines reining ability during the performance of many of the jobs common to ranch life. The horses race at top speed, stop, turn, or spin quickly. They work a rope properly with the rider either mounted or on foot.

All of these classes are included in adult shows. The Quarter Horse association recommends that adult shows include some youth classes.

Part of the youth program the Quarter Horse people promote includes tips to prospective horse owners. Some of these are worth listing here. So if your son or daughter just cannot do without a horse, check out some of these points. First, it is a good idea to know where you are going to keep your horse. This has become an increasingly important problem in suburban and urban areas. However, within the last few years many boarding stables have developed where, for a moderate monthly fee, your horse can be stabled. Most of these stables also supply training for both horse and rider. Of course if you live in the country this problem does not exist.

But let's start at the beginning. Keep in mind that horses differ just as widely as humans do. The better ones have quick reflexes and good dispositions. Do not feel that you have to select a young horse. Older horses have more experience, more training, and are usually easier to handle. This is also true of mares and geldings rather than stallions. It is a good idea to have the horse examined by a competent veterinarian before you buy. He will be able to tell you whether your horse has bad eyes, splay feet, straight shoulders, flat withers, ringbones, cow hocks, or a host of other defects that will make your animal difficult to live with.

Bloodlines can only really act as guidelines for the individual buying a horse. If a horse comes from a good family he is likely to have the good characteristics of that family (and he may have some of the bad ones). Usually because in registered horses many generations have been spent in breeding out the faults, they are likely to be better buys than unregistered animals. You cannot win a contest or a race with a pedigree—that takes a horse.

But over many generations it has been found that fast horses have a tendency to produce fast horses and smart ones to produce smart ones. So if you plan to do a lot of showing or use your horse for very specific purposes check on some of the available registered animals in your vicinity.

Is there any advantage in having a gelding instead of a mare? This is a tough question. Geldings may be a bit more settled or gentle, and as they become better trained they usually increase in value. Of course, with a mare you have the advantage of being able to breed her and raise her foal.

Even before purchasing a horse you should learn something about how much the care and feeding are going to cost. This too will depend on whether you have some available pasturage or whether all of the horse's feed must be purchased.

Finally, the best advice is to read over the various qualities to look for in the horse of your choice— Arabian, Thoroughbred, Appaloosa, or Quarter Horse. Then consult any knowledgeable horseman you know, select the horse you think you want, and have a qualified veterinarian look him over.

It is good to remember there is no perfect horse. Each breed will exhibit certain characteristics and all will have some factors in common. The Quarter Horse must be considered an all-purpose animal, but if you are selecting him purely for racing you would probably select a slightly different Quarter Horse from the one you would choose for showing or for overall ranch work. But we can describe an average good Quarter Horse. First, he should be neither a bulldog type, overmuscled and squat, nor should he be like a Thoroughbred, tall and delicately fashioned. He should be amply muscled, stand about fifteen hands high, and weigh around 1,150 pounds.

The head should be short yet well developed, with fairly short ears. His jaw should be set wide, his muzzle short. You can easily spot a horse with a bad head: long ears stick out, poorly developed jaws are obvious. A too heavy head can be quickly spotted. The eyes should be large and clear, reasonably far apart. Use your judgment to see whether

Short, alert ears

Short head

Flat face

Short, strong back

Firm, medium-long neck

Heavily muscled hindquarters

Heavily muscled forelegs
bulge to the breast
in a V shape

Short cannons

Tough, medium-size hoof

Average height: 14.3 hands

Average weight: 1,100 pounds

*Distinguishing Characteristics of the Quarter Horse*

they reflect intelligence. Look for sensitive, large nostrils. A horse needs them to breathe properly.

The neck is critical. An ideal Quarter Horse neck has a shallow poll, is well balanced (based on the size of the horse), and is set high on the breast with a depression where the neck slopes into the withers. The horse's proportion as well as the balance is thrown off if he is heavy through the poll and if the neck is set low on the breast. If the neck is too lean the horse is equally unbalanced.

Going down from the neck we follow the line from the withers to the croup. A Quarter Horse must have a good saddle-carrying back. His withers should be high enough to keep the saddle from slipping sideways. The shoulder blades should be long and slope to an angle of about forty-five degrees. Such sloping shoulders help absorb the total impact from the horse's forelegs. When you look at the horse he should seem to be well balanced. His front development, middle, and rear should be well proportioned. Like a table he should stand squarely on all four legs. The body of the Quarter Horse should have a short top-line and a long under-line. He then has strength in his back because the bridge from the withers to the hip is short, yet the longer length from front legs to flanks allows for a long stride. If the animal's compact body is well formed see that his legs are straight and well muscled. His legs, which even on the Quarter Horse are long compared to the size of his body, give him his speed.

Viewed from the front the horse should have medium-wide shoulders at the point, with well-shaped legs forming a strong-muscled, apparent "V" between the legs at the body. The legs then should be in a straight line from the point of the shoulders through the center of the knee to the center of the hoof, and they should be well balanced. The knee joint must be full, well rounded, and centered on the cannon bone as well as tapered into the cannon bone. The leg tendons should be visibly separated.

The Quarter Horse pastern should be short enough to be strong but long enough to be flexible. It must provide a good cushioning for the pressure the hoof has to bear. From hoof to fetlock to pastern a chain reaction occurs that makes it possible for a horse to pound along and have the shock cushioned before it reaches the knee. The condition of the horse's hoofs and legs will tell not only whether he will be a good performer but how long he is likely to be serviceable. It is important that the hoofs be neither too large nor too small, but average in size and tapering in slightly at the heel. When he is working or performing, the Quarter Horse places great demand on his leg muscles. He should be heavily muscled but never bunched or muscle bound. Rather, he should have long, solid muscle lines.

It is obvious that the horse should be neither pigeon-toed nor bowlegged. If a knee turns out it causes the foot to toe out. Sooner or later the concussion between the foot and the ground will cause soreness and eventually unsoundness. Again, look for straight legs with wide-set hocks.

These are some of the points a good Quarter Horse man looks for. Not all always hold true. Sometimes a horse whose conformation leaves much to be desired turns out to be a champion sprinter or a great cutting or working horse.

The Quarter Horse has come a long way from his origin on the tracks of Colonial America and the haciendas and *ranchos* of Mexico. He is the fastest-growing breed in the world.

*On a mesa in Texas cattle country, relaxed cowboy riding
"point" on alert Quarter Horse plans direction the herd will take.*

# QUARTER HORSES IN THE MODERN WEST

Part mustang, part Arabian, part Thoroughbred—this is the Quarter Horse, a wise and successful conglomerate of many early Arabian bloodlines. Named for his ability as a quarter-mile racer in pioneer days, he has furnished the most important breeding stock for development of the present-day cow horse. Yet he also is significant on pari-mutuel Quarter Horse tracks where he regularly sets records. He is the most popular breed among young Westerners as a riding horse in a line that runs from *Janus, considered the foundation sire, and which lists such famed stallions as Steel Dust and Peter McCue.

*Early morning sun is reflected on coats of horses of the* remuda. *Horse wrangler, right, is roping the stock that*

*will work the cows that day. Such herds of horses are moved along ahead of the cattle to supply mounts on cattle drive.*

*A good wrangler can snare a moving horse on almost each toss of the lariat. Once roped, horses are easily led out of herd.*

*While wrangler still ropes day's mounts (see noose above the horse at right), cowboy prepares to saddle Quarter Horse.*

*Almost obscured by rising dust from cattle on 6666 Ranch,
Quarter Horse and cowboy are seen riding "on swing" at upper*

*right. Horses keep the cattle on trail by cutting, sprinting, spinning, and using other like skills seen normally only at rodeos.*

*Almost hidden in a draw, behind a tangle of mesquite,*
*a well-trained cow pony forces stragglers back into main herd.*

*Riding "swing," cowboy turns the cattle to keep them on the*
*main trail. Such herds often cover more than 20 miles a day.*

*Leaning at almost 45 degrees, champion Cutting Horse*
*Shu Twist with champion Matlock Rose shows his dexterity.*

## The Cutting Horse

Alert enough to head off a fast-running calf, brave enough to face down a bull yearling, quiet enough to move through a nervous herd of cattle without disturbing them, tireless enough to work 16-hour days—that is the Cutting Horse. He is a special kind of athlete, exhibiting steel nerves, infinite patience, and split-second reflexes. He was developed during the 450 years that ranching evolved in the West, first in Mexico, then in the U. S. Southwest and the Far West. Now he is indispensable to the rancher, and he has also become a rodeo and stock-show star performer. As a contestant, with an expert rider, the Cutting Horse competes for half a million dollars in prize money each year. But whether in the arena or on the range he combines "horse sense" with a special "cow sense" to earn his golden oats.

*Cutter Bill, most famous of all Cutting Horses, performs in huge arena named for him at Rex Cauble Ranch, Denton, Texas.*

*Cutter Bill heads off calf. Forefeet are in air while his hindquarters are balanced to move in the opposite direction.*

*The rider's lariat is about to drop over the yearling's head. The horse has raised his head and settled body to take the pull.*

*With first noose around calf's neck, second rider prepares to rope hindquarters. Two men can throw yearling in 8 seconds.*

*Close-up shows yearling stretching rope while second rider
drops the noose under hind legs and quickly pulls back on it.*

*Hind legs awry, yearling is dropped to ground for inspection or for branding. Horses are trained to not pull hard and injure.*

*After an inspection, yearling trots away. For successful calf roping, a well-trained horse is a cowboy's insurance.*

*Yearlings rounded up for branding graze with herd under jagged peaks near Wolf, Wyoming, on Wyoming-Montana line.*

*Branding is essential, and Quarter Horses are ideal workers for it. Note how rope is neither too slack nor too taut.*

# The Producers

While great sires get most of the credit in magazines, books, and newspapers, the dams that produce champions are considered by breeders to be as valuable as the stallions. Indeed in the Quarter Horse world, fillies and mares hold track records for speeds as fast or faster than the marks of stallions and geldings. In the past ten years fillies that would go on to become important producers of champions have won almost as many races (including the All-American Futurity) as stallions and geldings have. In the photograph below are three of the greatest all-time producers of the Quarter Horse. At the left is Monita, which retired as the all-time top money-winning Quarter Horse in 1955 and is rated AAA. One of her offspring,

*Great Quarter Horse producers, Monita, Josie's Bar and Gold Angel, are outlined against lake on Melvin Hately farm.*

*Foal by champion Triple Chick frolics beside Paula Laico. She is also dam of All-American Futurity winner Laico Bird.*

Chicamona, earned $111,671 before retiring. Monita is now twenty-two years old. Her latest foal was sired by champion Triple Chick. In the center is Josie's Bar, another AAA star retired from racing in 1957. Both she and a daughter, Go Josie Go, were world-champ racers. Her colts have earned $155,155. She is sixteen years old, with a recent foal by Go Man Go. At the right is Gold Angel, now nineteen years old, producer of the great race mare, Miss Gold Angel, which won $107,556. Latest foal was sired by champion Go Man Go. Looking fit, all carrying foals, these magnificent producers are shown in the deep grass at the Briarwood Farm near Purcell, Oklahoma.

*Well-grown foal ready for weaning grazes with dam on the extensive plains at Pitchfork Ranch in the Texas Panhandle.*

*An all-time great stallion, Go Man Go was world champ in years 1955, '56, and '57. His get have been consistent winners.*

# The Stallions

It is no longer pertinent whether present Quarter Horse studs trace to the stallions that ran on the quarter-mile tracks of the East—before and after the American Colonies declared their independence—or on the short straightaways of the Spanish Dons in New Spain. They have proven they can run a quarter of a mile faster than any other horse and that they are unexcelled at handling cattle. And they have proven their ability to stamp their get with their own qualities of speed and agility. Like the renowned Thoroughbred sires, today's esteemed Quarter Horse studs command prices exceeding half a million dollars, and owners receive stud fees of $5,000 and more.

*Triple Chick, here at Briarwood Farm near Purcell, Okla., is another sire of champions, and is a son of famed Three Bars.*

*First horse named supreme champion was Kid Meyers, winner at halter, racing, roping, and as a Western pleasure horse.*

*Power to spare shows in girth, shoulders, dynamic bone and
muscle structure of 6666 Ranch champ stallion Big Reward.*

*Speed enough to qualify in the AAA class (which means he has run the one-quarter-mile in less than 21 seconds) is apparent.*

*Style and fine conformation show in his well-held short head, well-balanced neck, his saddle-strong back, and high-set tail.*

*Top track for Quarter Horses is Ruidoso Downs in the small town of Ruidoso, New Mexico. The season is May to September.*

*World's fastest Quarter Horses compete at Ruidoso Downs,
but numerous races for Thoroughbreds also are scheduled there.*

*Richest race in world is All-American Futurity, for
Quarter Horses only, with the top finishers dividing $600,000.*

*In small town gymkhanas throughout West, as many girls as boys compete in barrel-racing, pole-bending, and other feats.*

*Youths start early as gymkhana classes begin for 12-year-olds and under. This girl is racing against time to the finish line.*

*Young contestant makes a flying start. She will have to circle six poles, then race to the finish as shown.*

*Hair streaming in breeze, Valley Center, California, girl
runs against clock at the end of popular pole-bending event.*

*Waiting for their event to be called, three young riders relax at California City of Hope International Horse Show.*

*Youths under 14 line up before crowd while judge observes. Event, called Western pleasure, has most number of entrants.*

## Judging

*Youngest entry in a Western pleasure class in Los Angeles shows excellent control as she puts her horse into a canter.*

To a ten-year-old contestant in a Quarter Horse youth show the judge is a great and mystic person to be reverently looked up to. He knows more about Quarter Horses and their ways than the contestants do. And this knowledge is respected. All Quarter Horse judges must be experienced horsemen as well as students of breeding and conformation. A good judge looks at the whole horse and compares it to the picture he carries in his mind of the ideal Quarter Horse. He looks for soundness, quality, disposition, and the horse's ability to perform the tasks set. The judge avoids personal contact with contestants and horses prior to their entry into the ring. Do not be afraid. He is there to judge, not criticize.

*Spanish and U.S. flags flying, Caballeros del Camino Real
—Southwestern businessmen and ranchers—begin annual trek.*

*Snaked out in single file, Caballeros make a striking pattern
as they ride over the California hills to Mission San Luis Rey.*

# THE APPALOOSA

The road to the Nez Percé country leads through tall white pines that glitter like silver as the brilliant sun's rays illuminate them. Along the trail, multicolored syringa blossoms — white, pink, purple — glow on either side. It is a clean, crisp, cool, high land. Bluebirds are in every bush and tree. The fish go to spawn in the Salmon River, called by the Indians the River of No Return. It is the land of the Big Lost River, the Clearwater, and the Snake, which winds like a glistening, blue-green ribbon through the deeper green meadows. In the streams throughout northwest Idaho there are trout that weigh fifty pounds. The valleys are surrounded by the Sawtooth, Clearwater, and Bitter Root Mountains. Historic place names like Potlatch, Lewiston, White Bird, Spalding, Steptoe, and Lapwai lie along the riverbanks.

There is evidence that eohippus, the prehistoric horse which disappeared so long ago in the Western Hemisphere, lived in this region. In 1961, at Wilson Butte Cave on the Snake River plains of southern Idaho, archeologist Ruth Grubn found bones of horses which carbon 14 dating proved to be fifteen thousand years old. Evidence of man's occupation of this region has not been assigned to a date as early as that. But findings are considerable that the remote ancestors of the Nez Percé lived in the region nine thousand years to ten thousand years before Christ, and possible earlier.

This is the traditional home of the Nez Percé Indians and of the horses they have bred for two hundred and fifty years — the Appaloosas. This horse's name comes from a small clear stream, the Palouse, that runs along the northern border of Idaho, near the Washington border and not far north of the Oregon line. The little river meanders along, finally dumping itself with a great splash through the Palouse Falls into the Snake River in southeast Washington. Along the Palouse, north and south of it, the Nez Percé Indians have lived for many generations. It was a country that hid them well from their traditional enemies, the Blackfeet, who were to the northwest, and it gave them access to the fish-filled rivers that flowed to the Columbia.

They saw no white men, except an occasional trapper, until Lewis and Clark pushed their way across the difficult terrain leading into the Nez Percé homeland.

There are several conjectures about how the river got its name — or what the name meant. French traders and fur trappers, who came into the region in considerable numbers after Lewis and Clark, may have named the river. It is said they called it Pelouse, which has been translated as "with green banks." But a more likely explanation seems to be the Nez Percé word *peluse*, which means an object protruding from the water. There is such a jagged shaft of rock which rises high above the waters of the Snake River where the Palouse empties into it. Such a landmark could very possibly have given the river its name. It was a Nez Percé, Joseph Black Eagle, who gave this information to Francis Haines, the distinguished Western historian.

Indians living along the Palouse riverbank were called by travelers, and the later settlers, Palouse Indians — and indeed at some time they may have called themselves that. Their horses were then called Palouse horses, and this easily was developed into "a Palouse," as it was explained to me by Caleb Carter, one of the elders of the tribe still living in the Palouse River region.

It was in this colorful country that I had a rendezvous with Jesse Redheart. I was to meet this grandnephew of the noted Chief Joseph at his ranch on the Clearwater River, where he had agreed to tell me what he could of the history of his people and where he would pose for photographs with one of his prime Appaloosa stallions. We met on a sand spit along the Clearwater River a few miles east of Lewiston.

At this point no road, no trail, is visible. The country seems untouched by man. As I approached, I was first conscious of the magnificent Appaloosa horse pawing impatiently at the edge of the water. Mounted on him, sitting very straight-backed and patient was a lithe Indian dressed in full parade regalia. This was Jesse Redheart. His grandmother was the sister of Chief Joseph. Jesse wore a warbonnet of black and white turkey feathers decorated in the front by a shorter row of dyed red feathers. From the beaded headband streamed white ermine tails. These had been inherited first by his father and his grandfather, and they are among Jesse's most prized possessions. His buckskin trousers and jacket also were adorned with beads colored like those in the headband — white and blue and red and yellow — and his moccasins were similarly embellished.

The stallion, a large, strong-backed gray and spotted Appaloosa, wore a wide and elegant collar in which the white background beads dominated and in which red beads formed four flowing slashes. Jesse did not use a saddle. He sat instead on an exquisitely beaded blanket topped by a bearskin. On the beaded covering, which was over the horse's withers, the white again dominated, and here the design was red and black. The bearskin was trimmed in red. He rode without bridle and conventional bit, and his reins were handmade lines looped through the horse's mouth. Jesse Redheart and his grand stallion were stately figures, standing there on the banks of the Clearwater, looking much as their ancestors had one hundred years earlier.

We rode down to Jesse's ranch, which hugs a curve of the river so closely that it is only a few steps from his ramshackle barn to the river's edge. We walked to the open barn door, and just inside it was a high overstuffed living-room chair in battered condition. Here, Jesse explained to me, he would sit in the afternoons and watch the river flow by when his work was finished. I joined him in the doorway, seating myself on the doorsill, and we talked about Jesse's present life and the life in that region in those years between the white man's arrival and today.

First Jesse told me about the ermine tails that decorated his warbonnet. They had come down to him through Chief Joseph's sister and her husband, Jesse's grandfather. They frame Jesse's face in the same way that similar ermine tails framed the face of the Sioux Chief who was known as Rain-in-the-Face, but whose name was actually Face-like-a-Storm, in the famous photograph made of him in the mid-nineteenth century. Jesse told me the ermine tails worn on the headband were older than any of his people could remember and had been worn by chiefs for many generations.

Then we talked about the Appaloosa horse. The spotted horse which was developed by the Nez Percé into the Appaloosa breed was brought into the United States by the early Spanish settlers. Such horses were highly prized in Andalucía in Spain and in Austria. There they were cherished as ceremonial and parade horses and were ridden by nobles, princes, and kings. How did they happen to come from Austria as well as Spain to the New World? In 1519 Carlos V became emperor of the Holy Roman Empire. This grandson of Isabel and Fernando inherited Austria, the Tyrol, and parts of Germany from his paternal grandfather, Maximilian. From his maternal grandmother, Queen Isabel, he acquired Castilla, León, Navarra, and all the Spanish possessions in the New World. There is no question that among the thousands of horses exported to his possessions in the New World during the next thirty years was a sprinkling of the precious spotted horses, to be ridden by nobles in the New World and then bred to be used by their sons and daughters.

Into New Spain also came "color breeds," and it is probable that the Appaloosas were so considered until the present breed was developed. One of the most important of these color breeds was the Palomino, which still occupies a special niche in Western history. Like the Appaloosa, the Palomino was a favorite of European and Asiatic nobility. He too had infusions of Arabian and Barbary blood. In future generations the Palomino would also have infusions from the American saddlebred horse, the Quarter Horse, and the Thoroughbred. The ideal Palomino is known for his distinctive yellow-gold hue which is best de-scribed as the color of a new gold coin.

Another unique color design favored by the Indians was the Pinto, and his antecedents also trace to Europe and Asia. The word Pinto is derived from the Spanish word *pintado* which means painted. Like the Palomino and the Appaloosa, Pinto markings are distinct color factors which are usually dominant genetically and are not the result of chance breeding. But of all the colorful horses, the spotted horse is the one the Nez Percé made their own.

In the first chapter we have outlined how these horses came into the hands of the Indians that occupied the region that is now the southwestern border of the United States. From what is now New Mexico the horses spread rapidly to the North and Northwest. They were for the most part stolen from the Spanish by Indians, either individually or in mass raids. No moral stigma was attached to the stealing of horses, for these intruders were the enemy. If their horses could be used against them, so much the better. It is most likely that the Nez Percé, who did not range far from their homeland, secured their horses from the more adventurous Cayuse Indians who had so many horses that the word "cayuse" came to mean horse, or Indian horse. Most authorities agree that it would have been around 1730 or later before the Nez Percé began to breed their own animals.

That the Nez Percé over the next generations practiced selective breeding was apparent when the Lewis and Clark Expedition marched through that country. Meriwether Lewis, a Virginian who had bred horses, wrote in his daily journal on Saturday, February 15, 1806: "Their horses appear to be of an excellent race; they are lofty, eligantly [sic] formed, active and durable; in short, many of them look like fine English coarsers [sic] and would make a figure in any country. Some of those horses are pied with large spots of white irregularly scattered and intermixed with a black, brown, bey [sic] or some other dark color. . . ."

Why did the Nez Percé choose the spotted

*On his homestead in Nez Percé country three miles from Lenore, Idaho, Jesse Redheart poses with his wife and four of his six children. He has given up riding bucking horses in the regional rodeos but trains and breeds his own Appaloosas.*

*A true old-timer, Phil Types represents the progressive Nez Percé Indian. Phil lives on the reservation at Lapwai in northwestern Idaho, where he is vice-chairman of tribal affairs. When not attending Indian business he breeds horses.*

horse? The reasons are not difficult to find. They liked bright colors, and along with other tribes regularly painted some of their horses. But painting a horse was a tedious process and during the sweat of racing or the heat of battle the paint could disappear. To be able to identify other members of their band by the kind of horse they were riding would be a great advantage when the opposing cavalry attacked. So the reasons for breeding the Appaloosa were not solely esthetic but also realistic. He was a horse of distinguished appearance and one a man could be proud of — with the ability to withstand the pounding over the hard earth and jagged rocks.

An early Northwest missionary, Henry Harmon Spalding, in his diary, which is one of the most important original documents describing life in the Northwest, told how Indians gathered to trade after the Sunday church meeting:

"The Pondarays first brought into the circle their robes & laid in heaps their value for a horse. The N.P. [Nez Percé] then led up a horse to each bunch, & if the Pdys, thought the horse worth his robes &c, he put his rope on him & led him off & the N.P. took the robes, &c. Some 10 horses were traded in this way. Usually 3 robes and 1 Appishmore, [an apishamore, a saddle blanket of buffalo calve skins] or 2 robes & 1 gun or 2 robes, 2 App. & a shirt were given for a horse. This trade convinced me that the Nez P. are not the only sharp traders in the world."

But the development of the Appaloosa among the Nez Percé was not to run a smooth course. A series of almost incredible coincidences split the tribe and gave the two segments almost completely different ways of life; the horses contributed to the division.

Around 1825 some Canadian fur traders arranged to have two young Indians sent to the Red River Mission School of Canada for education in the white man's ways. These were two braves from the Spokan and Kutenai tribes, neighbors of the Nez Percé. Sometime shortly after this, three Nez

Percé youths also attended the same school in Canada. It is probable that some of the elders thought it would be wise to learn as much as possible of the ways of the white man. Next, four Nez Percé traveled with a party of fur traders to St. Louis. There they explained that they wanted to learn more about the white man. They had come for education. Instead, they were to be given religion and the white man's moral code. The Protestant churches, and the Catholic as well, took up the idea that here at last was an Indian group seeking salvation in the white man's manner.

It did not take very long for the first missionaries to find their way across the country to the unexplored Northwest. In 1836 Dr. Marcus Whitman with his young blonde wife Narcissa founded a mission in the Cayuse country, near the present city of Walla Walla, Washington. Young Mrs. Whitman created a great deal of excitement among Indians and trappers as she, the first white woman ever to cross the United States, made the momentous journey. The Whitmans were followed within a year by the Reverend Henry Harmon Spalding and his wife Eliza. They settled in the middle of the Appaloosa country at Lapwai, which is now the Lapwai Indian Reservation, and was then Fort Lapwai.

The coming of the missionaries broke the Nez Percé into two groups. It was a friendly division, however. The more sedentary of the group elected to become slowly Christianized, to farm, and to live in a manner prescribed by the missionaries. Because the Reverend Spalding and other religious leaders felt that the breeding of horses for racing and hunting was immoral, the Nez Percé who came under the missionaries' influence gave up their mounts. But outside the domination of the missionaries, farther down the Palouse River, the remaining group of Nez Percé continued to live as their ancestors had lived, hunting and fishing and raising their spotted horses.

Settlers followed the missionaries and slowly moved into the Indian country. New treaties were made but they were abandoned as new settlers took over or squatted upon Indian land. Yet no major trouble occurred until 1847. Then a group of Cayuse Indians, probably feeling that the Whitmans were encouraging settlers to move into their lands, killed Dr. Whitman, his wife, and ten other Americans at the mission. This was eleven years after the Whitmans had settled in the Northwest. The massacre brought soldiers. And their arrival marked the beginning of the end of the Nez Percé power and the diminishing of the popular spotted horses.

The Spaldings fled shortly after the Whitman massacre. But before they departed they had established a considerable influence on a young man whose son was destined to become a great hero of the Nez Percé.

At the mission school was a young brave whom the Reverend Spalding called Joseph. The youth's father was a Cayuse, but his mother was a Nez Percé and the young man himself had grown up to be a tribal spokesman. After the Spaldings had left the region, Joseph was selected as one of the Nez Percé chiefs to attend the great treaty conference in 1855 at Walla Walla, Washington. This treaty reserved the area of the Nez Percé band, the Wallowa Valley along the Snake River, for the exclusive use of the Nez Percé.

For the duration of this treaty, which unfortunately was not long, the Nez Percé cooperated in every way with the white military and the settlers around them. But in 1863, only eight years after the treaty, a new pact was negotiated. This ceded the Wallowa Valley to the United States government for the use of settlers. Joseph and his band did not participate in this treaty and protested that the other Nez Percé who had done so had acted without authority. He felt that his rights, and those of his people, granted in 1855, had been revoked.

Joseph died, and his son, called Thunder-Rolling-over-the-Mountains, and known to the whites as Young Joseph, took charge of affairs in 1871. Young Joseph seems to have been a popular, brave,

and reasonable man. He was later to be known as Chief Joseph. He had a broad face, deep-set eyes, an almost straight nose, and he wore his long hair in braids. He preached peace to all of his tribe and to all of the people around him. Joseph's band was made up entirely of horse breeders and cattle grazers. He belonged to the group that had split away from the missionary-influenced Indians and lived farther south in an almost hidden valley.

Young Joseph made a statement in later years describing his position regarding the second treaty. He was quoted as saying:

"My father was not there. He said to me: 'When you go into council with the white man, always remember your country. Do not give it away. The white man will cheat you out of your home. I have taken no pay from the United States. I have never sold our land.' In this treaty [Chief] Lawyer acted without authority from our band. He had no right to sell the Wallowa [winding water] country. That had always belonged to my father's own people, and the other bands had never disputed our right to it. No other Indians ever claimed Wallowa."

And in another statement:

"If we ever owned the land we own it still, for we never sold it. In the treaty councils the commissioners have claimed that our country had been sold to the Government. Suppose a white man should come to me and say, 'Joseph, I like your horses and I want to buy them.' I say to him, 'No, my horses suit me, I will not sell them.' Then he goes to my neighbor, and says to him: 'Joseph has some good horses. I want to buy them, but he refuses to sell.' My neighbor answers, 'Pay me the money, and I will sell you Joseph's horses.' The white man returns to me, and says, 'Joseph, I have bought your horses, and you must let me have them.' If we sold our lands to the Government, this is the way they were bought."

But the onward push of the white man's civilization did not permit peace for Chief Joseph and his band. At last, to avoid conflict, he agreed to settle on the Lapwai reservation in the spring of 1877.

As the Nez Percé began their move to the reservation trouble erupted with the whites. Some of the younger Nez Percé raided the settlers that had moved in and killed eighteen of them. From this time there was no possibility of peace. The military began preparations to attack. Joseph gathered his forces to resist.

In sadness rather than in anger he said later:

"I was deeply grieved. . . . I knew that their acts would involve all my people. I saw that the war could not then be prevented. The time had passed. I counseled peace from the beginning. I knew that we were too weak to fight the United States. We had many grievances, but I knew that war would bring more. . . . I would have given my own life if I could have undone the killing of white men by my people.

"I know that my young men did a great wrong, but I ask, Who was first to blame? They had been insulted a thousand times; their fathers and brothers had been killed; their mothers and wives had been disgraced; they had been driven to madness by the whisky sold to them by white men; they had been told by General Howard that all their horses and cattle which they had been unable to drive out of Wallowa were to fall into the hands of white men; and, added to all this, they were homeless and desperate.

"I blame my young men and I blame the white men. I blame General Howard for not giving my people time to get their stock away from Wallowa. I do not acknowledge that he had the right to order me to leave Wallowa at any time. I deny that either my father or myself ever sold that land. . . . It may never again be our home, but my father sleeps there, and I love it as I love my mother. I left there, hoping to avoid bloodshed."

Maneuvering his people and herds of horses in a masterly fashion, he fought a dozen skirmishes against superior forces. Officers who opposed them had nothing but praise for the skill, valor, and ingenuity of the Indians. The credit must not go to the chief alone. He was flanked by such famous warriors as his brother, Ollokot; by Looking Glass; and by White Bird, one of his lieutenants who at the last moment managed to break away and reach Canada with a small band of Nez Percé.

Chief Joseph also tried to reach Canada. But notice of his movements was telegraphed ahead and an overwhelming force cut him off. By this time he had crossed the almost impassable Bitter Root Mountains, gone twice across the Rockies, through the difficult Yellowstone area, across the Missouri River to the Bear Paw Mountains, and within thirty miles of the Canadian line.

There he stood at bay for two days before surrendering. His words are among the most moving and perhaps best known of any Indian oration:

"Tell General Howard I know his heart. What he told me before I have in my heart. I am tired of fighting. Our chiefs are killed. Looking Glass is dead. Too-hul-hul-sote is dead. The old men are all dead. It is the young men who say yes or no [that is, vote in council]. He who led on the young men is dead [Joseph's brother, Ollokot]. It is cold and we have no blankets. The little children are freezing to death. My people, some of them, have run away to the hills, and have no blankets, no food; no one knows where they are—perhaps freezing to death. I want to have time to look for my children and see how many of them I can find. Maybe I shall find them among the dead. Hear me, my chiefs. I am tired; my heart is sick and sad. From where the sun now stands I will fight no more forever."

The only condition for his surrender was that he and his people be allowed to return to the reservation at Lapwai. General Howard agreed on behalf of the government, but this promise, as others had been, was broken. The Nez Percé were shipped first to Bismarck, North Dakota, then to Fort Leavenworth, Kansas. There they were settled in the lowlands of the Missouri River in a climate and terrain as unlike their homeland as can be imagined. Later they were moved into the Indian Territory near the Salt Fork of the Arkansas River.

In 1883, six years after the surrender, twenty-nine of the Nez Percé were allowed to return to Idaho. Then in 1885 Joseph with 150 of his followers was allowed to move to the Colville Reservation at Nespelem, Washington. One hundred and eighteen of his people were resettled on the Lapwai Reservation near their original home. The San-Poil Indians who occupied the Colville Reservation did not welcome the Nez Percé but the government insisted that they stay there.

Over the years Chief Joseph petitioned the government to allow him to move back to the Wallowa Valley. He lived out his life with dignity on the Nespelem Reservation watching horses racing and is said to have enjoyed gambling on the fleet Indian ponies. That he thought a great deal about the 1,100 horses and one hundred saddles that he surrendered to the United States forces is indicated by the fact that he has often been quoted as saying, "Somebody has got our horses."

He made a trip to New York to ride in a parade past Grant's tomb in 1897. Four years before he died he was allowed to make a short visit to his homeland but was forced to return to the Colville Reservation where he died in 1904. Yet the loss of their horses in war and the death of their chief did not destroy the tradition of the Appaloosa as the Nez Percé mount. A few managed to keep a favorite stallion and mare and remain on the edge of the reservations in the Idaho, Washington, and Oregon areas. But the great herds of Appaloosas were dispersed and the breed was virtually lost to the region for the next fifty years.

Very slowly from the turn of the century Appaloosas began to be sought out for circuses and Wild West shows and as parade horses. Those marked outstandingly brought excellent prices. Buffalo Bill Cody rode an Appaloosa in his Wild West show that traveled all over the world. The famous French painter Rosa Bonheur depicted that legendary Westerner on an Appaloosa. And Henri Toulouse-Lautrec painted a Parisian circus scene featuring an Appaloosa and bareback rider.

As the spotted horses began their slow come-back by way of the circus and the wild West show, they were commencing an equally slow but definite return along the banks of the Palouse. At least one Indian, named Sam Fisher, had continued to breed Appaloosas in the region slightly southwest of the Chief Joseph country. A few white settlers also were interested in the spotted horses. For instance, Guy Lamb and Floyd Hickman continued to breed the best and oldest stock of Appaloosas in the West. From their work came the Toby line which, through Knobby, Little Dan, Old Blue, and other horses, traces unofficially to the earlier Nez Percé Appaloosas.

Building on this foundation, a group of horsemen met in 1938 in Oregon to form the Appaloosa Horse Club. Their purpose was to collect records and data giving substance to their knowledge of Appaloosas. Their further purpose was to issue certificates of registration to animals that they felt would be fit foundation stock and to standardize the breed of spotted horses known historically as the Appaloosa. The club grew slowly until after World War II. Then in September, 1947, headquarters were moved to Moscow, Idaho. The club's activities multiplied. Young George Hatley, a knowledgeable horseman and breeder of horses, became secretary. And in 1950 the Appaloosa Horse Club was approved by the National Stallion Board. All registered Appaloosas are licensed as purebred. And now many shows other than Appaloosa have Appaloosa classes.

How old was the spotted horse in history? Where did he come from? What kind of people owned and bred early spotted horses? How was he represented in ancient as well as modern times by artists in various countries? These were just a few of the questions the Appaloosa Horse Club wanted to answer. And through unusual cooperation, those questions were answered. An exhibit of the art of the spotted horses was collected from all over the world by the Amon Carter Museum of Western Art under the direction of Mitchell A. Wilder. Mr. Wilder, after conceiving the idea, received the full collaboration of the Appaloosa Horse Club and especially of its distinguished historian, Dr. Francis Haines. Out of this unprecedented exhibition came an extensive visual history of the spotted horse. But even more was added when Dr. Haines undertook to write the text for a book that contained pictures from the exhibition and which was published by the University of Texas Press for the Amon Carter Museum and the Appaloosa Horse Club.

The exhibit showed a remarkable procession of the spotted horses beginning with those of Peche-Merle in southwestern France, where cave artists of the upper Paleolithic period, between eight thousand and twenty thousand years before Christ, scraped away the cave wall facing and drew or painted upon it two spotted horses. The parade of colorful animals continued to a vase from Mycenae. This vessel was found beside a wall between the tombs of Aegisthus and Clytemnestra on the island of Crete. It shows that even in the fourteenth century B.C. men drove chariots and that harnessed to those chariots were horses with spots.

On the walls of an Egyptian noble's tomb of the early fifteenth century B.C. is painted a harvest scene which includes a chariot with a prancing spotted horse. It is probable that the painting represented those things the people felt would be the most useful to the deceased government official in his afterlife. From Egypt the exhibit moved to a mosaic from Carthage. In it a rider is waving or holding up an arm to catch his falcon. The spotted horse seems to have been branded on the right hip. Its spots, however, are all over the body.

Also seen is a tomb horse from the T'ang Dynasty, which existed from 618 A.D. to 906 A.D. These decorated statuettes of horses were substituted for real horses that previously had been buried with their masters ever since the Shang Dynasty originated the practice. The statuette of the horse is said to date from the seventh century A.D. and is one of the earliest representations of horses marked with the spotted rump blanket and round spots similar to the Appaloosa of today.

From later China was shown a portion of a scroll painted between 1254 and 1322 A.D. The horse is spotted all over. The procession of horses from China showed that spotted mounts were valued in several dynasties. In one early scroll from the Museum of Fine Arts in Boston, spotted horses are shown with their Tartar riders bareback. From the many ancient Chinese scrolls and paintings at the exhibition it becomes obvious that spotted horses were comparatively common in China over a lengthy span of years. Scrolls showing horses with their grooms are especially frequent during the thirteenth and fourteenth centuries.

Horses of the Appaloosa type with spotted blankets are shown in an unusual miniature of the mid-fifteenth century. A battle in Persia is represented by an attack of Tamerlane and his Mongol hordes. Both sides in the battle are using some mounts similar to today's Appaloosas.

Another battle of great interest is shown in the Heiji Monogatari "The Burning of the Sanjo Palace." In a scene where the emperor of Japan was being abducted, a rider on a spotted horse chases a fleeing chariot. Throughout this long narrative scroll, spotted horses appear.

But based on the exhibition's visual evidence, the spotted horse was also well known throughout Europe in the Middle Ages. In a French miniature from the fifteenth century, a spotted horse is prominent in the foreground. An earlier medieval drawing in an illustrated manuscript shows a rider on a fully spotted horse fleeing from a tiger whose cub the man has stolen. The exhibition illustrated riding schools of the seventeenth century by including prints of spotted horses performing some of the exercises done by the Lippizaners. Perhaps the most unusual print in the exhibition shows a young tiger horse near Delft, Holland. This creature is marked similarly—though the artist has exaggerated the design slightly—to Chief Handprint, one of the important Appaloosa stallions of recent years.

This is only a sampling of some of the pictures in this extraordinary exhibition. The visual proof that spotted horses existed throughout Europe and Asia over many millenniums is overwhelming and conclusive. By no means are all the displayed spotted horses similar to present-day Appaloosas, but their motifs are similar and in some cases the total conformation is not unlike that of today's Appaloosa. The modern Appaloosa is shown in nineteenth-century paintings by Alfred Jacob Miller and by Oglala Sioux and Crow Indian paintings. The exhibition and the book also include a painting by famed cowboy artist Charles M. Russell, who arrived in Montana in 1880. The Appaloosa is prominent in his "Watching for the Smoke Signal."

A more recent example of the Appaloosa in art came about in late 1968 when Miss Doris Lindner of the Worcester Royal Porcelain Company of England made a special trip to the United States to model the Appaloosa stallion, Imboden's Driftwood Bob, in clay. Soon the Royal Porcelain Company will release a limited edition of five hundred copies of porcelain figures, along with Miss Lindner's other museum pieces that include bulls and stallions. Miss Lindner has exhibited her work in the Royal Academy at London, and one of her most important creations was an equestrian statue of Queen Elizabeth, ordered by the Queen Mother. The Appaloosa has gone a long way in art.

But not all spotted horses are Appaloosas. So what is an Appaloosa and what is not? One distinguishing feature is a wide forehead. Another is a white sclera encircling the eye, giving the eye prominence and adding distinctiveness to the head's appearance. The Appaloosa is unique in that the white around his eye is like that of a human. On other breeds the white does not show. The ears of the Appaloosa are pointed and of medium size. His neck has a clean-cut throatlatch and a large windpipe that blends into a deep chest. Like the Quarter Horse and the Arabian, he has long, sloping shoulders and his withers are prominent and well defined.

A considerable number of the other features of a good Appaloosa are shared with other breeds of horses. His forearm is well muscled, long, wide, and tapered to a broad knee. His cannons are short, wide, and flat. They end in wide, smooth, strongly supported fetlocks. His pastern is long and sloping. The hoof is rounded and wide at the heel. His hoofs are usually striped. When the horse is viewed from the front a perpendicular line from the shoulder point should fall upon the center of the knee, the cannon, the pastern, and the hoof. A side view should show a perpendicular line dropping from the center of the elbow joint to the center of the knee and pastern joints and back of the hoof.

The back should appear short and straight, the loin short and wide. The underline is long with the flank well let down. Hips are smooth, long, sloping, and muscular. The thighs are long, muscular, and deep, giving the quarters a smooth, well-rounded appearance. The gaskins are long, wide, and muscular, extending to clean, clearly defined, wide straight hocks. The back feet are a trifle narrower than the front. The hoof is dense, having a large elastic frog, strong bars, concave sole, and wide heel. It is said to be of unusual durability.

From behind, a perpendicular line from the point of the buttocks should fall upon the center of the hock, cannon, pastern, and hoof. From the side, a perpendicular line from the hip joint should pass through the center of the hoof and divide the gaskins in the middle. And the perpendicular line from the point of the buttocks should run parallel with the line of the cannon. A short rattail is generally preferred.

But even if the horse has all of these qualifications he still is not an Appaloosa for registration purposes unless he shows Appaloosa coat markings. These markings may be few or many. But an Appaloosa must have spots. In addition he must have the white encircling the eye. Under registration requirements is an important note: "To be registered, a horse must be easily recognizable as an Appaloosa." There is, however, a provision for registering stock for breeding purposes only. Such stock does not necessarily have to have all of the Appaloosa qualifications but must have some. Such stock cannot be shown and can be used only for breeding. *The Appaloosa Registry Handbook* points out that the breeding stock provision is for horses possessing Appaloosa breeding and characteristics such as the white encircling the eye, the striped hoofs, and partly colored skin, but that do not have a typical Appaloosa coat pattern making them "easily recognizable" as Appaloosas. They are not eligible for show, race, or exhibition.

Now, what is *not* an Appaloosa? Horses carrying draft, pony, albino, paint, or Pinto blood are not acceptable. There also are many roans that are not acceptable. The best rule is the one that simply says the horse must be recognizable as an Appaloosa. The Appaloosa Horse Club makes available pamphlets showing pictures of acceptable patterns and of the kinds of designs in roans, paints, and Pintos that are not.

Among other studies the Appaloosa Horse Club has supported has been one on genetics. Another deals with the coloring of horses. In an interesting analysis, the hippologist B. S. Dystra of Holland has pointed out that spotted coloration as well as stripes were originally protective aids in early horses. Although present-day zebras are often born with spots that develop into stripes — and although Appaloosas occasionally are born with spots that later develop into a kind of striped pattern — Dystra does not believe there is any direct connection between the zebra and the Appaloosa. He points out, however, that both had a remote common ancestor that was more or less striped. He warns that unless new blood from spotted horses of either warm- or cold-blooded types is introduced — unless inbreeding occurs — stripes can reappear as they did on the early ancestor of the horse. But so far, recurrence of stripes has not become a major problem.

New blood is constantly being used to improve the Appaloosa. We have mentioned breeding to Thoroughbreds. But one of the outstanding Appaloosa stallions, Red Eagle, comes from a purebred Arabian sire that dates to the Kellogg stock and before that to the Crabbet Stud in England. On the tail-female side his dam comes from a long line of Appaloosas. Red Eagle has proven to be a very important Appaloosa progenitor. Silky Sullivan, the one-time famous California Thoroughbred racing stallion, has an important son by an Appaloosa mare with typical Appaloosa markings. He is also called Silky Sullivan and in 1969 began his racing career.

Another unusual Appaloosa is Honey Toe, one of the grand champions but which happens to be of registered Quarter Horse parentage on both sides. Yet there is no question about Honey Toe having all the qualifications of an Appaloosa, traits which of course come from an earlier ancestor.

Although circuses and wild West shows did a great deal to popularize the Appaloosa at the turn of the century, the motion picture has done more within the last few years. No one who has ever seen it is likely to forget the performance of Cojo Rojo as Marlon Brando's horse in *The Appaloosa*. The horse worked entirely from hand signals, and few retakes were necessary. In fact, he won the top award as actor of the year and received the annual animal Oscar from the American Humane Society.

Coming up soon will be another Appaloosa movie, and with the horse, Joker's Cold Cash, will be Appaloosa owner-rider Becky Zeller of Houston, Texas. They have just been signed for a film tentatively entitled *Valerie Scorby and the Big Port*. The film features such well-known actors as Karl Malden, John Cassavetes, Walter Pidgeon, and Gena Rowlands. In addition to Appaloosa stars in films there have been some great Appaloosa supporting players.

But whether as actor, performer, racehorse, cattle horse, or trail horse, the Appaloosa has without question proven himself over many generations. At the beginning of 1969 more than 104,000

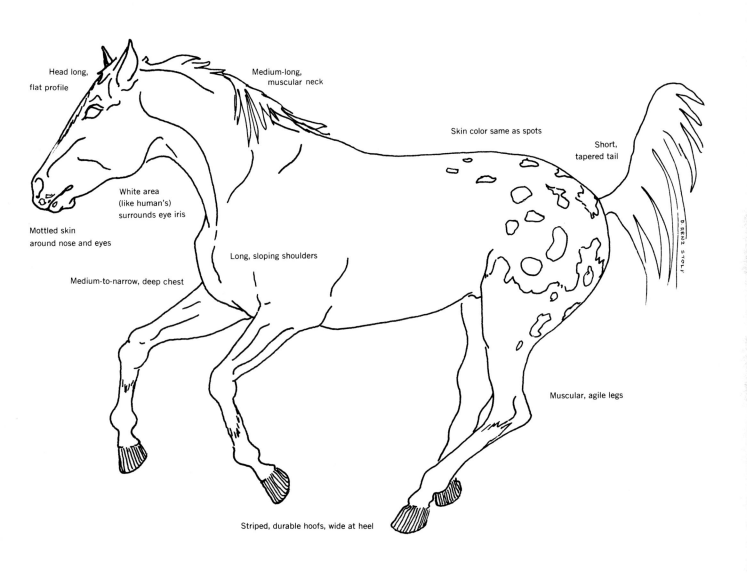

Head long,
flat profile

Medium-long,
muscular neck

Skin color same as spots

Short,
tapered tail

White area
(like human's)
surrounds eye iris

Mottled skin
around nose and eyes

Long, sloping shoulders

Medium-to-narrow, deep chest

Muscular, agile legs

Striped, durable hoofs, wide at heel

Average height: 14.2 to 16 hands

Average weight: 900 to 1,150 pounds

*Distinguishing Characteristics of the Appaloosa*

Appaloosas were registered — many more than were ever owned by the Nez Percé Indians. The club has 25,000 members, and 110 regional organizations are scattered around the country.

Of the hundreds of trail rides every year in the Western states, none exceed in scenic grandeur and historical interest the Appaloosa Horse Club's annual adventure across the Chief Joseph War Trail. The rides have been made in sequential segments of one hundred miles each, the first in the summer of 1965. They will continue each summer until the entire trail, which extends some 1,400 miles, is covered.

In the Wallowa Valley near Joseph, Oregon, along a deep blue lake that once teemed with silver salmon, the first riders covered the one hundred miles through almost virgin terrain, flushing deer and elk along the way. The trail took them through Lightning Creek Canyon and finally to Dug Bar on the west bank of the Snake River. This was the fording where the Nez Percé lost nine hundred horses in the swift-running stream. Because of the fast current caused by heavy rainfalls, Chief Joseph ordered that some horses be kept on the Oregon side. However, white men attacked the guards of the separated group and drove off additional horses and cattle. These were the first losses the Nez Percé suffered.

The second ride a year later began on the Idaho side of the Snake River near Grave's Creek, Idaho. It continued through country white with camas blossoms and green with groves of ponderosa pine. From the town of Cottonwood the riders moved along Tolo Lake and camped where the first battle of the Nez Percé war was fought near Grangeville. Then the trail wound southward through the White Bird Battlefield, named for the most violent and dangerous of Joseph's chiefs. The U. S. Cavalry was badly defeated in this engagement, losing thirty soldiers killed and many wounded. The Indians suffered no losses. There the horsemen rode along the flats of the Salmon River and across the Joseph Plains. The going was rough on trail riders and

horses. Only the endurance of the hard-hoofed Appaloosas kept the expedition moving. The riders returned to Grave's Creek, completing the same circle Chief Joseph and his tribesmen made to confuse the U. S. Cavalry almost one hundred years earlier.

The Indians who earlier traveled this route ate lightly and carried as little with them as possible. But the trail riders of today have a chuck truck that keeps ahead of the group. From it are served generous Western-style breakfasts of eggs, sausages, ham, pancakes, syrup, and all the coffee and milk that a hungry rider can drink. The total advance crew on the ride includes a baggage-trunk man who carries tents, bedrolls, and suitcases supplied by the riders so that these items are available at every overnight camp. The cooks and the food wagon take along propane refrigeration equipment and propane gas stoves. Riding with the group are a veterinarian and a physician. On most of the rides the distinguished historian Dr. Francis Haines has accompanied the party, often giving historical talks at night around the campfire.

On each ride the terrain varies. Fortunately, the Chief Joseph War Trail has never become a commercial or built-up region. Most of the trail has changed little in the past one hundred years. It is even possible for considerable periods to stay within the shade of the high cedar and fir trees.

The third trail ride began near the village of Keuterville southwest of Cottonwood. There the riders saw the Indians harvesting the camas root, which is a tuber somewhat like an onion. Then they rode across the breaks of the Salmon River where dark and threatening basalt bluffs line the sides of the river's tributary.

The horsemen rode through an area where a butte extends dramatically upward. It is now called Mount Misery. Here a group of soldiers were surrounded while driving away a band of horses they had stolen from the Indians. The Nez Percé recaptured their mounts and held the soldiers captive for some eighteen hours. But they did not further molest the soldiers, permitting them to find their way back to the fort near Grangeville. From Grangeville the riders crossed the Camas Prairie, up through Kooskia and to the magnificent Weippe Prairie within sight of the Clearwater River.

The fourth and most dramatic segment of the ride began near Weippe and moved slowly across the almost impassable Lolo Trail to Lolo Pass. This was the same trail on which Lewis and Clark in 1805 were forced to kill and eat their horses. Even in July when the fourth ride was made, snow drifts spotted the trail. Because of the wilderness of this high country it is one of the most extraordinary scenic regions in the West.

Describing the country, George B. Hatley quoted the cowboy artist Charles M. Russell:

"You can see what man made from the seat of an automobile, (but) the only way to see what God made is from the back of a horse."

The fifth ride went north of Fort Fizzle, which in 1877 was hurriedly constructed of entrenchments and barricades. The soldiers who built it had been working on Fort Missoula, but with word of Chief Joseph's flight they hurried to a site five miles west of Lolo, and started building. Joseph and his braves overran the new fort with apparent ease on July 28, 1877, and it became known thereafter as Fort Fizzle. From Fort Fizzle the trail runs south near the town of Darby. The 1970 ride will begin at Packer Meadows and end at Big Hole Battlefield, site of a crucial engagement between the United States and the Nez Percé.

At the rate of one hundred miles per year it may take fourteen to sixteen years to complete the ride. Each of the one hundred-mile segments is covered in approximately five days. On some days the riders travel fifteen miles, on others as many as twenty-five or thirty. Both men and women make the trip, and anyone is welcome who supplies his own registered Appaloosa and pays $60 for feed for his horse and himself. The rider must, however, be over twelve years old and must be mounted on a mare or gelding. It has been found that stallions are likely to be too troublesome to handle on such a long journey.

In 1877, by the way, the Nez Percé covered twice as many miles daily as the pleasure riders do.

It would probably have come as no great surprise to Chief Joseph if he had made contact in his later years with such a caravan. The portable dance floor, Western musicians, and square dancing under the stars might have interested him. For after his defeat Joseph had been entertained by the ladies of Bismarck and Fort Lincoln, North Dakota. The Bismarck *Tribune* of November 21, 1877, reprinted the ladies' invitation:

"To Joseph, Head Chief of Nez Perces.

"Sir: — Desiring to show you our kind feelings and the admiration we have for your bravery and humanity, as exhibited in your recent conflict with the forces of the United States, we most cordially invited you to dine with us at the Sheridan House, in this city. The dinner to be given at 1-1/2 P.M. to-day."

Joseph and his chiefs were said to enjoy the luncheon and especially his favorite food, the salmon which was served by the good ladies. That the ladies of the present are still interested in Chief Joseph is illustrated by the fact that over half of the participants on the Chief Joseph War Trail rides are women.

These are a few of the topics Jesse Redheart and I discussed as we sat in his doorway watching the Clearwater River roll by. Jesse told me the difference between a white blanket, a spotted blanket, a frosted blanket, a snowflake, a snowstorm, a leopard, a polka dot, and a good many other kinds of Appaloosa horse markings. He also mentioned the hand print, which is the arrangement of five dark spots in the pattern of a man's hand. There are all kinds of spots too: shadow spot (a dark spot with a lighter border encircling it), squaw spots, leaf spots, raindrop, paintbrush, and pepper.

An Appaloosa with a flashy coat marking is referred to as being wild-colored or, sometimes, loud-colored. When an Appaloosa foal is solid-colored at first and later develops Appaloosa markings he is said to be "coloring up" or "coloring out." The partly colored skin around the Appaloosa's nose and mouth is called freckled or mottled. And if he has dark stripes down the frontal bones of the head he is said to be wearing a mask.

The Appaloosa's sparse tail is referred to as rat-tail, shavetail, and finger tail. His fast easy walk is known as the "Indian shuffle."

Jesse and I got to know each other pretty well as the breeze grew cooler across the river and the shadows began to slant long through the doorway, so before I left I told him a story that had been told to me the previous day by an Appaloosa breeder. He had said he had put a smart Thoroughbred stallion in with his Appaloosa mare and left them for a while. When he returned, the Thoroughbred looked mighty lonesome and was standing in one end of the pasture; the Appaloosa was in the other. So he went up to the Thoroughbred and said, "What's wrong?" "Well," replied the Thoroughbred, "I've been in here now for a full twenty-four hours and I haven't been able to get that mare to take off those wild pajamas."

Jesse laughed, but I figured he had probably heard the story three or four times before. Anyway, it was the only funny Appaloosa story I had heard.

I rode down to Lenore, where Jesse's wife and children live on the reservation. There Jesse showed me some more of his horses and all six of his children. All of them ride well, even the smallest girl. They take care of the stock, and in the afternoons they ride over the golden mountains.

Those Nez Percé Indians surely knew what they were doing when they raised Appaloosas in the high country of Idaho, Washington, and Oregon—and some of them still do.

APPALOOSAS
IN THE
MODERN WEST

Most colorful of all recognized breeds is the Appaloosa, a rangy horse with a coat pattern that immediately identifies him. His head is shaped more like the Barbary horse's than the Arabian's. His eyes have white around the irises, like a human's. He has a mottled pink and black nose and a short tail. Some are covered with egg-shaped spots, although most have a rump blanket of those spots. Yet he has a rugged kind of beauty. In color the Appaloosa is more closely related to the zebra than are other breeds, for among zebras the young sometimes have spotted coats.

The Appaloosa's coat pattern appeared in European cave paintings more than twenty thousand years ago. In ancient Asia and Africa, spotted horses were sought extensively and were recorded in sculpture, ceramics, and painting. But the modern Appaloosa has been bred since 1730 by the Nez Percé Indians who live on the Palouse River in northwest Idaho. It was from this vast and rugged land, a land still primitive, that the name evolved: a horse from the Palouse country, or, an Appaloosa.

*In a lush and vast pasture near Potlatch, Idaho, an outstanding Appaloosa producer exercises her frisky foal.*

*Nursing foal shows few spots, but spots will become more visible as it grows. Skin is reverse color of the spots.*

*These foals by Spud-Nik Jr., on Sun Bar Training Ranch at Poway, California, display almost identical markings.*

*Foals romp in high grass. Once confined to Northwest, Appaloosas now are very popular throughout the West.*

*Showing excellent Appaloosa conformation, foals exhibit typical medium-large heads, muscular necks, "rattails."*

*Powerful necks entwined, colts maneuver for position.
In play they often strip the skin with long sharp teeth.*

*A rough wrestling match develops. Colt on left is using
weight and hindquarter muscles to force the other to its knees.*

*Biting and kicking, Appaloosa colts test their strength, agility, and aggressiveness. Colt in the foreground has fastened his teeth on his opponent's neck. Loser usually slinks away but awaits chance to surprise his rival and even the score.*

*On the trail, Debbie Slocum lets champion mare Fräulein show Appaloosas are sure-footed as she avoids obstacle.*

*Champion stallion Doll's Toby shows mettle in exercise with owner-trainer Karen McPherson of Moscow, Idaho.*

*On Nez Percé reservation in Idaho, Jesse Redheart, grandnephew of Chief Joseph, raises Appaloosas and children.*

*In his grandfather's trappings, Jesse takes daughter for a ride near Lewiston, Idaho. Jesse has twenty-eight Appaloosas.*

By the time Chief Joseph of the Nez Percé was forced to surrender to an overwhelming force of U.S. Cavalry in 1877, his people had been breeding Appaloosas for more than 150 years. He surrendered 1,100 horses. These and others rounded up in the region were sold to white horse traders. Forced onto reservations, the remaining Nez Percé were forbidden to breed or discouraged from breeding horses. Only in recent years have the Nez Percé returned to the raising of the "lost" breed. Such a breeder is Chief Joseph's grandnephew, Jesse Redheart, shown on these pages. His grandmother was Chief Joseph's sister.

*Riding Indian fashion, without saddle, Jesse Redheart*
*has as bridle a single strand of rope knotted around muzzle.*

*Now retired to stud, Apache King was a great racing Appaloosa, winning 15 out of 18 starts as a three-year-old.*

Racing stallion Double Patch, photographed at Coeur d'Alene, Idaho, was trained by Joe King of Boise, Idaho.

Pari-mutuel racing of Appaloosas is new but catching on in West. Coeur d'Alene summer meet is one of biggest.

*On Parvin Ranch, young Calvin Parvin, riding Comanche's Snowflake, loops his rope over an agile Hereford yearling.*

Nez Percé Indians raced their Appaloosas along the banks of the Palouse and Snake rivers more than two hundred years ago, but pari-mutuel racing of these colorful horses dates only from 1962. Since then purses have increased more than ten times while the number of horses running is up from twenty-two to over four hundred. Fans like to see them go, and this rangy horse with the spotted hip blanket is being bred increasingly for speed. A recent example is Joker's Moneka, which in twenty-two races won fifteen, was second five times, and showed twice. She was bred to Top Deck, the Thoroughbred which fathered Quarter Horses Go Man Go and Decketta. Their colt Ledge Deck won all six races he entered, including the Worldwide Futurity at Albuquerque. But breeders are careful to keep the spots. Without them a horse cannot be a registered Appaloosa.

Champ Appaloosa Cutting Horse Tobeeanna, with Roy
Parvin up, out-jumps and out-thinks yearling just cut from herd.

Spots prominent, Appaloosas round a far turn. Fern-
dale, California, has one of the biggest Appaloosa race meets.

*Two Nez Percé old-timers are Caleb Carter and Phil Types. They live at Lapwai where Types breeds Appaloosas.*

Nez Percé tribal leader Phil Types tells exciting stories of the old days when big encampments were held every month, and each Sunday there would be a horserace. According to Types, different tribes of Nez Percé would breed for different colors or patterns. Types says: "When horses were our only transportation it was a good way of life." He now breeds Appaloosas on the reservation at Lapwai, Idaho.

Caleb Carter, respected for his age and knowledge, recalls when Indians from a distant tribe thought the horses had been painted. He also speaks of a fine herd of Appaloosas traded from the Mormons and says some Indians still call Appaloosas "Maumon Sekum," Mormon horses. Indians used to swap two to four good ordinary mounts for a spotted one, says Carter. He adds: "It has not been too long ago that I have heard a traveler say, 'There goes a Palouse horse.'"

# ACKNOWLEDGEMENTS _____

It is always a pleasure to express my thanks to the many people who have contributed their assistance and advice on a book. It is a pleasant task for two reasons. First, it signifies the book is finished. But more important, it allows me to relive the encounters and adventures experienced while the book was in preparation. I will long remember the many trips through Arizona, California, Idaho, Montana, New Mexico, Oklahoma, Oregon, Texas, Washington, and Wyoming, and the helpful men and women, experts in their fields, whom I met.

I am especially indebted to Reverend Floyd Schwieger of Lovell, Wyoming, whose knowledge of the haunts and habits of the wild horse herds in the Pryor Mountain range along the Wyoming-Montana border made it possible for me to photograph those magnificent but elusive animals. Mrs. Charles "Chuck" Wagner, whose husband is also an expert on the free running horses, kindly made many arrangements for me in Wyoming and acted as long distance telephone contact between the Reverend Schwieger and me. I am grateful for the information about the United States government program to protect the range of these "wild" horses, data supplied by John Killough of the U. S. Department of the Interior in Cheyenne. Thanks also to my friend Tony Bevinetto of the Wyoming Travel Commission.

The Thoroughbred picture in the West would not have been complete without the counsel of Louis R. Rowan, owner of Summit Lake Farm and former president of the California Thoroughbred Breeders Association. The general manager of the association, Colonel W. F. Koester, was also most helpful. I recall with pleasure the sunny spring days on the El Peco Ranch of George A. Pope, Jr., touring the extensive spread in a golf cart photographing stallions, mares, and yearlings in the company of his cooperative ranch manager Louis Coelho. At Flag Is Up Farm in Solvang, California, one of the newest and most elaborate horse establishments in the West, owned by Hastings Harcourt and Marvin Roberts, I was shown every courtesy and was given excellent assistance in photographing their modern breeding, training, and hospital facilities.

At Corona Breeding Farm, entertainer Desi Arnaz cheerfully gave me permission to photograph the great stallion Nashville, which posed like a professional model. Few Thoroughbred farms are more beautiful than Granja Vista Del Rio, on rolling hills and in a river valley near Corona, California. There, Bert C. Altfillisch, owner-manager, guided me about the modern facilities which include a full-size training track complete with sound effects to simulate race conditions. At Rancho Lilac near Escondido, California, I have long enjoyed conversations about horses and Indians with Colonel Irving Salomon. And at Vista Hermosa Farm in Rancho Santa Fe, California, Gabor Renner gave freely of his time and expertise as I visited the ranch to photograph the outstanding stallion Crazy Kid. The Thoroughbred picture could not be completed without essential information supplied by Rex Ellsworth, one of California's most knowledgeable breeders and former owner of the immortal Swaps and of that little gray dandy, Determine.

Quarter Horse country extends throughout the Western states (and much of the East, South, and North). Through the friendly and efficient intervention of Garford Wilkinson and Don Jones of the American Quarter Horse Association in Amarillo, Texas, I met some of the colorful breeders, owners, and managers of the great cattle and horse ranches of the Southwest. In Guthrie, Texas, as a guest of Jay Pumphrey at the famous 6666 Ranch (part of the Burnett Estates), I was able to join the working cowboys on a cattle drive, eat with them from the chuck wagon, and photograph horses and cattle on foot, from a pickup truck, and from the broad back of a Quarter Horse that stood as steady as a tripod.

No Texas hospitality could exceed that of Jay Pumphrey and Mrs. Anne Burnett Windfohr at the 6666. But Rex Cauble, owner of Cutter Bill and the Rex Cauble ranches of Denton, Texas, equaled it. There Mr. Cauble performed on Cutter Bill and also arranged to have Matlock Rose, famous Cutting Horse champion rider, ride Cutter Bill to demonstrate the training, agility, and response of that great horse.

In Oklahoma I was the guest of Melvin Hatley on his Briarwood Farm. I then visited A. B. Green's adjacent farm, called Green Pastures, where Mr. Green reminisced about old days in the Quarter Horse game. Additional information on Quarter Horses was gathered from Frank Vessels, distinguished Quarter Horse breeder, and from my old friend Walt Wiggins, who made my visit to the Ruidoso Downs track and the All-American Futurity Race both interesting and rewarding.

My informal interview with Marion Flynt, former president of the National Cutting Horse Association, was held in the boot-fitting department of Ryon's famous Western emporium in Fort Worth, Texas. Flynt's knowledge of the Cutting Horse, based on many active years in the saddle and as first president of the National Cutting Horse Association, was indispensable.

My friends among Arabian horse owners and breeders are many. First on the list is Mrs. Gladys Brown Edwards of Riverside, California, who has devoted her life to writing about, judging, and painting the Arabian horse. Mrs. Edwards was most generous with her time and advice and excellent

Arabian Horse library. At California State Polytechnic College in Pomona, Norman K. Dunn, associate professor and manager of the Arabian Horse Department, kindly read my manuscript. With his knowledgeable students, including Judy Halleran who posed for the Eastern-style riding pictures, he assisted me with research material and made it possible for me to photograph the outstanding breeding stock on the Kellogg-Voorhis Campus. Interviews with Dr. R. H. Packard, veterinarian at Cal Poly, were most instructive.

Miss Sheila Varian of Varian Arabians at Arroyo Grande, California, is one of the West's best-known breeders and trainers. She spent many days remembering anecdotes, demonstrating breeding techniques, and herding her award-winning horses for me to photograph. At Greengate Farms in the hills above San Luis Obispo, California, Jay Stream cooperated by putting his champion Arabians through their paces for my color camera.

In Arizona, I am indebted to Dr. Eugene E. LaCroix of Lasma Arabians near Scottsdale. Both Dr. LaCroix and his sons, Eugene and Raymond, gave me their full cooperation. So did his well-trained horses. In the shade of tall eucalyptus trees, "Frisco" Mari of La Puente, California, long-time breeder of Arabian horses, regaled me with information about the breed. His three daughters also contributed some good stories. My special thanks to Jim Alderson, breeder and trainer of Arabians and Quarter Horses and once trainer of the famous Arabian performing stallion Poly Royal.

Although the Appaloosa is widespread in the West, and in the United States generally, his homeland is still the Snake River valley where the states of Idaho, Washington, and Oregon meet. In the rugged grandeur of this area, I met with George B. Hatley, executive secretary of the Appaloosa Horse Club. After traveling about the country and developing an itinerary, I continued my peregrinations over the spacious countryside with Don Walker, editor of the *Appaloosa News*, meeting such interesting and helpful horse breeders as Jesse Redheart, descendant of Chief Joseph, and also meeting Jesse's wife and children; Phil Types, vice-chairman of the Nez Percé Reservation at Lapwai; and Caleb Carter, one-time football star of the Carlisle Indian School. I also photographed some of the fine Appaloosa stock on the ranch of Palmer Wagner at Garfield, Washington, and I received excellent cooperation from Roy Parvin on the Parvin Ranch and from the Randall Jack Stables near Moscow, Idaho. The photo of the saddle on Page 181 was provided by Ryon's.

Current information regarding certain horse blood tests being made was kindly supplied to me by Dr. Clyde Stormont and Miss Yoshiko Suzuki of the University of California at Davis. Marshall B. Kroh, secretary of the Caballeros del Camino Real (he is of Twin Pines Ranch, San Luis Rey, California) and his company of horsemen made me welcome as I traveled with them on their big ride of the year, the El Camino trek, which starts at Pala Mission in Pauma Valley, California, and ends at San Luis Rey Mission in San Luis Rey, California. I am especially grateful to the staff at the San Diego Public Library; to Dr. Louis Kenney, head librarian of San Diego State College; to Jan Love of San Diego; to Nelson Fisher of San Diego; and to Charles Halleran and Judy Halleran of California State Polytechnic College. In Spain, I owe thanks to the director and the staff of the Biblioteca del Archivo General de Las Indias, in Sevilla. For the photograph on Page 159 I am grateful for permission from the historical collection of Title Insurance and Trust Company of San Diego, California.

*Bradley Smith*
*La Jolla, California*

We wish to thank the following authors and publishers for their permission to use quotations in this book:

Dave and Mary Roberts Coolidge, "The War God's Horse Song," *The Navajo Indian*, Houghton Mifflin Co.

Sewell Ford, *Black Eagle Who Once Ruled the Ranges*, reprinted from *The Personality of the Horse*, Crown Publishers, Inc., 1963.

Bob Gray of *Horseman* magazine, *Great Horses of the Past*, Vol. 1, pp. 100-101, Cordovan Corp., 1967, Houston, Texas.

J. Frank Dobie, *The Mustangs*, Little, Brown and Company.

Ramon F. Adams, *Western Words*, University of Oklahoma Press.

Robert Glass Cleland, quoting Thomas D. Mott, *The Irvine Ranch of Orange County, 1810-1950*, Huntington Library.

Nelson C. Nye, *The Complete Book of the Quarter Horse*, A. S. Barnes and Co., Inc.

Louis Taylor, *BITS, Their History, Use and Misuse*, Harper & Row, 1966.

# BIBLIOGRAPHY

Adams, Ramon F.,
*Western Words: A Dictionary of the*
*Range, Cow Camp and Trail,*
University of Oklahoma Press, 1969

Alamán, Lucas,
*Historia de Méjico,* (5 vols.)
Mexico City, 1849-1852

Altamira, Rafael,
*A History of Spain,*
D. Van Nostrand Company, 1949

American Heritage,
*The Great West,*
American Heritage Publishing
Company, Inc., 1965

*Indians,*
American Heritage Publishing
Company, Inc., 1961

**The American Racing Manual,**
Triangle Publications, Inc., 1968

Bandelier, Fanny,
*The Journey of Álvar Núñez Cabeza*
*de Vaca and His Companions,*
New York, 1904

Beebe, Lucius, and Charles Clegg,
*U. S. West—The Saga of Wells Fargo,*
E. P. Dutton & Co., Inc., 1949

Bieber, Ralph P.,
*Southwest Historical Series,* (12 vols.)
Glendale, California, 1938

Brackett, R. W.,
*The History of San Diego County*
*Ranchos,*
Union Title Insurance and
Trust Company, 1951

Brown, M. H.,
*The Flight of the Nez Percé,*
G. P. Putnam's Sons, 1967

Browne, J. Ross,
*Adventures in the Apache Country,*
New York, 1869

Catlin, George,
*Letters and Notes on the Manners,*
*Customs and Condition of the*
*North American Indians,*
London, 1841

Chamberlain, Samuel E.,
*My Confession,*
New York, 1956

Chard, Thornton,
*Endurance Rides of the Early 60's,*
Journal of Heredity, XVII, January, 1926

Cleland, Robert Glass,
*The Irvine Ranch of Orange County,*
The Huntington Library, 1953

Cortés, Hernán,
*Cartas de Relación de la*
*Conquista de Méjico,*
Mexico, 1908

Dale, Edward Everett,
*The Range Cattle Industry,*
University of Oklahoma Press, 1960

Davies, R. Trevor,
*The Golden Century of Spain, 1501-1621,*
Macmillan, 1954

*Death Valley National Monument,*
U. S. Government Printing Office, 1955

Denhardt, Robert Moorman,
*The Horse of the Americas,*
University of Oklahoma Press, 1947

*Spanish Horses and the New World,*
The Historian, University of
New Mexico, 1938

*The Quarter Horse,* (Vol. 3),
The American Quarter Horse Assn., 1950

Denhardt, Robert Moorman,
and Helen Michaelis,
*The Quarter Horse,* (Vol. 2),
The American Quarter Horse
Association, 1945

De Voto, Bernard,
*The Year of Decision 1846,*
Boston, 1943

Díaz del Castillo, Bernal,
*The Bernal Díaz Chronicles,*
(tr. and ed. by Albert Idell)
New York, 1956

*The Conquest of New Spain,*
(tr. by J. M. Cohen)
Penguin Books, 1965

Dobie, J. Frank,
*The Mustangs,*
Little, Brown and Company, 1952
*A Vaquero of the Brush Country,*
Grosset & Dunlap, 1929

Dodge, Col. Richard Irving,
*Our Wild Indians: Thirty-Three Years'*
*Personal Experience Among the*
*Red Men of the Great West,*
Hartford, Connecticut, 1883

Drucker, Philip,
*Indians of the Northwest Coast,*
The Natural History Press, 1963

Emory, Lieut. Col. W. H.,
*Notes of a Military Reconnaissance*
*from...Missouri to San Diego,*
Ex. Doc. No. 41, 30th Congress,
1st Session, Washington, D.C., 1848

Engel, Fritz-Martin,
*Life Around Us,*
(tr. by J. R. Foster)
Thomas Y. Crowell Company, 1965

Foreman, Grant
*Pioneer Days in the Early Southwest,*
Cleveland, Ohio, 1926

Fowler, Jacob,
*The Journal of Jacob Fowler,*
(ed. by Elliott Coues)
New York, 1898

Graham, R. B. Cunninghame,
*The Horses of the Conquest,*
London, 1930

Gray, Bob,
*Great Horses of the Past,* (Vol. 1)
Cordovan Corporation, 1967

Grinnell, George Bird,
*The Cheyenne Indians:*
*Their History and Ways of Life,*
Yale University Press, 1923, II

*The Indian,* (2 vols.)
D. Appleton & Company, 1897

Hackett, Charles Wilson,
*Pichardo's Treatise on the*
*Limits of Louisiana and Texas,*
University of Texas Press, 1941

Haines, Francis,
*Appaloosa,*
University of Texas Press, 1963

*Red Eagles of the North,*
Portland, Oregon, 1939

*Where Did the Plains Indians*
*Get Their Horses?*
American Anthropologist, Vol. 40,
1938, and *The Northward Spread of*
*Horses Among the Plains Indians*

Herold, A. Ferdinand,
*The Life of Buddha,*
(tr. by Paul C. Blum)
Charles E. Tuttle Company, 1954

Horgan, Paul,
*Conquistadors in*
*North American History,*
Farrar Strauss and Co., 1963

Hunter, John Warren,
*Nine Years with the Apaches
and Comanches*,
pamphlet, 1906

Irving, John Treat,
*Indian Sketches Taken During a
U.S. Expedition to Make Treaties With
the Pawnee and Other Tribes in 1833*,
New York, 1888

Johnson, John J.,
*The Introduction of the Horse
into the Western Hemisphere*,
The Hispanic Historical Review,
XXIII, Nov., 1943

Josephy, Alvin M., Jr.,
*The Nez Percé and the Opening
of the Northwest*,
Yale University Press, 1965

Lewis, Meriwether,
*The Lewis and Clark Expedition*, (3 vols.)
J. B. Lippincott Company, 1961

*The Life of the Admiral Christopher
Columbus by His Son Ferdinand*,
(tr. and ed. by Benjamin Keen)
Houghton Mifflin, 1959

Lowie, Robert H.,
*Indians of the Plains*,
The Natural History Press, 1963

*The Lyman Wight Colony in Texas*,
(compiled by J. Marvin Hunter)
The Bandera Bulletin, Bandera, Texas

*The Manuscript Journals of
Alexander Henry and David Thompson*,
(ed. by Elliott Coues)
New York, 1897

McBeth, Frances Turner,
*Lower Klamath Country*,
Anchor Press, 1950

McClintock, William A.,
*Journal of a Trip Through Texas and
Northern Mexico in 1846-1847*,
Southwestern Historical Quarterly,
XXXIV, 1931

Merriman, Roger Bigelow,
*The Rise of the Spanish Empire in the
Old World and in the New*, (4 vols.)
Macmillan, 1918-1934

Middleton, John W.,
*The Regulators and Moderators and
The Shelby County War*,
Frontier Times Publishing House,
Grand Prairie, Texas, 1953

Morison, Samuel Eliot,
*Admiral of the Ocean Sea: A Life of
Christopher Columbus*, (2 vols.)
Atlantic Monthly Press, 1942

Morris, Desmond,
*The Mammals*,
Harper & Row, 1965

*Mustangs and Cow Horses*,
(ed. by Dobie, Boatright and Ransom)
Texas Folklore Society, 1940

*Narratives of the Career of
Hernando de Soto*,
(ed. by Edward Gaylord Bourne)
New York, 1922

Nye, Nelson C.,
*The Complete Book of the Quarter Horse*,
A. S. Barnes and Co., Inc., 1964

*Original Journals of the
Lewis and Clark Expedition*,
(ed. by Reuben Gold Thwaites)
New York, 1905

Oviedo y Valdés,
Gonzalo Fernández de,
*Historia General y Natural de las
Indias Islas y Tierra-Firme
del Mar Océano*,
Editorial Guarania, Madrid, 1944-45

*The Personality of the Horse*,
(ed. by Brandt Aymar and
Edward Sagarin)
Crown Publishers, Inc., 1963

Prescott, William H.,
*The Conquest of Mexico and
The Conquest of Peru*,
Random House, Inc., 1957

*Readings in Latin American Civilization,
1492 to the Present*,
(ed. by Benjamin Keen) 1955

Reese, Herbert H.,
*The Kellogg Arabians*,
Borden Publishing Company, 1958

Robinson, G. C.,
"Mustangs and Mustanging in
Southwest Texas" in
*Mustangs and Cow Horses*,
Texas Folklore Society, 1940

Roe, F. G.,
*From Dogs to Horses Among the
Western Indian Tribes*,
Transactions of the Royal Society of
Canada, 1939, Third Series,
Section II, Vol. XXXIII.

Ross, Alexander,
*The Fur Hunters of the Far West*,
London, 1855

Taylor, T. U.,
*The Lee-Peacock Feud*,
Frontier Times Publishing House, Inc.,
reprinted from Frontier,

Vol. 3, No. 8, 1926

*Thoroughbred Racing in the U.S.A.*,
Thoroughbred Racing
Protective Bureau, Inc., 1950

Timmons, William,
*Twilight on the Range*,
University of Texas Press, 1962

*Travels and Explorations of the Jesuit
Missionaries in New France, 1610-1791*,
Cleveland, Ohio, 1900

Vega, Garcilaso de la,
*The Florida of the Inca*,
(tr. and ed. by John and Jeannette Varner)
University of Texas Press, 1951

Wagner, H. R.
*The Rise of Hernán Cortés*,
University of California Press, 1944

Wentworth, Lady,
*The Authentic Arabian Horse
and His Descendants*,
London, 1945

*Thoroughbred Racing Stock and
Its Ancestors*,
London, 1938

Wilhelm, Paul, Duke of Wuerttemberg,
*Journey to North America, 1822-1824*,
South Dakota Historical Collections,
XIX, 1938

Williams, R. H., and John W. Sansom,
*The Massacre on the Nueces River*,
Frontier Times Publishing House,
Grand Prairie, Texas

Wilson, Gilbert L.,
*The Horse and Dog in Hidatsa Culture*,
Anthropological Papers of the
American Museum of Natural History,
1924, Vol. XV, Part II

Wissler, Clark,
*The Influence of the Horse in the
Development of Plains Culture*,
American Anthropologist, Vol. 16,
New Series, Jan.-March, 1914

Worcester, D. E.,
*Spanish Horses
Among the Plains Tribes*,
Pacific Historical Review, XIV,
Dec., 1945

*The Spread of the Spanish Horses
in the Southwest*,
New Mexico Historical Review, XIX,
July, 1944

Zeuner, Frederick E.
*A History of Domesticated Animals*,
Harper & Row, 1963

# INDEX _____

*Page numbers in italics refer to a caption.*

This text is set in Bodoni Book, a modern type designed by master craftsman Giambattista Bodoni in Italy during the 1790's. Lithography and color separations are by Frye & Smith, Ltd., of San Diego, California. Typography is by Linotron, a division of Frye & Smith. Art production is by Image, also a division of Frye & Smith. The paper, prepared specially for this edition, is white Camelia Matte Book.